THE ARMED FORCES OFFICER

Edition of 1950

US Department of Defense

Introduction and notes copyright © 2013 by the Quiet
Creek Corporation, publishers, Twentynine palms, CA.
sales@thequietcreek.com

1 3 5 7 9 8 6 4 2

ISBN-13: 978-0-9883696-3-4
ISBN-10: 098836963X

Library of Congress Control Number: 2013947423

CONTENTS

Introduction by the Publisher

The Armed Forces Officer gets better with age. I first read it as a young second lieutenant in the early 1980s. But I didn't really read the *The Armed Forces Officer*; I more or less (less) glanced through the thing in a poor attempt to speak intelligently should I be asked. I was never asked and didn't pick it up again for several years.

When I did pick it up again, I had just completed a tour at the Joint Staff in Washington, DC. Then a newly minted lieutenant colonel, I decided to take another look at *The Armed Forces Officer*. This time, though, my motivation for reading it was internal. Precisely what it was, I'm not sure; perhaps the Joint Staff's way of diminishing optimism caused me to seek a greater understanding of what it was to be an officer, indeed what it was to be an American in the service of my country. As I read *The Armed Forces Officer*, it quickly dawned on me that it is much more than a how-to guide for junior officers. Rather, it is a series of candid, timeless essays on the nature of the people who occupy the ranks of the military services.

The Armed Forces Officer's author understood that our military is not just a collection of machines, processes, and regulations, but a very human endeavor whose proper understanding requires acknowledging that humans and nothing else are what make our military the complex, potent, and wonderful organization that it is—a truth that can be applied to any organization, military or civilian, composed of people and all their mysterious complexities.

The author of course was S. L. A. Marshal; his first edition was published in 1950 and was forged from his and others' collective wisdom and decades of experience.

Several subsequent editions appear after the 1950 edition, each correcting details as time affected the military. S. L. A. Marshall crafted those subsequent editions until his death in 1979.[1] In 2002 a consortium of sorts was created to develop a new *The Armed Forces Officer*. That effort resulted in the current edition, which, while excellent in its own way, is completely different in tone, structure, and organization from the original.

---

1. US Department of Defense, *The Armed Forces Officer* (Washington, DC: Department of Defense, 2006).

As for my 1950 edition (printed by the Marine Corps Association tion well after 1950), it is now highlighted and underlined, the spine is broken, and there are notes in the margins. All of my defacing points to where I've found wisdom, truths, and profound insight into the nature of the men and women who make up our armed services. It is a wonderful book. Enjoy.

Robert Davis
Colonel, USMC (ret)

CHAPTER ONE

THE MEANING OF YOUR COMMISSION

Upon being commissioned in the Armed Services of the United States, a man incurs a lasting obligation to cherish and protect his country and to develop within himself that capacity and reserve strength which will enable him to serve its arms and the welfare of his fellow Americans with increasing wisdom, diligence, and patriotic conviction.

This is the meaning of his commission. It is not modified by any reason of assignment while in the service, nor is the obligation lessened on the day an officer puts the uniform aside and returns to civil life. Having been specially chosen by the United States to sustain the dignity and integrity of its sovereign power, an officer is expected so to maintain himself, and so to exert his influence for so long as he may live, that he will be recognized as a worthy symbol of all that is best in the national character.

In this sense the trust imposed in the highest military commander in the land is not more than what is encharged the newest ensign or second lieutenant. Nor is it less. It is the fact of commission which gives special distinction to the man and in turn requires that the measure of his devotion to the service of his country be distinctive, as compared with the charge laid upon the average citizen.

In the beginning, a man takes an oath to uphold his country's Constitution against all enemies foreign and domestic, to bear true faith and allegiance, and to discharge well and faithfully the duties of office. He does this without any mental reservation.

Thereafter he is given a paper which says that because the President as a representative of the people of this country reposes "special trust and confidence" in his "patriotism, valor, fidelity, and abilities," he is forthwith commissioned.

By these tokens, the Nation also becomes a party to the contract, and will faithfully keep its bond with the man. While he continues to serve honorably, it will sustain him and will clothe him with its dignity. That it has vouched for him gives him a felicitous status in our society. The device he wears, his insignia, and even his garments identify him directly with the power of the United States. The living standards of himself and of his family are underwritten by Federal statute. Should he become ill, the Nation will care for him. Should he be disabled, it will stand as his guardian through life. Should he seek to advance himself through higher studies, it will open the way.

Other than the officer corps, there is no group within our society toward which the obligation of the Nation is more fully expressed. Even so, other Americans regard this fact with pride, rather than with envy. They accept the principle that some unusual advantage should attend exceptional and unremitting responsibility. Whatever path an American officer may walk, he enjoys prestige. Though little is known of his intrinsic merit, he will be given the respect of his fellow citizens, unless he proves himself utterly undeserving.

This national esteem for the corps is one of the priceless assets of American security. The services themselves so recognize it. That they place such strong emphasis upon the importance of personal honor among officers is because they know that the future of our arms and the well-being of our people depend upon a constant renewing and strengthening of public faith in the virtue of the corps. Were this to languish, the Nation would be loath to commit its sons to any military endeavor, no matter how grave the emergency.

The works of goodwill by which those who lead the national military forces endeavor to win the unreserved trust of the American people is one of the chief preservatives of the American system of freedoms. The character of the corps is in a most direct sense a final safeguard of the character of the Nation.

To these thoughts any officer who is morally deserving of his commission would freely subscribe. He will look beyond the letter of his obligation and will accept in his own heart the total implications of his new responsibility.

So doing, he still might see fit to ask: "But to what do I turn my thoughts? How do I hold myself so that while following the line of duty, I will also exemplify those ideals which may inspire other men to make their best effort?"

It is suggested that there is a one-word key to the answer among the four lofty qualities which are cited on every man's commission.

That word is *Fidelity*.

As for patriotism, either a man loves his country or else he would not seek commission at its hands, unless he be completely the rascal, pretending to serve in order to destroy.

Valor, on the other hand, can not be fully vouchsafed,[1] since it is not given to any man to know the nature and depth of his personal courage.

Abilities vary from man to man, and are partly what heredity and environment have made them. If nature had not imposed a ceiling, mere striving would make every man a genius.

But Fidelity is the derivative of personal decision. It is the jewel within reach of every man who has the will to possess it.

Given an officer corps composed throughout of men who would make the eternal try toward bettering their professional capacities and furthering the working efficiency and harmony within all forces, the United States would become thrice-armed though not producing one new weapon in its arsenals.

Great faith, rightness of mind, influence over other men, and finally, personal success and satisfaction come of service to the ideals of the profession. Were these strengths reflected throughout the officer body, it could well happen that because of the shining example, the American people would become more deeply conscious of the need to keep their own fibers strong than has been their disposition throughout history.

Accepting these truths as valid, a man still must know where he stands before making a true reckoning of his line of advance. This entails some consideration of himself (a) as to the personal standard which is required of him because of his position in relation to all others (b) as to the reasons in common sense which make this requirement, and (c) as to the principles and philosophy which will enable him to play his part well.

The military officer is considered a gentleman, not because Congress wills it, nor because it has been the custom of people in all times to afford him that courtesy, but specifically because nothing less than a gentleman is truly suited for his particular set of responsibilities.

This is not simply a bit of self-adulation; it is distinctly the American tradition in the matter. The Nation has never attempted to draw its officers from a particular class. During World War II, thousands of men were commissioned in our forces who had enjoyed little opportunity in their earlier environments. They were sound men by nature.

---

1. The Oxford English Dictionary defines vouchsafe as: "To confer or bestow (some thing, favour, or benefit) *on* a person."

They had courage. They could set a good example. They could rally other men around them. In the eyes of the services, these things count more than any man's blood lines. We say with Voltaire, "Whoever serves his country well has no need of ancestors."

On the other hand, from the time of the Colonies, this country has despised press gangs, floggings, martinetism,[2] and all of the other Old World military practices which demeaned the rank and file. Its military system was founded on the dignity of man, just as was its Constitution. The system has sought ever since to advance itself by appealing to the higher nature of the individual. That is why its officers need to be gentlemen. To call forth great loyalty in other people and to harness it to any noble undertaking, one must first be sensible of their finer instincts and feelings. Certainly these things at least are among the gentle qualities which are desired in every military officer of the United States:

1. Strong belief in human rights.

2. Respect for the dignity of every other person.

3. The Golden Rule attitude toward one's daily associates.

4. An abiding interest in all aspects of human welfare.

5. A willingness to deal with every man as considerately as if he were a blood relative.

These qualities are the epitome of strength, not of softness. They mark the man who is capable of pursuing a great purpose consistently in spite of temptations. He who possesses them will all the more surely be regarded as a "man among men." Take any crowd of new recruits! The greater number of them during their first few days in service will use more profanity and obscenity, talk more about women and boast more about drinking than they have ever done in their lives, because of the mistaken idea that this is the quick way to get a reputation for being hard-boiled. But at the same time, the one or two men among them who stay decent, talk moderately and walk the line of duty will uniquely receive the infinite respect of the others. It never fails to happen!

---

2. From the Oxford English Dictionary: "the spirit or action characteristic of a martinet."

There is the other matter about how a man should feel toward his own profession. Simply to accept the fact that the bearing of arms is a highly honorable calling because the book says so should not suffice one's own interest in the matter, when a little personal reflection will reveal wherein the honor resides.

To every officer who has thought earnestly about the business, it is at once apparent that civilization, as men have known it since the time of the Greek City States, has rested as a pyramid upon a base of organized military power. Moreover, the general possibility of world cultural progress in the foreseeable future has no other conceivable foundation. For any military man to deny, on any ground whatever, the role which his profession has played in the establishment of everything which is well-ordered in our society, shows only a faulty understanding of history. It made possible the birth of the American system of freedoms. Later, it gave the nation a new birth and vouchsafed a more perfect union.

Likewise, we need to see the case in its present terms. One may abhor war fully, despise militarism absolutely, deplore all of the impulses in human nature which make armed force necessary, and still agree that for the world as we know it, the main hope is that "peace-loving nations can be made obviously capable of defeating nations which are willing to wage aggressive war." Those words, by the way, were not said by a warrior, but by the eminent pacifist, Bertrand Russell. It does not make the military man any less the humanitarian that he accepts this reality, that he faces toward the chance forthrightly, and that he believes that if all military power were stricken tomorrow, men would revert to a state of anarchy and there would ensue the total defeat of the forces which are trying to establish peace and brotherly love in our lives.

The complete identity of American military forces with the character of the people comes of this indivisibility of interest. To think of the military as a guardian class apart, like Lynkeus[3] "born for vision, ordained for watching," rather than as a strong right arm, corporately joined to the body and sharing its every function, is historically false and politically inaccurate. It is not unusual, however, for those whose task it is to interpret the trend of opinion to take the line that "the military" are thinking one way and "the people" quite another on some particular issue, as if to imply that the two are quite separate and of different nature.

---

3. An ancient Greek argonaut renowned for his excellent vision.

This is usually false in detail, and always false in general. It not only discounts the objects of their unity but overlooks the truth of its origins.

Maybe they should be invited to go to the root of the word. The true meaning of "populus," from which we get the word "people," was in the time of ancient Rome the "armed body." The pure-blooded Roman in the days of the Republic could not conceive of a citizen who was not a warrior. It was the arms which a Roman's possession of land enabled him to get that qualified him to participate in the affairs of state. He had no political rights until he had fought. *He was not of the people; they were of him!* Nor is this concept alien to the ideals on which the Founding Fathers built the American system, since they stated it as the right and duty of every able-bodied citizen to bear arms.

These propositions should mean much to every American who has chosen the military profession. A main point is that on becoming an officer a man does not renounce any part of his fundamental character as an American citizen. He has simply signed on for the post graduate course where one learns how to exercise authority in accordance with the spirit of liberty. The nature of his trusteeship has been subtly expressed by an Admiral in our service: "The American philosophy places the individual above the state. It distrusts personal power and coercion. It denies the existence of indispensable men. It asserts the supremacy of principle."

An understanding of American principles of life and growth, and personal zeal in upholding them, is the bedrock of sound leading in our services. Moral and emotional stability are expected of an American officer; he can usually satisfy his superiors if he attains to this equilibrium. But he is not likely to satisfy himself unless he can also achieve that maturity of character which expresses itself in the ability to make decisions in detachment of spirit from that which is pleasant or unpleasant to him personally, in the desire to hold onto things not by grasping them but by understanding them and remembering them, and in learning to covet only that which may be rightfully possessed.

An occasional man has become wealthy while in the services by making wise investments, through writings, by skill at invention, or through some other means. But he is the exception. The majority have no such prospect. Indeed, if love of money were the mainspring of all American action, the officer corps long since would have disintegrated. But it is well said that the only truly happy people on earth are those who are indifferent to money because they have some positive purpose which forecloses it. Than the service, there is no other environment which is more conducive to the leading of the full life by the individual who is ready to accept the word of the philosopher that the only security on earth is the willingness to accept insecurity as an inevitable part of living. Once an officer has made this passage into maturity, and is at peace with himself because the service means more to him than all else, he will find kinship with the great body of his brothers-in-arms. The highest possible consequence can develop from the feelings of men mutually inspired by some great endeavor and moving forward together according to the principle that only those who are willing to serve are fit to lead. Completely immersed in action, they have no time for smallness in speech, thought or deed. It is for these reasons that those who in times past have excelled in the leadership of American forces have invariably been great Americans first and superior officers second. The rule applies at all levels. The lieutenant who is not moved at the thought that he is serving his country is unlikely to do an intelligent job of directing other men. He will come apart at the seams whenever the going grows tough. Until men accept this thought freely, and apply it to their personal action, it is not possible for them to go forward together strongly. In the words of Lionel Curtis: "The only force that unites men is conscience, a varying capacity in most of them to put the interests of other people before their own."

The services are accustomed to being hammered. Like other human institutions, they are imperfect. Therefore the criticisms are not always unjust. Further, there is no more reason why the services should be immune to attack than any other organic part of our society and government.

The service officer is charged only to take a lively interest in all such discussions. He has no more right to condemn the service unfairly than has any other American. On the other hand he is not expected to be an intellectual eunuch, oblivious to all of the faults in the institution to which he gives his loyalty. To the contrary, the nature of that loyalty requires that he will use his force toward the righting of those things which reason convinces him are going wrong, though making certain that his action will not do more damage than repair.

His ultimate commanding loyalty at all times is to his country, and not to his service or his superior. He owes it to his country to speak the truth as he sees it. This implies a steadying judgment as to when it should be spoken, and to whom it should be addressed. A truth need not only be well-rounded, but the utterance of it should be cognizant of the stresses and objectives of the hour. Truth becomes falsehood unless it has the strength of perspective. The presentation of facts is self-justifying only when the facts are developed in their true proportion.

Where there is public criticism of the services, in matters both large and small, the service officer has the right and the duty of intervention only toward the end of making possible that all criticism will be well-informed. That right can not be properly exercised when there is nothing behind it but a defense of professional pride. The duty can be well performed when the officer knows not only his subject--the mechanism itself--but the history and philosophy of the armed services in their relation to the development of the American system. Criticism from the outside is essential to service well-being, for as Confucius said, oftentimes men in the game are blind to what the lookers on see clearly.

The value of any officer's opinion of any military question can never be any greater than the extent and accuracy of his information. His ability to dispose public thought favorably toward the service will depend upon the wisdom of his words rather than upon his military rank and other credentials. A false idea will come upon a bad fate even though it has the backing of the highest authority.

Only men of informed mind and unprejudiced expression can strengthen the claim of the services on the affections of the American people.

This is, of itself, a major objective for the officer corps, since our public has little studious interest in military affairs, tends ever to discount the vitality of the military role in the progress and prosperity of the nation and regards the security problem as one of the less pleasant and abnormal burdens on an otherwise orderly existence.

It is an explicable contradiction of the American birthright that to some of our people the military establishment is at best a necessary evil, and military service is an extraordinary hardship rather than an inherent obligation. Yet these illusions are rooted deep in the American tradition, though it is a fact to be noted not without hope that we are growing wiser as we move along. In the years which followed the American Revolution, the new union of States tried to eliminate military forces altogether. There was vast confusion of thought as to what freedom required for its own survival. Thomas Jefferson, one of the great architects of democracy, and still renowned for his "isolationist" sentiments, wrote the warning: "We must train and classify the whole of our male citizens, and make military instruction a regular part of collegiate education. We can never be safe until this is done."

None the less, the hour came when the standing Army was reduced to 80 men. None the less, the quaint notion has survived that an enlightened interest in military affairs is somehow undemocratic. And none the less, recurring war has invariably found the United States inadequately prepared for the defense of its own territory.

Because there has been a holdover of these mistaken sentiments right down to the present, there persists in many military officers a defensive attitude toward their own profession which has no practical relation to the strength of the ground on which they are enabled to stand. Toward any unfair and flippant criticism of the "military mind" they react with resentment, instead of with buoyant proof that their own minds are more plastic and more receptive to national ideals than those of any other profession. Where they should approach all problems of the national security with the zeal of the missionary, seeking and giving light, they treat this subject as if it were a private game preserve.

It suffices to say of this minority that they are a barnacle on the hull of an otherwise staunch vessel. From such limited concepts of personal responsibility, there can not fail to develop a foreshortened view of the dignity of the task at hand. The note of apology is injected at the wrong time; the tone of belligerency is used when it serves no purpose. When someone arises within the halls of government to say that the military establishment is "uneconomic" because it cuts no bricks, bales no hay and produces nothing which can be vended in the market places, it is not unusual to hear some military men concur in this strange notion. That acquiescence is wholly unbecoming.

The physician is not slurred as belonging to a nonproductive profession because he contributes only to the care and healing of the body, and through these things to the general well-being of society. Respect for formal education, organized religion and all of the enterprises built up around the dissemination of ideas is not the less because the resultant benefit to society is not always tangible and saleable. Hence to say that that without which society could not endure in its present form is "uneconomic" is to make the word itself altogether meaningless.

In that inner power of courage and conviction which stems from the spiritual integrity of the individual, lies the strength of democracy. As to their ability to produce toward these ends, the military services can stand on the record. When shortly after World War II, a census was taken among the returned men, 60 percent said that they had been *morally strengthened* by their military service in the American uniform. About 30 percent had no opinion or felt that military life had not changed them one way or the other. An insignificant minority considered themselves damaged. This is an amazing testimony in light of the fact that only a small fraction of American youth is schooled to believe that any spiritual good can come of military service. As to what it signifies, those who take a wholly materialistic view of the objects of the Republic are entitled to call the military establishment "uneconomic." The services will continue to hold with the idea that strong nationhood comes not of the making of gadgets but of the building of character.

Men beget goodwill in other men by giving it. They develop courage in their following mainly as a reflection of the courage which they show in their own action. These two qualities of mind and heart are of the essence of sound officership. One is of little avail without the other, and either helps to sustain the other. As to which is the stronger force in its impact upon the masses of men, no truth is more certain than the words once written by William James: "Evident though the short-comings of a man may be, if he is ready to give up his life for a cause, we forgive him everything. However inferior he may be to ourselves in other respects, if we cling to life while he throws it away like a flower, we bow to his superiority."

Theodore Roosevelt once said that if he had a son who refrained from any worthwhile action because of the fear of hurt to himself, he would disown him. Soon after his return to civilian life, Gen. Dwight D. Eisenhower spoke of the worthwhileness of "living dangerously." An officer of the United States armed forces can not go far wrong if he holds with these ideas. It is not the suitable profession for those who believe only in digging-in and nursing a soft snap until death comes at a ripe old age. Who risks nothing gains nothing.

Nor should there be any room in it for professional smugness, small jealousies, and undue concern about privilege.

The regular recognizes as his peer and comrade the officer from any of the civilian components. That he is a professional does not give him an especial eminence, but simply a greater measure of responsibility for the success of the total establishment. Moreover, he can not afford to be patronizing, without risking self-embarrassment, such is the vast experience which many reservists have had on the active field of war.

Toward services other than his own, any officer is expected to have both a comradely feeling and an imaginative interest. Any Army officer is a better man for having studied the works of Admiral Mahan and familiarized himself with the modern Navy from first-hand experience. Those who lead sea-going forces can enlarge their own capacities by knowing more, rather than less, about the nature of the air and ground establishments. The submariner can always learn something useful to his own work by mingling with airmen; the airman becomes a better officer as he grows in qualified knowledge of ground and sea fighting.

But the fact remains that the services are not alike, that no wit of man can make them alike, and that the retention by each of its separate character, customs and confidence is essential to the conserving of our national military power. Unification has not altered this basic proposition. The first requirement of a unified establishment is moral soundness in each of the integral parts, without which there can be no soundness at all. And on the question of fundamental loyalty, the officer who loves every other service just as much as his own will have just as much active virtue as the man who loves other women as much as his own wife.

CHAPTER TWO

FORMING MILITARY IDEALS

Any stranger making a survey of what Americans are and how they get that way would probably see it as a paradox that within the armed establishment the inculcation of ideals is considered the most vital of all teaching, while in our gentler and less rigid institutions, there is steadily less emphasis on this subject.

He would be entitled to the explanation that it is not so done because this has always been the way of Armies, Navies, and other fighting forces, or because it is universal in the military establishments of the twentieth century, but because nothing else would better suffice the American military system under present conditions.

There are two main reasons why.

The first is that we are an altogether unregimented people, with a strong belief in the virtues of rugged individualism and in the right of the average man to go along about as he pleases, so long as he does not do actual injury to society. Voluntary group cooperation rather than absolute group loyalty, developing from a strong spiritual bond, is the basic technic[1] of Americans in their average rounds. It is enough to satisfy the social, political and economic needs of a democracy, but in its military parts, it would be fatally weak. There would be no possibility of achieving an all-compelling unity under conditions of utmost pressure if no man felt any higher call to action than what was put upon him by purely material considerations.

Military ideals are therefore, as related to this purpose, mainly an instrument of national survival. But not altogether so, since in the measure that they influence the personal life and conduct of millions of men who move in and out of the services, they have a regenerative effect upon the spiritual fiber of the Nation as a whole.

There is the second and equally important reason that, whereas wars have sometimes been fought for ideal causes, as witness the American Revolution and Civil War, war itself is never ideal, and the character of our people is such as to insist that from our side, its brutalities be minimized. The barbarian who kills for killing's sake and who

---

1. The Oxford English Dictionary defines "technic" as "Pertaining to art, or to an art…"

scorns the laws of war at any point is repugnant to the instincts of our people, under whatever flag he fights. If we did not have some men of this type among us, our penitentiaries would not be filled. The ravages which they might commit when all of the barriers are down on the battlefield can be prevented only when forces as a whole believe that armed power, while not ideal in itself, must be made to serve ideal ends.

To speak of ethics in the same breath with war may seem like sheer cant and hypocrisy. But in the possibility that those who best understand the use and nature of armed power may excel all others in stimulating that higher morality which may some day restrain war lies a main chance for the future. The Armed Services of the United States do not simply do lip service to such institutions as United Nations. They encourage their people to take a deep personal interest in every legitimate activity aimed to bulwark world peace. But while doing this, they keep their powder dry.

Military ideals are not different than the ideals which make any man sound in himself, and in his relation to others. They are called military ideals only because the proving ground is a little more rugged in the service than elsewhere. But they are all founded in hard military experience; they did not find expression because some Admiral got it in his head one day to set an unattainable goal for his men, or because some General wished to turn a pious face toward the public, professing that his men were aspiring to greater virtue than anything the public knew.

The military way is a long, hard road, and it makes extraordinary requirements of every individual. In war, particularly, it puts stresses upon men such as they have not known elsewhere, and the temptation to "get out from under" would be irresistible if their spirits had not been tempered to the ordeal. If nothing but fear of punishments were depended upon to hold men to the line during extreme trial, the result would be wholesale mutiny and a situation altogether beyond the control of leadership. So it must be true that *it is out of the impact of ideals mainly that men develop the strength to face situations from which it would be normal to run away.*

Also, during the normal routine of peace, members of the Armed Services are expected to respond to situations that are more extensive, more complex, and take longer to reach fulfillment than the situations to which the majority of men instinctively respond. Even the length of the enlistment period looks like a slow march up a 60-mile grade. Promotion

13

is slow, duty frequently monotonous. It is all too easy for the individual to worry about his own insignificance and to feel that he has become lost in the crowd. Under these conditions a man may go altogether bad, or simply get lazy and rock with the grain. But nothing except a strong belief in the ideals he is serving will make him respond to the larger situation and give it his best effort. Ideals have the intensely practical end of strengthening men for the better discharge of duties which devolve upon them in their day-to-day affairs.

What is the main test of human character? Probably it is this: that a man will know how to be patient in the midst of hard circumstance, and can continue to be personally effective while living through whatever discouragements beset him and his companions. Moreover, that is what every truly civilized man would want in himself during the calmer moments when he compares critically what he is inside with what he would like to be. That is specifically the reason why the promulgation of military ideals is initially a problem in the first person, singular. The Armed Services have in one sense a narrow motive in turning the thoughts of younger leaders toward a belief in ideals. They know that this is a lubricant in the machinery of organization and the best way to sweeten the lives of men working together in a group toward some worthwhile purpose. But there is also a higher object. All experience has taught that it is likewise the best way to give the individual man a solid foundation for living successfully amid the facts of existence, irrespective of his situation. The military system of the United States is not committed to grinding out warriors *per se*, but to the training of men in such manner that they will be able to play a better part anywhere, and will find greater satisfactions in what they do. All the time, when the service seeks to emphasize to its ranks what is the "right thing to do," it is speaking of that course of conduct which in the long run is most necessary and useful to the individual.

As to what one man should seek in himself, in order to be four-square with his own life and all others who are related to his personal situation, it is simple enough to formulate it, and to describe what constitutes maturity of character. In fact, that can be done without mentioning the words "patriotism" and "courage", which traditionally and rightly are viewed as the very highest of the military virtues.

No man is truly fit for officership unless in the inner recess of his being he can go along with the toast known to every American schoolboy:

"My country, in her intercourse with other nations may she always be in the right! But right or wrong, my country!" And he will never do a really good job of supporting her standards if, when the clutch comes, he is lacking in intestinal fortitude.

But there is this to be said about the nature of courage and patriotism, in the same breath that we agree they are essential in an officer of the fighting establishment--neither of these qualities of itself carries sufficient conviction, except as it is the product of those homelier attributes which give dignity to all action, in things both large and small, during the course of any average work day.

When Dr. Johnson remarked that patriotism is the last refuge of a scoundrel he was not belittling the value of love of country as a force in the lives of men, but to the contrary, was pointing out that a profession of patriotism, unaccompanied by good works, was the mark of a man not to be trusted. In no other institution in the land will flag-waving fall as flat as in the Armed Services when the ranks know that it is just an act, with no sincere commitment to service backing it up. But the uniformed forces will still respond to the real article with the same emotion that they felt at Bunker Hill and Manila Bay.

There is a Civil War story from one of the campaigns against Stonewall Jackson in the Valley. A Confederate who had had his leg shot away turned on his pallet to regard a Union private who had just lost an arm, and said to him, "For what reason did you invade us and make all this trouble?" The boy replied simply: "For the old flag." That may sound like sentiment from a distant past. But turn to the story of Major Devereux and the Marine defense of Wake Island. He wrote that the "music" had always gone sour, and had invariably broken down when he tried to play "The Colors." But on the morning of Pearl Harbor, when the flag was raised, the garrison already knew that the war was on. And for some reason which no man could account for, the bugler rose to the occasion, and for the first time, every note came straight and true. Devereux said that every throat tightened and every head went higher. Yet Devereux was a remarkably unmelodramatic fighting man.

But to get back to those simpler virtues which provide a firm foundation for patriotism and may become the fount of courage, at least these few things would have to be put among the fundamentals:

1. A man has honor if he holds himself to a course of conduct, because of a conviction that it is in the general interest, even though he is

well aware that it may lead to inconvenience, personal loss, humiliation or grave physical risk.

2. He has veracity if, having studied a question to the limit of his ability, he says and believes what he thinks to be true, even though it would be the path of least resistance to deceive others and himself.

3. He has justice if he acknowledges the interests of all concerned in any particular transaction rather than serving his own apparent interest.

4. He has graciousness if he acts and speaks forthrightly, agrees warmly,disagrees fairly and respectfully, participates enthusiastically, refrains from harboring grudges, takes his reverses in stride, and does not complain or ask for help in the face of trifling calamities.

5. He has integrity if his interest in the good of the service is at all times greater than his personal pride, and when he holds himself to the same line of duty when unobserved as he would follow if all of his superiors were present.

The list could be longer, but for the moment, we can let it go at that. These standards are not counsels of perfection; thousands of officers have adhered to them. But it should be said as well that if all leaders at the lower levels in all of the services were to conform in the same way, the task of higher command would be simplicity itself. The cause of much of the friction in the administrative machinery is that at all levels there are individuals who insist on standing in their own light. They believe that there is some special magic, some quick springboard to success; they mistakenly think that it can be won by bootlicking, apple-polishing, yessing higher authority, playing office politics, throwing weight around, ducking the issues, striving for cheap popularity, courting publicity or seeking any and all means of grabbing the spotlight.

Any one of this set of tricks may enable a man to carry the ball forward a yard or two in some special situation. But at least this comment can be made without qualification: Of the men who have risen to supreme heights in the fighting establishment of the United States, and have had their greatness proclaimed by their fellow countrymen, there is not one career which provides any warrant for the conclusion that there is a special shortcut known only to the smart operators. True enough, a few men have gained fairly high rank by dint of what the late Mr. Justice Holmes called "the instinct for the jugular"--a feeling for when to jump, where to press and how to slash in order to achieve somewhat predatory personal ends. That will occasionally happen in any walk of life. But from Washington, Wayne, and Jones down to Eisenhower, Vandegrift, and Nimitz, the men best loved by the American people for their military successes were also men with greatness of soul. In short, they were idealists, though they likely would have disclaimed that label, since it somehow connotes the visionary rather than the intensely practical man.

But it isn't necessary to look at the upper brackets of history to find the object lesson. The things that any man remembers about his own father with love and reverence have to do with his forbearance, his charity toward other men, his strength and rightness of will and his readiness to contribute of his force to the good of other people. Or if not his father, then it may be an uncle, a neighbor or one of his schoolmasters.

In one way, however, it illuminates but half the subject to reflect that a man has to find purpose in himself before he can seek purpose in any of the undertakings of which he is a part or in the society of which he is a member. No man is wholly sufficient unto himself even though he has been schooled from infancy to live according to principles. His character and the moral strength from which he gains peace of mind need constantly to be replenished by the force of other individuals who think and act more or less in tune with him. His ability to remain whole, and to bound back from any depression of the spirit, depends in some measure on the chance that they will be upgrading when he is on the downswing. To read what the wisest of the philosophers have written about the formation of human character is always a stimulating experience; but it is better yet to live next to the man who already possesses what the philosophers are talking about. During World War II, there were quite a few higher commanders relieved in our forces because it was judged, for one reason or another, that they had failed in battle. Of the total number, there were a few who took a reduction in rank, went willingly to a lower post in a fighting command, uttered no complaint, kept their chins up, worked courageously and sympathetically with their commands, and provided an example of manhood that all who saw them will never forget. Though their names need not be mentioned, they were imprinted with the real virtue of the services even more deeply than many of their colleagues who had no blemishes on their records. Their character had met the ultimate test. The men who had the privilege of working close to them realized this and the sublime effect of this personal influence helped strengthen the resolve of many others.

Because there is so much at stake in the matter, the services cannot depend solely upon such influence as would be exerted on their affairs by the occasional idealist, but must work for that chain reaction which comes of making the inculcation of military ideals one of the cardinal points of a strong, uniting inner doctrine. It is altogether necessary that as a body, the power of their thought be shaped along ideal lines. The ideal object must be held high at all times, even though it is recognized that men are not perfect, and that no matter how greatly they may aspire, they will occasionally fail. Nor is the effort to lead other men to believe in the transcendent importance of goodwill made less effective because the leader has a conscience about his own weakness, *provided he has the good sense not to flaunt it*. He need not be a paragon of all the virtues to set an example which will convince other men that his ideas are worth following. No man alive possesses perfect virtue, which fact is generally understood. Many an otherwise ideal commander is ruthless in his exactions upon his staff; many a petty officer, who has won the absolute love of all men with whom he served, has found himself in the middle because he couldn't think straight about his debts. But these things do not lessen the impact upon men of thinking together about common ideals and working together toward the fulfillment of some high obligation. The pursuit of ideals culminates in the experience of mutual growth. If that were not so, men who have served the arms of the United States would not continue to have a special respect for the uniform, and an extra reverence for the flag, for years after they have passed from the service. These emotions are not the consequence of habit, but come of having known the comradeship of other men whom they loved and respected, who shared these same thoughts, and believed in the same body of ideals.

Any normal man loves his country and it is natural in him to regard highly the symbols through which this affection is expressed. An American child of kindergarten age already feels an emotional attachment for the national emblem. The recruit who has just entered upon service can begin to understand that his regard for his uniform must be a far different thing than what he felt about his civilian dress, since it is identified with the dignity of the Nation. His training in military ideals starts at this point, and for the main part is carried forward subtly, by transfer of this same feeling to all other objects associated with his military life. His perseverance in the care of weapons, in keeping his living quarters orderly and in doing his full share of work is best insured, not through fear of punishments, but by stimulating his belief that any other way of going is unworthy of a member of a fighting service.

Precision in personal habits, precision in drill and precision in daily living are the high road to that kind of discipline which best insures cool and collected thought and unity of action on the field of battle. When men, working together, successfully attain to a high standard of orderliness, deportment and response, each to the other, they develop the cohesive strength which will carry them through any great crisis. For this reason mainly, military life is far more exacting than civil life. But the services hold that what is best for the many can be achieved without cramping the personal life or blighting individuality and initiative. Within the frame of our system, we can achieve obedience and discipline without destroying independence and impulse.

This is idealism, though we seldom think about it in that light. Further, it is all the better that in the beginning these impressions are developed obliquely, rather than through the direct approach of reading a lecture on ideals and ethics, since it means that the man is assisted to reach certain conclusions by himself, and as Kant has said, those things which a man learns pretty much on his own become the ideas that he is least likely to forget.

Looking at this subject in its largest aspect, it should be perfectly clear that any institution must know what its ideals are before it can become coherent and confident, and that there must be present in the form of clearly available ideas an imaginative conception of the good at which the institution aims.

This is fully recognized in the American armed establishment. For many years, the program of indoctrinating military ideals has been inseparably linked with instruction in democratic ideals, teaching as to the American way of life and clear statement of the policies and purposes of the Government of the United States in its relations with all others powers and peoples.

Moreover, it is an accepted principle in all services that this mission can not be carried forward competently except by those officers who are directly in charge of forces. It is not a job for chaplains or orientation specialists, because it cannot flourish unless it is in the hands of those leaders whom men know well and in whom they place their confidence. When men are well led, they become fully receptive to the whole body of ideas which their leaders see fit to put before them.

There are two points which follow, as a matter of course.

An officer's ability to talk effectively on these or other subjects to his men can be no better than his information, irrespective of his zeal or of his own firm belief in the ideals of his country and service.

All other things being equal, his effectiveness will depend on the extent to which he participates in all of the other affairs of organization. If he is remote from the spirit of his own unit, and indifferent to the varying activities which enter into the building of that spirit, he will not have a sympathetic audience when he talks to men about the grand objectives of organization. There is something terribly incongruous about a man talking to troops on the ideal purposes of the military service if all they see of him convinces them that he is loyal only to his own rank and his pay check. It can be said without any qualification that when an officer's interest in the unit is limited strictly to those things which *have to be done* in line of duty, even though he attends to them truly and well, he will never have a strong hold on the sympathy and imagination of his men. When he takes an enthusiastic part in the sports program of the ship, the company, the squadron or the battalion, even though he has no natural talent for sport, when he voluntarily helps in furthering all activities within the unit which are designed to make leisure more enjoyable, and when he is seen by his men attending religious exercises, his magnetism is increased. It was noteworthy during World War II that church attendance among enlisted personnel took a tremendous bound forward when it was seen that their officers were present at church services. This provided tremendous support to those chaplains who were intent not only on praising the Lord but on passing moral ammunition to all ranks so that they would be better prepared for the ordeal ahead.

Recognizing that instruction in the duties of citizenship, and providing information which will enable Americans to have a better understanding of their national affairs, is part of the arch of morale and of a strong uniting comradeship, the Armed Services nevertheless hold that the *keystone of the arch, among fighting forces, is the inculcation of military ideals and the stimulation of principles of military action.* Unless orientation within the services is balanced in this direction, the military spirit of all ranks will suffer, and the forces will deteriorate into an assembly of Americans who, whatever their enthusiasms for the nation, will lack an organized capacity to serve it efficiently along the main line of resistance.

To round out any discussion of how military ideals are formed, much more needs to be said about the nature of courage on the battle-field and, in preparation for it, about the winning and meaning of loyalty within the Armed Services and how instruction on these points and all related matters is best advanced within the organization.

But the object of this chapter is to define certain governing principles. The substantive parts of the subject can be more clearly presented further along in the book.

CHAPTER THREE

RESPONSIBILITY AND PRIVILEGE

There is a common saying in the services, and elsewhere, that greater privileges grow out of larger responsibilities, and that the latter justifies the former. This is part truth and part fable.

In military organization, as in industry, business, and political life, the more important a man's position, the more lavish he is likely to be in his office appointments and living arrangements, and the greater the care that is apt to be taken in freeing him of trifling annoyances.

But that is only partly because of the need for him to conserve his time and energy. When men are successful, they like the good things of life. Why deny it? Not one individual in 10,000 would aspire to power and authority if it meant living like a hermit.

There is no way that the military establishment can denature human nature, and change this determining condition. Nor is there any reason why it should wish to do so. Its men, like all others, develop a sense of well-being from those advantages, many of them minor, which attend, and build prestige, both in private and in official life. The incentive system by which our country has prospered has always recognized that privilege is a reward for effort and enterprise. The American people have always accepted that reasonable, harmless privileges should attend merit. It is by enhancing the prestige of leaders and by making their positions attractive that the Armed Forces get better officers and men.

One of the keenest-minded Americans of our time has said: "Responsibilities are what devolve upon a person, and privileges are what he ought not to have, but takes." In a perfect universe, that would be a perfect truth. But men being as they are, prideful and desirous of any mark of recognition, privileges are the natural accompaniment of rank and station, and when not wilfully misused, may contribute to the general welfare. At all levels, men will aspire more, and their ambition will be firmer, if getting ahead will mean for them an increase in the visible tokens of deference from the majority, rather than simply a boost in the paycheck. To complain about this quality in human nature is as futile as regretting that the sun goes down.

However, since it is out of the abuse of privilege that much of the friction between authority and the rank-and-file arises, the subject can't be dropped at that point. What puts most of the grit into the machinery isn't that privileges exist, but that they are exercised too often by persons who are not motivated by a passionate sense of duty. For it is an almost inviolable rule of human behavior that the man who is concerned most of all with his responsibilities will be fretted least about the matter of his privileges, and that his exercise of any rightful privilege will not be resented by his subordinates, because they are conscious of his merit.

We can take two officers. Lieutenant "A" enters the service with one main question in mind: "Where does my duty lie?" So long as he remains on that beam, he will never injure the morale of the service by using such privileges as are rightfully his as an officer. But in the mind of Lieutenant "B" the other idea is uppermost: "What kudos do I get out of my position?" Unless that man changes his ways, he will be a trouble-maker while he remains in the service, a headache to his fellow officers and a despoiler of those who are under him.

In recent years, we have learned a lot about American manpower. We have seen enough of the raw material under testing conditions to know that, with the exception of the occasional malcontent who was irreparably spoiled before he left home, American young men when brought into military organization do not resent rank, and are amenable to authority. Indeed, they expect that higher authority will have certain advantages not common to the rank-and-file, because that is normal in our society in all of its workday relationships.

But they do not like to have their noses rubbed in it by officers who, having no real moral claim on authority, try to exhibit it by pushing other people around. And when that happens, our men get their backs up. And they wouldn't be worth a hoot in hades if they didn't.

Even as privilege attends rank and station, it is confirmed by custom, and modified by time and environment. What was all right yesterday may be all wrong tomorrow, and what is proper in one set of circumstances may be wholly wrong in another.

Take one example. In Washington's Continental Army, a first lieutenant was court-martialed and jailed because he demeaned himself by doing manual labor with a working detail of his men. Yet in that same season, Major General von Steuben, then trainer and inspector of all the forces, created a great scandal and almost terminated his usefulness by trying to rank a relatively junior officer out of his quarters. Today both of these usages seem out of joint. Any officer has the *privilege* of working with his men, if he needs exercise, wishes to see for himself how the thing is done, or feels that an extra hand is needed on the job at a critical moment. As for any notion that his quarters are his permanent castle no matter who comes, he had best not make an issue of the point!

But to emphasize it once again, duty is the great regulator of the proper exercise of one's rights. Here we speak of duty as it was meant by Giuseppe Mazzini, Italy's great patriot of the early Nineteenth Century, when he said: "Every mission constitutes a pledge of duty. Every man is bound to consecrate his every effort to its fulfillment. He will derive his rule of action from the profound conviction of that duty." For finally the key lies in this, that out of high regard for duty comes as a natural flow that sense of proportion which we call common sense.

Adjustment and dignity in any situation are impossible when minds are bent only on a code of conduct rather than on action which is consistent with the far objectives. In the early stages of World War II, it was not unusual to see a junior officer walking on the public sidewalk, hands free, and looking important, while his wife tagged along, trying to keep step, though laden like a pack mule. This was because someone had told him that it was not in keeping with an officer's dignity to be seen heavily burdened. In the nature of things, anyone so lacking in gallantry as that would stimulate very little respect for the officer corps.

Actually, in these times, there are relatively few special privileges which attend officership, and though the war brought perhaps a few excesses, the post war trend has been in the other direction.

Normally, an officer is not expected to buck a chow line, or any other queue in line of duty, if he is sensibly in a rush. The presumption is that his time is more valuable to the service than that of an enlisted man. Normally, an officer is not expected to pitch a tent or spend his energy on any hand labor incidental to housekeeping. Normally, he has greater freedom of action and is less bound by minor restrictions than the ranks.

But the accent in these things is decidedly on the word *normally*. If a mess line were in an area under general fire, so that added waiting meant extra danger, then only a poltroon would insist on being fed first. And while an officer wouldn't be expected to pitch a tent, he would dig his own foxhole, unless he was well up in grade. At that, there were a few high commanders in World War II who made it a point of pride to do their own digging from first to last. Greater "freedom of action," too, can go out the window, for conditions arise, particularly in war, when freedom of action can not be permitted anyone except the very top authority. When a general restriction is clamped down, the officer caught violating it is in more serious jeopardy than the enlisted offender.

As the entire body of this book is directed toward the consideration of the fundamental responsibilities in officership, the special comments in this chapter will relate mainly to propositions not stated elsewhere.

Though it has been said before, even so, it can be said again: It is a paramount and overriding responsibility of every officer to take care of his men before caring for himself. From the frequent and gross violation of this principle by badly informed or meanly selfish individuals comes more embarrassment to officer-man relationships than perhaps from all other causes put together. *It is a cardinal principle!* Yet many junior officers do not seem to understand that steadfast fidelity to it is required, not lip service. "And of this," as Admiral Mahan would say, "comes much evil." The loyalty of men simply cannot be commanded when they become embittered by selfish action.

Then how deeply does this rule cut? In line of duty, it applies right down to the hilt! When a command is worn, bruised, and hungry, officers attend to their men's creature comforts and make sure that all is going well, before looking to their own needs. If an officer is on a tour with an enlisted man, he takes care that the man is accommodated as to food, shelter, medical treatment or other prime needs, before satisfying his own wants; if that means that the last meal or the last bed is gone, his duty is to get along the hard way. If a command is so located that recreational facilities are extremely limited, and there are not enough to go around, the welfare of the ranks takes priority over the interests of their commissioned leaders; in fact, it would be more correct to say that the welfare of men *is* the prior interest of the officer.

These few concrete illustrations show, in general, what is expected. Once the main idea is grasped, the way of its total application becomes clear. Officers do not go around playing pigtail to enlisted men. But they build loyalty by serving the men first, when all concerned are following a general line of duty together.

It is an incumbent responsibility on all officers to maintain the dignity of the uniform and prevent anyone from sullying it. This means not only the dress of person, but the uniform wherever it is worn publicly by any man of the United States forces. Where the offense is committed by a member of some other service and the disgrace to the uniform is obvious, it is the duty of the officer to intervene, or to bring about intervention, rather than to walk out on the situation. This calls for judgment, tact, nerve. The offense must be real, and not simply an offense against one's private sensibilities. But indecencies, exhibitionism and bawdiness of such a nature that if done on a reservation would warrant trial of the individual for unbecoming conduct will justify intervention by the officer under public circumstances.

Similarly, any officer has a responsibility to any enlisted man who is in personal distress, with no other means of ready help. Suppose they just happen to meet in a strange community. The enlisted man's credentials are shown to be *bona fide*. But he has had his pocket picked, or has lost his wallet, or has just missed the train that would have carried him back from his leave on time, and he doesn't know what to do. For any officer to brush-off a forthright request for aid or advice under such circumstances is an unofficerly act. Likewise, if one suspects, just from appearances, that the man is in trouble and somewhat beyond his depths, it will be found that, far from resenting a kindly inquiry, he will mark it to the credit of the whole fighting system.

To say that an officer owes a fellow officer no less consideration than this is to state the obvious. Officers meeting in transit usually get into conversation; it is a habit that adds much to one's professional education. When an officer is getting into a strange town, or arriving at a new post, anything done by a fellow officer to help him get oriented, or to make things friendly and easy for him, furthers the comity of the corps. Between officers of differing services these small courtesies are particularly appreciated. Nor does the matter end there. Within Unit A, the officers have the responsibility of continuing support to the officers of Unit C, Unit B, and so on. Though they are in a sense competing, each trying to build higher than the other, they must never forget that the basic technique of organization is cooperation. What "A" knows that has helped his unit, or whatever he can do to assist "B" and "C" without materially depriving himself, it becomes his official and moral obligation to transmit. An officer can never understand his own command problem very well unless he knows, at least a little, of how things are going in other units. And the statement can be reversed. He cannot judge the problems of other people unless he tries passionately to understand his own people.

There are many other minor articles within what is sometimes called the "unwritten code" which help to regulate life in the services, and to sweeten it.

But what counts most is not the knowing of the rule but the sharing of the spirit which gives it meaning and makes its proper administration possible.

CHAPTER FOUR

PLANNING YOUR CAREER

The main purpose of this book is to stimulate thought and to encourage the average young officer to seek truth for, and in, himself. It is never a good idea to attempt a precise formula about matters which are by nature indefinite and subject to all number of variable factors.

Thus with respect to career planning, despite all of the emphasis put upon that subject in modern America, it would be plain error to infer that any man can become all-wise, as to the direction which he should take with his own life, simply by steeping himself in all of the information which is to be had on this subject.

That might qualify him to give top-lofty advice to all others on how to make the start up the right ladder, and he would win a reputation as a personnel expert, which in itself is no mean assignment. But in all probability, he would still be doing better by himself than by any other individual.

American library shelves are stacked with such books as "Planning Your Future," "New Careers for Youth," and "The Problem of Vocational Guidance." The pages are laden with sage counsel and bromidic expressions. But their chief public value is that they enabled a writer, his publisher and the bookseller to get a little further ahead in life.

Reflecting the trend elsewhere in the national life, the Armed Services are equipped to give their forces the advantage of career management principles, and to assist their men to plan their professional careers. The opportunities and the job qualifications can be described. Also, somewhat more thoroughly than is done in civil life, the establishment's system of record-keeping throws a partial light on the aptitudes of the individual. The qualified man is soon known by his "spec number" or maybe two numbers. It might seem therefore that things are so well-regulated that the prospect of every man finding his niche is better than even.

The fact remains that the majority of individuals spend the greater part of their lives doing something other than that which would bring out their best quality and give them the greatest satisfaction, mainly because accident, in one form or another, put them into a particular channel, and inertia kept them there.

A boy builds model airplanes. His hobby being a force in his youthful years, he becomes a pilot, and then discovers to his shocked amazement that he does not have his heart in machines but in the management of men. A man who has lived his life among guns, and who enjoys the feel and the working of them, enters the service and permits himself to be made a food procurement specialist, having run that kind of business in civil life only because he had inherited it from his father. An officer assigned to a weapons detail finds it hard going. And the fact that he takes a delight in writing a good paper still does not signal to him that this is his main field and he should exploit it to the fullest!

To what do these things point? In particular, to this, that despite all of the help which may be provided by outside agencies, finding the straight thoroughfare in work is mainly a problem of searching self-examination and personal decision. The impression which any other person may have of our talents and possibilities is largely formed by what we say, think and feel about ourselves.

This does not require that constant introspection which is found in Cecil Forester's nervous hero, "Captain Horatio Hornblower." That man doubtless would have died of stomach ulcers before winning his second stripe. It is not a matter of, "How do I look to someone else?" but of, "What do I know about myself?" The kind of work which one likes best and does with the greatest facility, the avocational study which is pursued because it provides greater delight than an encharged responsibility, the talent which one had as a youth but was dropped because of the press of making a living, the task which looks alluring though one has lacked either the chance, or the courage, to try a hand at it--these are among the more fertile points of inquiry.

Weighing it out, the service officer has an unrivaled opportunity for fruitful experiment.

In the first place, he has made the fundamental decision to serve his country in the profession of arms. The meaning of that decision should not be lost on him. It is by nature patriotic. But if he regards his inheritance simply as a snug berth and the best way to provide "three squares" to himself and family throughout a lifetime, he is neither soundly patriotic nor intelligently selfish.

After signing on the line for his country, the individual's duty to himself is to strive by every honorable means to move ahead of his competition by growing more knowledgeable and better qualified. *It is the inherent right of every officer to request such service as he believes will further his advancement,* and far from discouraging the ambitious man, higher authority will invariably try to favor him. In no other mode of life are older men so ready to encourage the willing junior.

Gen. H. H. Arnold, the great air leader of World War II, is an inspiring case study with respect to several of these points. He wrote in "Global Mission" how he considered quitting the Army in disgust upon being commissioned in infantry, following graduation, so deeply was his heart set upon service in cavalry. But something held him to the assignment. Some years later he tried to transfer to ordnance because the prospect for advancement looked better. While still ruminating on this change, he was offered a detail to the newly forming aviation section of the signal corps, and took it, not because he had a clear vision of the future, but because it looked like a chance to get ahead. Thus, almost inadvertently, he met the opportunity of which came his world fame.

This emphasizes another peculiar advantage belonging to the young officer who is trying to orient himself toward the line of greatest opportunity. In civil life, the man who flits from job to job is soon regarded as a drifter and unstable. In the military establishment an ability to adjust from job to job and to achieve greater all-around qualification by making a successful record in a diversified experience becomes a major asset in a career. Generalship, in its real sense, requires a wider knowledge of human affairs, supported by specialized knowledge of professional techniques, than any other great responsibility. Those who get to the top have to be many-sided men, with skill in the control and guidance of a multifarious variety of activities. Therefore even the young specialist, who has his eyes on a narrow track because his talents seem to lie in that direction, is well advised to raise his sights and extend his interest to the far horizons of the profession, even while directing the greater part of his force to a particular field.

After all, variety is the spice of life, as well as a high road toward perfection. Of Princeton's 1932 class, 161, or 59 percent, were in the armed services during World War II. Questioned after the war 70 percent of the total number replied that military service was interesting, broadening, and profitable. But the main point was that they said in overwhelming number that its great lure was that *they were doing something new.* They liked it because it gave them a legitimate excuse to quit their jobs and attempt something different. In the services, a man may give vent to this natural desire without impairing his record, and if he is young and not at all certain what is his favorite dish, the more he broadens his experience, the more likely it becomes that he will sharpen his view of his own capabilities.

The possible hard consequence of looking at service opportunity through any one lens is epitomized in one paragraph of a reclassification proceedings on an officer relieved during World War II while serving as assistant division commander:

"Through no fault of his own, General Blank has never served with   troops since he was a captain during World War I. He has been unable to keep pace with the problems of a commander on the   battlefield of today. He is unqualified for command of troops due   to lack of practical experience."

It is hard to imagine a more dismal ending for a career than that of the man who aspires to rank, without having any honest concept of its proportionate moral responsibilities, particularly when the lives of others are at stake.

So when we say that "career planning" is a springboard to personal success within the military establishment, it is not with the narrow meaning that any officer should proceed to limit his field of interest, decide quickly and arbitrarily where he will put his plow and run his furrow, and then sit down and plot a schedule of how he proposes to mount the success ladder rung by rung. That might suit a plumber, or tickle the fancy of an interior decorator, but it will not conserve the strength of the officer corps. Its consequence would be to stereotype the thinking faculties of a professional whose inner power flows from the questing imagination, eager curiosity and versatility of its individuals. Intense specialization, to the exclusion of all peripheral areas of knowledge, warps the mind and limits the useful action and influence of its owner. Dr. Vannevar Bush was a greater scientist on the day he made his decision to explore the sphere of military knowledge, and greater still when he applied himself to literature.

There are few men of great talent who initially have an unswerving inner conviction that they possess the final answer, as to themselves. They may feel reasonably sure about what they would like to do, though still reserving an honest doubt about the validity of their instincts and of their power to compete. Even long and successful experience does not always allay this doubt. Said Washington, on being appointed

31

Commander-in-Chief: "I beg it may be remembered by every man in this room that I this day declare with the utmost sincerity, I do not think myself equal to the command I am honored with." Assurance, or by its other name, self-confidence, is only a continuing willingness to keep coming back and trying, without fear of coming a cropper, but with a care to the constant strengthening of one's own resources. The motto of Admiral Robert E. Peary: "I will find a way or make one," is not over-bold; any officer can afford to paste the words inside his own hat. But in the hard game with which Peary's fame is forever linked, there were countless errors, an occasional hit, and at last a run.

The health and progressive spirit of the services come of the many-sided officer who can make not one career for himself but three or four. Had officers from all services been unwilling to go into the industrial workshops and scientific laboratories of the Nation to try their hands at wholly new lines of work, had successful cavalrymen been unable to evolve as leaders of armored forces, had ship captains and ensigns disdained taking to the air, had foot soldiers refused the risks of parachuting and naval officers not participated as observers with the infantry line to further SFC (ship fire control) we would have run out of wind before winning World War II.

Some months after the war ended, the Secretary of the Navy, recognizing the dilemma which confronted thousands of men who were asking whether the wave of the future would be to the specialist or to the all-around man, sent a message which applied not less to the officers of every service:

It is intended that the highest posts will be filled by officers   of the highest attainments, regardless of specialty. Be assured,   whatever may be your field of endeavor, that your future as an   officer rests, as it always has, in your hands. The outstanding   officer will continue to be he who attacks with all of his energy   and enthusiasm the tasks to which he is assigned and who grows in   stature and understanding with his years and with his experience.   Responsibility comes to him who seeks responsibility. It is this   officer, regardless of his field of effort, who will be called to   high command.

There is not a chief of service who would shade the general tone of this paragraph if asked to put before his own officers the one rule which, most closely followed, would most surely bring success. Nothing need be added to it and nothing should be taken away; it states the case.

At the same time, and as the message itself implies, specialization, like sex and the automobile, is here to stay. In the service, perforce, even the balanced, all-around man has his specialty. In the beginning, true enough, he may aspire only to being a soldier, marine, sailor or airman. That is good enough in the cocoon stage. But ultimately he emerges with the definite coloring of a ground fighter, a gunner, an engineer officer, a signals man, a submariner, a weapons man, a navigator, an observer, a transport officer or something else. If his tact, bearing and quick pick-up suggest to his superiors that he may be good staff material, and he takes that route, there are again branch lines, leading out in roughly parallel directions, and embracing activities in the fields of personnel, intelligence, operations, supply and military government. And each one of these main stems has smaller branches, greatly diversified. The man with a love for logistics (and few have it) might some day find himself running railroads or managing a port. The engineer could become a salvage officer working a crew of deep sea divers, or as easily a demolitions expert running a company of dynamiters. The expert in communications? His next task might be setting up a radio station near the North Pole or helping perfect radio control of troops over a 50-mile area.

It is in these things that the privilege of free choice arises, for despite the popular theory that in the services you take what you are given and like it, the placement of officers according to their main aptitudes and desires is a controlling principle of personnel policy. It is recognized throughout the military establishment that, in general, men will do their best service in that field where they think their natural talents are being most usefully employed.

Among the combat line commanders in World War II there were doctors, dentists and even a few ministers. They could have had places in their regular corps, but they were permitted to continue with the duty of their own choice.

Concerning the main problem of the officer, in fitting himself for higher command, the controlling principle is well expressed in the words of a distinguished educator, Wallace B. Donham: "The hope of the wisdom essential to the general direction of men's affairs lies not so much in wealth of specialized knowledge as in the habits and skills required to handle problems involving very diverse viewpoints which must be related to new concrete situations. Wisdom is based on broad understanding in perspective. It is common sense on a large canvas. It is never the product of scientific, technological, or other specializations, though men so trained may, of course, acquire it."

This puts just the right light on the subject. The military officer specializes strictly to qualify himself more highly in his main calling-- the management of men in the practice of arms. Becoming a specialist does not *ipso facto* make him a better officer, or win him preferment. It is part of the mechanism, though not the main wheel. As Admiral Forrest P. Sherman has so well said: "We are not pushed willy-nilly into special- ization; there is never an excess of the all-around, highly competent combat officer."

Concerning his choice, all general advice is gratuitous. Whatever might be written here would be worth far less than the counsel or sugges- tion of any superior, or for that matter, a colleague, who has observed his work closely over a long period, who has some critical faculty, and whose good will is beyond question.

Particularly, the *voluntary* advice of such a person is worth notice. That which is spontaneous usually has shrewd reason behind it. When counsel is deliberately sought, it may catch the consultant unaware, and in lieu of saying that which is well-considered, he may offer a half-baked opinion, rather than be disappointing. But when another person having one's trust, says: "Your natural line is to do thus-and-so," it is time to ask him why, and check his reasoning with one's own. Worth just as much earnest consideration is his negative opinion, his strong feeling that what one is about to undertake is not particularly suitable.

As for the man himself, it remains to survey thoughtfully the whole range of possibilities, to keep the mind open and receptive to impressions, to experiment but take firm hold in so doing, to tackle each new task with as much enthusiasm as if it were to be his life work, to ask for difficult assignments rather than soft snaps and to be calmly deliber- ate, rather than rashly hasteful, in appraising his own capabilities.

Self-study is a lifetime job. A great many engineers didn't realize that they were born to make nuclear fission possible until there was a three-way wedding between science, industry and the military in 1940. Many officers who have had a late blooming as experts in the field of electronics and supersonic speeds had lived out successful careers before these subjects first saw daylight.

As Elbert Hubbard said of it, the only way to get away from opportunity is to lie down and die.

CHAPTER FIVE

RANK AND PRECEDENCE

The regulations that govern precedence among officers of the same service and among the services in relation to each other have a very real utility not only in determining succession to command and as reminders of the authority to which all persons in the Armed Services are subject but in providing precedent for all official or ceremonial occasions in which officers or organizations of the several services may find themselves cooperating. It is easy to imagine the confusion that would result without such rules, especially if a junior commander of a senior service had to defend the right of his organization to occupy the place of honor ahead of a very senior commander with a detachment from a junior service. These regulations are also the arbiter in disputes arising between officers of equal rank who aspire to command of the same unit.

The legislation which separated the Air Force from the Army again raised the question of precedence in parades and ceremonies. Since the Air Force is the junior service, as to date of recognition, the change indicated the following parade order: (Reference, *Federal Register*, Volume 14, Number 160, August 19, 1949, page 5203)

1. Cadets, United States Military Academy.
2. Midshipmen, United States Naval Academy.
3. Cadets, United States Coast Guard Academy.
4. United States Army.
5. United States Marines.
6. United States Navy.
7. United States Air Force.
8. United States Coast Guard.
9. National Guard of the United States.
10. Organized Reserve Corps of the Army.
11. Marine Corps Reserve.
12. Naval Reserve.
13. Air Force National Guard of the United States.
14. United States Air Force Reserve.
15. Coast Guard Reserve.

16. Other training organizations of the Army, Marine Corps, Navy, Air Force, and Coast Guard, in that order, respectively.

During any period when the United States Coast Guard shall operate as a part of the United States Navy, the Cadets, United States Coast Guard Academy, the United States Coast Guard, and the Coast Guard Reserve, shall take precedence, respectively, next after the Midshipmen, United States Naval Academy, the United States Navy, and the Naval Reserve.

In any ceremony in which any or all of these components act together, the table of precedence in appropriate regulations determines their location in the column.

The ranks and insignia in the Armed Services have been substantially the same since 1883. During World War II there were newly established the five star ranks of general of the army and fleet admiral. After the first World War the rank of general-of-the-armies was created to honor General Pershing, who was permitted to choose the number of stars he would wear. He chose four. After the Spanish-American War the rank of admiral-of-the-navy was established for Admiral Dewey. No one has held this rank since.

On November 15, 1776, Congress established the ranks of admiral, vice-admiral, rear admiral and commodore corresponding to general, lieutenant general, major general, and brigadier general. It also established three grades of naval captains--captain of a 40-gun ship and upward to rank with colonel, captain of a 20 to 40-gun ship to rank with lieutenant colonel, captain of a 10 to 20-gun ship to rank with major, and lieutenant to rank with captain in the Army.

Although the top naval ranks were provided, the only two officers ever to attain a higher rank than captain prior to 1862 were Ezekiel Hopkins, whom Congress on December 22, 1775, commissioned with the rank of *C-in-C of the Fleet*, and Charles Stewart who was commissioned *Senior Flag Officer* by Congress in 1859. Hopkins and Stewart were called "commodore" as was any other captain who commanded more than one ship.

During our War of Independence, the Army had the rank of ensign and the Navy did not. The several Army ranks were then distinguishable by the color of the cockade, green for lieutenant, buff for captain, and pink or red for a field officer. As early as 1780 major generals wore two stars on their epaulettes and brigadier generals one. During our quasi-war with France, toward the end of the eighteenth century, Washington was commissioned lieutenant general, our first, and three stars were prescribed to be worn by him.

In the Army Register for 1813 the rank of ensign had disappeared but there were third lieutenants (as in the Soviet Army today) and coronets. In 1832 the eagle was adopted as the insignia of colonel in the Army and in 1857 the lieutenant colonel, captain, and first lieutenant wore the same insignia as today. These insignia were adopted some time in the interval between 1847 and 1857. The gold bar, insigne[1] of the second lieutenant, was authorized just prior to World War I.

The Navy has used the same shoulder insignia as the Army since the Civil War. However, shoulder insignia on blues were discontinued by the Navy in 1911 but the insignia were still prescribed on epaulettes. The Navy adopted the eagle for captain in 1852, twenty years after it had been approved by the Army for colonels.

In the first half of the last century the Navy List contained officers of four grades only. A captain wore three stripes, a master commandant, two (master commandant, established in 1806, was changed to commander in 1837;) and a lieutenant, one. A master had no stripe but three buttons instead. There were midshipmen too, but they were warrant officers and *aspirants* for commissioned rank as the present French term designates them.

Our first full general was U. S. Grant and our first full admiral, David D. Porter; both won their rank in the Civil War. In that war there was a large increase in the Navy and more naval ranks were established. In 1862 ensign was provided in the Navy to correspond to second lieutenant; and the term lieutenant commanding became lieutenant commander. An ensign wore one stripe as now; an additional stripe was added for each rank till the rear admiral had eight. Since 1869 the senior officers have worn the same stripes as now prescribed. In 1883 the rank "master" was changed to lieutenant, junior grade.

The rank of commodore, which had been abolished, was temporarily revived during World War II. The rank of passed-midshipman was abolished about 1910; thereafter graduates of the Naval Academy were commissioned ensign. The rank of ensign had previously been attained

---

1. The Oxford English Dictionary lists "insigne" as an obsolete form of "ensign."

by passed-midshipmen after 2 years at sea and a successful examination at the end of that cruise. The only permanent change in recent years was the addition of aviation cadet to both the Air Force and Navy listings. The warrant rank of flight officer in the Air Force, which was created during the war, has now been abandoned, all the flight officers then holding warrants either being commissioned second lieutenants or separated. The naval rank of commodore was likewise dropped, and brigadier generals of the Army and Air Force now rank with admirals of the lower half.

The following are the present corresponding ranks in the Armed Services:

NAVY	MARINE CORPS	ARMY	AIR FORCE	COAST GUARD
Fleet Admiral		General of the Army	General of the Air Force	
Admiral	General	General	General	Admiral
Vice Admiral	Lieutenant General	Lieutenant General	Lieutenant General	Vice Admiral
Rear Admiral (upper half)	Major General	Major General	Major General	Rear Admiral (upper half)
Rear Admiral (lower half) and Commodore	Brigadier General	Brigadier General	Brigadier General	Rear Admiral (lower half) and Commodore
Captain	Colonel	Colonel	Colonel	Captain
Commander	Lieutenant Colonel	Lieutenant Colonel	Lieutenant Colonel	Commander
Lieutenant Commander	Major	Major	Major	Lieutenant Commander
Lieutenant	Captain	Captain	Captain	Lieutenant
Lieutenant (Junior Grade)	First Lieutenant	First Lieutenant	First Lieutenant	Lieutenant (Junior Grade)
Ensign	Second Lieutenant	Second Lieutenant	Second Lieutenant	Ensign
Commissioned Warrant Officer	Commissioned Warrant Officer	Chief Warrant Officer	Chief Warrant Officer	Commissioned Warrant Officer
Midshipman				Cadet
Warrant Officer	Warrant Officer	Warrant Officer Junior Grade	Warrant Officer Junior Grade	Warrant Officer

NAVY	MARINE CORPS	ARMY	AIR FORCE	COAST GUARD
Aviation Cadet			Aviation Cadet	

Officers of all the fighting service, whether regular or reserve, take precedence among themselves according to their dates of rank. Officers take command in their respective services in accordance with their dates of rank in the line, the senior, unless otherwise ordered, taking command, whether regular or reserve. The command of a task force or group composed of commands from two or more services devolves upon the senior commanding officer present in the force or group unless otherwise designated by the appropriate common senior, acting for the President.

The obvious exceptions to this are that officers outside the line (that is, commissioned in specialized branches or corps) cannot command line organizations. They may, however, in the Army and Air Force, command organizations within the structure of their own corps. Non-rated officers in the Air Force and Navy are not eligible to command tactical flying units. As a specialized case of command, the assigned first pilot and airplane commander of any aircraft continues in command even though a pilot senior in rank may be aboard.

Retired officers of the Army rank at the foot of active officers of the same grade; those of the Navy according to date of rank.

Changing personnel policies have been reflected by frequent revisions of the scale and grade given noncommissioned leadership. This subject should therefore be checked against current regulations. But as a rough guide, the following can be taken as the corresponding noncommissioned grades and rates in the services:

PAY GRADE	NAVY AND COAST GUARD	ARMY	AIR FORCE	MARINE CORPS
E-7	Chief Petty Officer	Master Sergeant	Master Sergeant	Master Sergeant
E-6	Petty Officer First Class	Sergeant First Class	Technical Sergeant	Technical Sergeant
E-5	Petty Officer Second Class	Sergeant	Staff Sergeant	Staff Sergeant
E-4	Petty Officer Third Class	Corporal	Sergeant	Sergeant
E-3	[A] Airman [A] Construction-man [A] Dentalman Fireman Hospitalman Seaman Stewardsman	Private First Classs	Corporal	Corporal
E-2	Apprentice	Priivate	Private First Class	Private First Class
E-1	Recruit	Recruit	Recruit	Recruit

[A] Does not apply to Coast Guard.

Enlisted insignia of rank are of cloth, sewn on the sleeve of the outer garment. Army chevrons are worn on both sleeves with the point up, and special devices may be incorporated within the chevron to indicate specialties. Chevrons for combat soldiers are blue on a gold background, and all others are gold on a blue background. Naval chevrons are worn point down. Air Force chevrons have no point, but are a compound reverse curve with the deepest part of the curve worn down; over this is imposed a star within a circle. Marine Corps chevrons are worn on both sleeves with the point up and are gold on a crimson background for the dress blue uniform, green on a red background for the forest green uniform, green on a khaki background for the khaki uniform, and for combat uniforms the chevrons are stenciled on the sleeves in black ink.

Army and
Marine Corps

Navy and
Coast Guard

Air Force

All military and naval personnel are addressed in official correspondence by their full titles. Off duty in conversations and in unofficial correspondence, officers are addressed as follows:

ARMY, AIR FORCE, MARINE CORPS

All general officers	General
Colonels and Lt. Colonels	Colonel
Majors	Major
Captains	Captain
Lieutenants	Mister or Lieutenant
Lieutenants in Medical Corps	Doctor or Lieutenant
All Chaplains	Chaplain
Army nurses	Nurse
Cadets	
(Official address)	Cadet
(Unofficial address)	Mister
Warrant Officers	Mister
All sergeants	Sergeant
Corporals	Corporal
Privates and Privates, First Class	Private Jones or Jones

When the name is not known, an Army private may be addressed as "Soldier," and in the Marine Corps the term, "Marine," is proper in such a case.

NAVY, COAST GUARD

All Admirals	Admiral
Commodores	Commodore

Captains	Captain
Commanders	Commander
Lieutenant Commanders, lieutenants, ensigns and midshipmen	Mister
All Chaplains	Chaplain
All medical officers (to commander)	Doctor

Except when in the presence of troops, senior officers frequently address juniors as "Smith" or "Jones" but this does not give the junior the privilege of addressing the senior in any other way than his proper title. By the same token, officers of the same grade generally address one another by their first or last names depending on the degree of intimacy. The courtesy and respect for others which govern the conduct of gentlemen are expected to prevail at all times.

Enlisted men are commonly addressed by their last names. Except in cases where the officer has a blood relationship or a preservice friendship with an enlisted man, the occasions on which an enlisted man can properly be called by his first name are extremely rare. Speaking face to face, it is proper to use either the last name, alone, or the title of rank, or the last name and any accepted abbreviation of the title. In calling First Sergeant Brown from among a group, it would be acceptable to call for "Brown" but better still "Sergeant Brown." In the Navy, the common practice in addressing Chief Pharmacists Mate Gale, for instance, would be either "Gale" or "Chief." On formal occasions, as in calling a senior enlisted man front and center at a formation, the full military title would be used: "Chief Bo's'ns Mate Gale and Master Sergeant Brown, front and center." The longer form of address would also be proper in directing a third party to report to Master Sergeant White.

A painstaking observation of the courtesies due to ranks of other services is more than a sign of good manners; it indicates a recognition of the interdependence of the services upon one another. Failure to observe or to recognize the tables of precedence officially agreed upon among the services is both stupid and rude. Any future war will see joint operations on a scale never before achieved, and its success will be dependent in large part upon the cooperation of all ranks in all services. Likewise, in combined operations, the alert officer will take it upon himself to learn and respect the insignia, relative ranks, and customs of his Allies. By exerting himself in the recognition of other ranks, by exacting adherence to the official tables of precedence, he contributes not only to his own stature as a professional soldier, sailor, marine or airman, but adds to the reputation of his service.

In the main requirements, military courtesy varies but little from nation to nation. During service abroad, an American officer will salute the commissioned officers and pay respects to the anthems and colors of friendly nations just as to those of his own country.

CHAPTER SIX

CUSTOMS AND COURTESIES

Mutual respect and courtesy are indispensable elements in military organization. The junior shows deference to the senior; the senior shows consideration for him. The salute is the ancient and universal privilege of fighting men. It is a recognition of a common fellowship in a proud profession. Saluting is an expression of courtesy, alertness, and discipline. The senior is as obliged to return it as the junior is to initiate it. In fact, in the Army particularly, it is not unusual to see the senior salute first. Interservice salutes should be exchanged as punctiliously as between members of a single service, for both services stand to gain or lose by the manner in which this act is performed.

The general rules governing saluting are based on common sense, good manners, and the customs of the times. For instance, soldiers actively engaged in sports are not required to salute, nor is any man leading a horse, since the sudden motion so near the horse's head might make it restive. There will always be occasions when it is inconvenient, impractical, or illogical to render or require the return of a salute. The intent of the regulation is not that it embarrass or demean the individual, but that it serve as a signal of recognition and greeting between members of the military brotherhood. According to regulations, in all services, the salute is initiated by the junior, and at any convenient distance that insures recognition, the least being about six paces. The form of the salute is the same in the Army, Navy and Air Force, and it is given either from the position of attention or at a walk. It is not given indoors except when reporting to another officer in an official capacity. In the Navy, it is customary for the junior initiating a salute to combine it with "Good morning, Sir," as a means of reinforcing its meaning as a greeting. Where this is done in the other two services, it is usually the result of a local directive expressing the wish of a particular commander. While it is expected that the junior will initiate such a greeting, there is no obligation upon him to do so, nor is there any reason that the senior may not say it first.

The Navy and Air Force require that the junior, when engaged in work that brings him in reasonably frequent contact with the same seniors during the course of the working day, salute each senior officer the first time that he is passed during the day, but not subsequently unless a change in circumstances requires it. In the Air Force an enlisted mechanic working on the line would salute the engineering officer and his assistants the first time he recognized them during the day. If he passed one of the same officers later in the day, for example in front of the post exchange, he would salute again. The Army requires that a salute be given and returned each time the junior passes the senior, unless circumstances dictate that it be temporarily suspended by common agreement. The Commanding Officer of a naval vessel is saluted whenever met.

Salutes are not mandatory on the driver of a vehicle, whether moving or idling at the curb, for the reason that the operator is presumed to need both hands for driving. Salutes are not exchanged between moving vehicles, between moving and halted vehicles, or between persons walking and persons riding in official cars except when it is obvious that the passenger is a senior, or when it is required as part of a ceremony. Official vehicles carrying general officers or flag officers will be clearly marked outside, and will be saluted. A salute is exchanged between persons in a parked vehicle and persons walking, unless the car is a bus or taxi. When two boats pass each other, the senior officer in each boat salutes without rising.

Aside from saluting, there are certain other customs that govern conduct around official vehicles. Since the place of honor is on the right, the junior not only walks on the left, but rides there as well. In entering a car, the junior enters first, followed by other members of the party in inverse order of rank, each seating himself so that the senior may take position on the right side. In leaving the car, the senior debarks first. However, if following this general procedure would necessitate any member of the party climbing over another, or in any other way cause an awkward situation, the senior may enter first and alight last.

The same rules govern for boarding and leaving small boats, except that the junior rides forward and the senior aft.

In boarding aircraft with a single hatch, the pilot enters first, followed by the copilot and other members of the crew. With the crew in place, other passengers enter according to rank, the senior first; he takes the seat of his choice if the aircraft is equipped with seats. In either transport or tactical aircraft, the senior officers generally ride as far forward as possible. In leaving the aircraft, the aircrew who handle deplaning normally leave first, followed by passengers in order of seniority.

The long association of the Air Force with the Army precludes any large body of custom and tradition that can be called peculiarly Air Force in origin or usage. In time undoubtedly a considerable body of distinctive official and social courtesies will grow, but at present most of the official and unofficial usages given here for the Army are understood to be applicable to the Air Force as well, and will be so treated.

The hand salute is required on all military installations and in occupied territories, whether on or off duty; in all official greeting in the line of duty both on and off the base; for ceremonial occasions; and in honoring the National Anthem, or color, or distinguished persons.

Since most military posts or bases are guarded on a twenty-four hour basis, the first official contact will be with the guard on the main gate. He may be a soldier or airman selected by roster and under the temporary control of the Officer of the Day, a Military Policeman wearing an MP brassard and under the command of the Provost Marshal, or a civilian guard either under the Provost or some other special staff agency of the Post or Base Commander. On the ordinary post or base, officers of other services will be admitted if wearing uniform, even when accompanied by civilian dependents. If the stay is of short duration, a "visitors" tag on the car may be sufficient; in other cases it may be necessary to secure a temporary pass from the Provost.

Except for civilian guards, who do not salute, and who will be readily identified in their police uniforms, the guard, if armed with a pistol or carbine will give a hand salute. During the hours for challenging (usually extending from a short time before darkness until after reveille the next morning) sentries on an Army post may require any officer to halt, give his rank and name, and advance for recognition. The challenging sentry stands at "raise pistol" or "port arms" until the challenged party has been recognized, after which he simply returns his weapon to the normal carrying position; if armed with a rifle, he executes "present arms" and holds it until the salute is returned.

On any post or base, the adjutant usually acts for the commanding officer in greeting the visitor and directing him to the various facilities of the base, although if the visit is to be of short duration--say, just for the purpose of seeing a friend--it would be impertinent to bother him. But if the visiting officer is reporting for temporary duty, or if he will be living in the immediate vicinity for some time on special detail and desires the use of post facilities, he is required to report to the adjutant.

Most posts and bases have not only a bachelor officers quarters, more popularly known by the abbreviation BOQ, where the visitor may obtain lodging, but also a Hostess House where the officer may stay with his dependents. These accommodations are usually under the supervision of the Billeting Officer, who makes the assignments and charges a nominal fee for the services provided. Other facilities that the visitor may use include the Officer's Club and dining room, the Post Exchange (corresponding to Navy Exchanges), and the post theater. Under certain conditions the visitor may secure permission from the adjutant or executive to make purchases at the Commissary, which deals in foodstuffs and other perishables.

Special dinners are served to the enlisted men on Christmas, Thanksgiving, July 4, New Year's Day and sometimes on February 22. The company commander and lieutenants of the company accompanied by their wives and families and other guests visit the dining room and kitchen just before Christmas dinner is served, often remaining for dinner as guests of the organization. In some companies the soldiers are permitted to invite their wives and other ladies to dinner. In some commands, the post commander accompanied by his staff and some of the ladies of the garrison visit all the dining rooms and kitchens just previous to dinner hour.

A newly arrived officer on a post and the adult members of his family are usually invited to be in the receiving line at the first regimental function after their arrival.

If you arrive at a post at which you expect to remain longer than 24 hours you should check with the post adjutant for rules on calling. The adjutant will also give the normal calling hours in effect at the post or station. You are usually expected to call on the post commander. If assigned to duty there, you would normally call on all of your intermediate commanders at their offices. These calls should be made immediately after the call on the post commander. If unable to wear uniform, an explanation should be made for appearing in civilian clothes.

When it is in keeping with local rules, as verified by the adjutant, you should follow the official visit by a social call on the post and intermediate commanders at their residence within 72 hours after your arrival. If the commander is married and his wife is present on the post, it is customary for you to make the visit accompanied by your wife. These calls should be formal and ordinarily last no longer than fifteen minutes.

You need not make other calls until the officers of the battalion, regiment or garrison have called on you except that as junior officer you should make the first call on field officers of your organization.

It is customary for all officers of a unit or garrison to call upon the commanding officer on New Year's Day. (Again the commanding officer's desire in this matter can be asked of his aide or adjutant.)

The visitor at the average Army and Air Force post will probably see few ceremonies other than retreat. This ceremony, which closes the official day, may be accompanied either by appropriate bugle calls, or by a parade with a military band. In the former case, the music will sound *To the Color*, and in the latter, the *National Anthem*, while the flag is being lowered. Retreat is held daily at a fixed time, usually about 1700 hours. Posts with saluting cannon fire one round at the designated hour. At the first note of either the *National Anthem* or *To the Color*, all dismounted persons face toward the color or flag and render the prescribed salute from attention; the salute is held until the last note of the music has been played. In the event the flag cannot be seen and the location of the flag staff is unknown to the person saluting, he faces toward the sound of the music.

At parades and reviews and on other occasions when uncased colors are carried, all military personnel salute at six paces distance and hold the salute until the color or standard is the same distance past. When personal honors are being rendered to general or flag officers at a review, all military personnel present and not in formation salute during the ruffles, flourishes, and march. When a cannon salute is given, personnel in the immediate vicinity conform to the actions of the person being saluted. No salute is required during the 48 gun salute to the Nation on the Fourth of July.

Military personnel also salute during the passing of a caisson or hearse in a military funeral. If attending the services at the grave side either as mourners or as honorary pallbearers, they stand at attention with the head-dress over the left breast at any time the casket is being moved, and during the service at the grave, including the firing of the volleys and the sounding of *Taps*. In cold or inclement weather, the head-dress is left on and the hand salute is rendered during the movement of the casket, the firing of the volleys, and the sound of *Taps*.

On ships having 180 or more men of the seaman branch, the side is attended by side boys for visiting officers of our Armed Services, except in civilian clothes, and for officers of the Foreign Service when they come on board and depart. This courtesy is also extended to commissioned officers of the armed services of foreign nations. Officers of the rank of lieutenant to major inclusive are given two side boys, from lieutenant colonel to colonel four side boys, from brigadier to major general six side boys, and lieutenant general and above eight side boys. Full guard and band are given to general officers, and for a colonel the guard of the day but no music.

During the hours of darkness or low visibility an approaching boat is usually hailed "Boat ahoy?" which corresponds to the sentry's challenge, "Who goes there?" Some of the answers are as follows:

ANSWER	MEANING: Senior in boat is:
"Aye aye"	Commissioned officer
"No no"	Warrant officer
"Hello"	Enlisted man
"Enterprise"	CO of U.S.S. Enterprise
"Third Fleet"	Admiral commanding Third Fleet

Similarly if the CO of the 13th Infantry is embarked or the CO of Fortress Monroe, the answers would be "13th Infantry" or "Fort Monroe."

On arrival, at the order, "Tend the side" the side boys fall in fore and aft of the approach to the gangway, facing each other. The boatswain's mate-of-the-watch takes station forward of them and faces aft. When the boat comes alongside the boatswain's mate pipes, and again when the visiting officer's head reaches the level of the deck. At this moment the side boys salute.

On departure, the ceremony is repeated in reverse, the bo's'ns mate begins to pipe and the side boys salute as soon as the departing officer steps toward the gangway between the side boys. As the boat casts off the bo's'ns mate pipes again. (Shore boats and automobiles are not piped.)

You uncover when entering a space where men are at mess and in Sick Bay (Quarters) if sick men are present. You uncover in the wardroom at all times if you are junior. All hands except when under arms uncover in the captain's cabin and country.

You should not overtake a senior except in emergency. In the latter case slow, salute, and say, "By your leave, sir."

Admirals and captains when in uniform fly colors astern when embarked in boats. When on official visits they also display their personal flags (pennants for commanding officers) in the bow. Flag officers' barges are distinguished by the appropriate number of stars on each side of the barge's hull. Captains' gigs are distinguished by the name or abbreviation of their ships surcharged by an arrow.

Where gangways are rigged on both sides, the starboard gangway is reserved for officers and the port for enlisted men. Stress of weather or expedience (in the discretion of the officer of the deck or OOD) may make either gangway available to both officers and men.

Seniors come on board ship first. When reaching the deck you face toward the colors (or aft if no colors are hoisted) and salute the colors (quarterdeck). Immediately thereafter you salute the OOD and request permission to come on board. The usual form is, "Request permission to come aboard, sir." The OOD is required to return both salutes.

On leaving the ship the inverse order is observed. You salute the OOD and request permission to leave the ship. The OOD will indicate when the boat is ready (if a boat is used). Each person, juniors first, salutes the OOD; then faces toward the colors, salutes and embarks.

The OOD on board ship represents the captain and as such has unquestioned authority. Only the executive and commanding officer may order him relieved. The authority of the OOD extends to the accommodation ladders or gangways. He is perfectly within his rights to order any approaching boat to "lay off" and keep clear until in his judgment he can receive her alongside.

The OOD normally conveys orders to the embarked troops via the Troop Commander but in emergencies he may issue orders direct to you or any person on board.

The *bridge* is the "Command Post" of the ship when underway, as the quarterdeck is at anchor. The officer-of-the-deck is in charge of the ship as the representative of the captain. Admittance to the bridge when underway should be at the captain's invitation or with his permission. You may usually obtain permission through the executive officer.

The *quarterdeck* is the seat of authority; as such it is respected. The starboard side of the quarterdeck is reserved for the captain (and admiral, if a flagship). No person trespasses upon it except when necessary in the course of work or official business. All persons salute the quarterdeck when entering upon it. When pacing the deck with another officer the place of honor is outboard, and when reversing direction each turns towards the other. The port side of the quarterdeck is reserved for commissioned officers, and the crew has all the rest of the weather decks of the ship. However, every part of the deck (and the ship) is assigned to a particular division so that the crew has ample space. Not unnaturally every division considers it has a prior though unwritten right to its own part of the ship. For gatherings such as smokers and movies, all divisions have equal privileges at the scene of assemblage. Space and chairs are reserved for officers and for CPO's, where available, and mess benches are brought up for the men. The seniors have the place of honor. When the captain (and admiral) arrive those present are called to attention. The captain customarily gives "carry on" at once through the executive officer or master-at-arms who accompanies him to his seat.

If you take passage on board a naval vessel you will be assigned to one of several messes on board ship, the wardroom or junior officer's mess. In off-hours, particularly in the evenings, you can foregather there for cards, yarns or reading. Generally a percolator is available with hot coffee.

The Executive Officer is ex officio the president of the wardroom mess. The wardroom officers are the division officers and the heads of departments. All officers await the arrival of the Executive Officer before being seated at lunch and dinner. If it is necessary for you to leave early, ask the head at your table for permission to be excused as you would at home. The seating arrangement in the messes is by order of seniority.

Naval Officers are required to pay their mess bills in advance. The mess treasurer takes care of the receipts and expenditures and the management of the mess. The mess chooses him by election every month. When assigned to a mess you are an honorary member. Consult the mess treasurer as to when he will receive payment for mess bills. Your meals are served by stewards who in addition, clean your room, make up your bunk, shine your shoes. This is their regular work for which they draw the pay of their rating. They are not tipped.

The Cigar Mess is the successor of the old Wine Mess. You may make purchases from this mess, for example, of cigarettes, cigars, pipe tobacco and candies. The cigar mess treasurer will make out your bill at the end of the month or before your detachment. Before you are detached be sure that the mess treasurer and the cigar mess treasurer have sufficient warning to make out your bills before you leave. Once a ship has sailed, long delays usually occur before your remittances can overtake it. The unpaid mess bill on board is a more serious breach of propriety than the unpaid club bill ashore because of the greater inconvenience and delay in settlement.

Passenger officers should call on the captain of the ship. If there are many, they should choose a calling committee and consult the executive officer as to a convenient time to call. The latter will make arrangements with the captain.

Gun salutes in the Navy are the same as in the Army, except that flag officers below the rank of fleet admiral or general of the Army are, by Navy regulations, given a gun salute upon departure only. By Army regulations gun salutes for the same officers are fired only on arrival.

The rules governing saluting, whether saluting other individuals or paying honor to the color or National Anthem, are the same for the Air Force as in the Army, with the minor exceptions already noted. Because a most frequent contact between the Air Force and the other services comes of the operations of air transport, an officer should know what is expected of him when he travels as a passenger in military aircraft.

It is assumed that the majority of officers visiting an Air Force base will arrive by air at the local military airfield. In addition to the Base Operations Officer, who is the commander's staff officer with jurisdiction over air traffic arriving and departing, the Airdrome Officer is charged with meeting all transient aircraft, determining their transportation requirements, and directing them to the various base facilities. General officers and admirals will usually be met by the Base Commander if practicable. RON (Remaining Over Night) messages may be transmitted through Base Operations at the same time the arrival notice is filed.

Pilots of transient aircraft carrying classified equipment are responsible for the safeguarding of that equipment unless it can be removed from the aircraft and stored in an adequately guarded area. Under unusual circumstances, it may be possible to arrange for a special airplane guard with the base commander.

Passengers from other services, who desire to remain overnight at an air force station should make the necessary arrangements with the Airdrome Officer, and not attach themselves to the pilot who will be busy with his own responsibilities. By the same token, passengers of other services who have had a special flight arranged for them should make every effort to see that the pilot and crew are offered the same accommodations that they themselves are using, unless the particular base has adequate transient accommodations.

Passenger vehicles are never allowed on the ramp or flight line unless special arrangements have been made with the Base Operations Officer; this permission will be granted only under the most unusual circumstances.

The assigned first pilot, or the airplane commander, is the final authority on the operation of any military aircraft. Passengers, regardless of rank, seniority, or service, are subject to the orders of the airplane commander, who is held responsible for their adherence to regulations governing conduct in and around the aircraft. In the event it is impractical for the airplane commander to leave his position, orders may be transmitted through the copilot, engineer, or flight clerk, and have the same authority as if given by the pilot himself.

The order of boarding and alighting from military aircraft--excluding the crew--will vary somewhat with the nature of the mission. If a special flight is arranged for the transportation of Very Important Persons, official inspecting parties, or other high ranking officers of any service, the senior member will enter first and take the seat of his choice, unless the aircraft is compartmented otherwise. Other members of the party will enter in order of rank, and precedence among officers of the same rank will be determined among the officers themselves. In alighting from the aircraft, the senior member will exit first, and the other members of the party will follow either in order of rank, or in order of seating, those nearest the hatch alighting first. The duties of the crew preclude their acting as arbiters in matters of precedence, and order of boarding and alighting will be decided among the members of the party.

In routine flights, officers will normally be loaded in order of rank without regard for precedence, except that any VIP will be on- and off-loaded first; in alighting, officers will leave as they are seated from the exit forward--officers seated near the hatch will debark first, and so on to those who are seated farthest forward. In the event civilian dependents are being carried, or an enlisted man accompanied by dependents, they will be loaded after any VIP and before the officers, and leave in the same sequence.

Aircraft carrying general or flag officers will usually be marked with a detachable metal plate carrying stars appropriate to the highest rank aboard, and will be greeted on arrival by the Air Force Base Commander, if the destination is an Air Force base. Other aircraft are usually met by the Airdrome Officer, who is appointed for one day only, and acts as the Base Commander's representative.

Other personnel on active duty, seeking transportation on navigation or training missions, should realize that the flight is at the pilot's convenience. While the pilot will usually agree to any reasonable request, he can not deviate from his approved flight plan simply to accommodate a passenger. By the same token, passengers should be prompt, observe all pertinent safety regulations, and remain in the passengers compartment of the aircraft unless specifically invited to the flight deck or pilot's compartment. Under instrument conditions--so-called "blind" flying--continuous movement of the passengers of the aircraft makes unnecessary work for the pilot in maintaining balance, trim, and his assigned altitude. Passengers who are abnormally active while in the air are sometimes called--with exasperation--"waltzing mice."

Since flights are somewhat dependent on weather, especially when carrying passengers, the decision of the pilot to fly or not to fly, or to alter his flight plan enroute will not be questioned by the passengers of whatever rank or service. Regulations governing the use of safety belts; wearing of parachutes; smoking during take-off, landing, fuel transfer, or in the vicinity of the aircraft on the ground are binding on all classes of passengers.

When airplanes participate in the funeral of an aviator, it is customary to fly in a normal tactical formation, less one aircraft, to indicate the vacancy formerly occupied by the deceased. The flight should be so timed that it appears over the procession while the remains are being carried to the grave. Care should be exercised that the noise of the flight does not drown out the service at the edge of the grave.

Other ceremonies, including Retreat and reviews, are the same for the Air Force as for the Army.

By custom; and because it is the natural way of an American, the officers of the host service accord more than their average hospitality to the individual from any other service who may be visiting or doing duty among them. Even the young officer, having this experience for the first time, and in consequence feeling a little strange about it, is not permitted to feel that way long. He quickly finds a second home, provided there is that in his nature which responds to friendship.

These amenities, carefully observed at all levels, contribute more directly to a spiritual uniting of American fighting forces than all of the policies which have been promulgated toward the serving of that object.

CHAPTER SEVEN

KEEPING YOUR HOUSE IN ORDER

In one of Lord Chesterfield's letters to his son there is to be found this bit of wisdom: "Dispatch is the soul of business and nothing contributes more to dispatch than method. Fix one certain hour and day in the week for your accounts, keep them together in their proper order, and you can never be much cheated."

Although that is good advice in any man's league, there is just a little more reason why the military officer should adopt a system of accounting whereby he can keep his record straight, his affairs solvent and his situation mobile than if he had remained in civil life.

He rarely, if ever, becomes permanently fixed in one location or remains tied to one group of individuals who know his credit, his ability, his past accomplishments and his general reputation. In the nature of his work, these things have to be reestablished from point to point, and if he personally does not take pains to conserve them, he can be certain only that no one else ever will.

On the whole, the attitude of the services toward the private affairs and nonduty conduct of their officers can be best set forth by once again employing Chesterfield's phrases: "If you have the knowledge, the honor, and probity which you may have, the marks and warmth of my affection will amply reward you; but if you have them not, my aversion and indignation will rise in the same proportion."

Reassignment to a distant station is of course a day-to-day possibility in the life of any military officer. Far from this being a general hardship, it is because the pattern of work and environment changes frequently, and the opportunity to build new friendships is almost endless, that the best men are attracted to the services. To vegetate in one spot is killing to the spirit of the individual who is truly fitted to play a lead part in bold enterprises, and for that reason there is something very unseemly and unmilitary about the officer who resists movement.

On the other hand, a move order is like a club over the head to the officer who hasn't kept his own deck clean, has made no clear accounting of himself and is out of funds and harassed by his creditors.

Concerning the evils of running into debt, there is hardly need for a sermon to any American male who has brains enough to memorize his general orders. As Mr. Micawber put it to David Copperfield, "The blossom is blighted, the leaf is withered, the god of days goes down upon the dreary scene, and--and in short, you are forever floored." The over-extension of credit is a not unknown American failing. It is now the nigh universal custom to overload the home with every kind of gadget, usually bought on time, and nearly all intended to provide the householder with every possible excuse for resisting human toil or for declining to use any personal ingenuity in making life interesting for his family. It is all good enough for those who must have it, but it is well for an officer to remember that the greater the accumulation, the less his chance of accommodating his personal establishment to the require-ments of the service. All moves are costly, even though the government pays most of the freight.

For these and many other reasons, the habit of systematic saving is an essential form of career insurance. The officer who will not deprive himself of a few luxuries to build up a financial reserve is as reckless of his professional future as the one who in battle commits his manpower reserve to front-line action without first weighing his situation.

In the old days, keeping up with the Joneses was almost a part of service tradition. If the colonel's lady owned a bob-tailed nag, the major's wife could be satisfied with nothing less than a bay. And so on and on. Things are no longer that way. They have become much more sensible.

There is one other kind of credit--the professional credit which an officer is entitled to keep with his own establishment. Junior officers are entitled to know that which their superiors are often too forgetful to tell them--that if they have made some especially distinct and worthy contribution to the service, it belongs in the permanent record. If, for example, an officer has written part of a manual, or sat on a major board or committee or provided the idea which has resulted in an improvement of materiel, the fact should be noted in the 201 file, or its equivalent. Such things are not done automatically, as many an officer has learned too late and to his sorrow. But any officer is within propriety in asking this acknowledgment from his responsible superior.

The legal assistance office in an officer's immediate organization will usually suffice his needs in the drawing of all papers essential to his personal housekeeping.

To make a will is merely good business practice, and to neglect it simply because one's holdings are small is to postpone forming the habits which mark a responsible person. Because of superstition and a reluctance to think about death, about three out of every four Americans die intestate. That is about as foolish as leading men into battle without designating a second in command. The Armed Services counsel all officers to take the more responsible view, and make it easy for their officers to do this duty without cost.

A power of attorney enables one person to take certain legal steps for another in his absence, and execute papers which would usually require his signature. When an officer is going on an extended tour overseas, his interests are apt to be left dangling unless he leaves such a power with his wife, mother, best friend or some other person, thereby avoiding loss of money and excess worry.

Any citizen may draw up a will in his own handwriting, and if it is properly attested, it will have some standing in court. Likewise, a power of attorney can be executed on a blank form. But it is foolish for a military officer to do these things halfway when the legal offices of the service are available to him, not only for performing the work, but for counseling him as to its effect.

There is one other step that the responsible man takes on his own. It is not likely that his wife or any other person knows at any one time the whole story of his interests, obligations and holdings, as to where goods may be stored, savings kept, insurance policies filed, what debts are owed and what accounts are receivable. In the event of his sudden death, next of kin would be at a loss to know whom and where to call to get the estate settled smoothly, and with all things accurately inventoried. So it is a practical idea to keep an up-to-date check list in ledger form, but containing all pertinent information whereby things may be made readily accessible. If for some private reason, it is preferred not to leave this with next of kin, it can be kept in a top drawer at the office, where it could scarcely escape attention.

A current inventory of household goods is also a safety and time-saving precaution. As changes occur, the list can be corrected and kept fresh. Then in case of a sudden move, there is almost nothing to be done in preparation for the movers, and in the event of loss anywhere along the line, one's own tables will provide a basis for recovery. Goods are not infrequently mislaid, lost, or damaged when shipped or warehoused, and the more authentic the description of the goods in question, the better the chances for the claim.

For any officer with dependents, insurance is of course a necessity. How much it should be, and what its form, are matters for his judgment and conscience, and according to his circumstances. The services do not try to tell a man how he should provide for his family. Men of honor need no such reminder, though they may be bothered by the question: "How much can I afford?" On that point, sufficient to say that it is *not* more blessed to be insolvent and worried about debts from being overloaded with insurance than for any other reason. Many retired officers supplement their pay by selling insurance. When a young service officer wants insurance counsel, he will find that they are disposed to deal sympathetically with his problem.

A few recurrent expenses, such as insurance premiums and bond purchases, can be met with allotments through the Finance or Disbursing Officer. The forms for the starting of an allotment are quite simple. When an officer is going overseas, if his dependents are not to follow immediately, an allotment is the best way to insure that they will get their income regularly. Overseas expenses are usually quite light, which means that the allotment may safely be made in larger amount than half the monthly pay. Under certain circumstances, it may also be arranged for allotments to be made to banks, as a form of steady saving.

Adverting for a moment to the question of what happens to a service officer when he becomes ridden by debt and plagued by his creditors, it is a fair statement that the generality of higher commanders are not unsympathetic, that they know that shrewdness and thrift are quite often the product of a broadened experience, and that their natural disposition is to temper the wind to the shorn lamb, if there are signs that he is making a reasonable effort to recover. When it becomes clear that he is taking the service for a ride and cares nothing for the good name of the officer corps, they'll send him packing. A man harassed by debt, and not knowing how to meet his situation, is always well-advised to go to his commander, make a clean statement of the case, and ask for his counsel.

Every officer should be absolutely scrupulous about keeping a complete, chronologically arranged file of all official papers having anything to do with his status, movements, duties, or possessions. That may seem burdensome, but it is well worth doing, since one never knows when an old paper will become germane to a current question or undertaking.

Likewise, receipts are necessary whenever one spends money on anything (for instance, travel) on which reimbursement is expected from the Government. Regulations are clear on this point--the Government simply will not give the individual the benefit of the doubt. No receipt; no check from the Treasury.

The military society is a little more tightly closed than a civilian society, particularly in posts, camps and stations. For that reason the pressure from the distaff side is usually a little heavier. Wives get together more frequently, know one another better, and take a more direct interest in their husbands' careers than is common elsewhere. That has its advantages, but also its headaches. There is an occasional officer who is so immature in his judgments as to permit his wife's feelings about a colleague or a colleague's wife to supervene in the affairs of organization. This is one way to ask for trouble.

Gossip is to be avoided because it is vicious, self-destructive, unmanly, unmilitary and, most of the time, untrue. The obligation of each officer toward his fellow officer is to build him up, which implies the use of moral pressure against whatsoever influence would pull him down. While the love of scandal is universal, and the services can not hope to rid themselves altogether of the average human failings, it is possible for any man to guard his own tongue and, by the example of moderation, serve to keep all such discussion temperate. Were all officers to make a conscious striving in this direction, the credit of the corps as a whole, and the satisfactions of each of its members in his service, would be tremendously increased. Besides, there is another point: gossip is the mark of the man insufficiently occupied with serious thought about his personal responsibilities. His carelessness about the destruction of the character of others is incidental to his indifference to those things which make for character in self.

As for the rest of it, we can turn back to Chesterfield, with whom we started. For how might any man state it more neatly than with these words:

"Were I to begin the world again with the experience which I now have of it, I would lead a life of real, not of imaginary pleasure. I would enjoy the pleasures of the table and of wine, but stop short of the pains inseparably annexed to an excess of either.

"I should let other people do as they would without formally and sententiously rebuking them for it. But I would be most firmly resolved not to destroy my own faculties and constitution in complaisance to those who have no regard for their own.

"I would play to give me pleasure, but not to give me pain. That is, I would play for trifles in mixed companies, to amuse myself and conform to custom. But I would take care not to venture for sums which if I won I would not be the better for, but if I lost, should be under a difficulty to pay."

CHAPTER EIGHT

GETTING ALONG WITH PEOPLE

The main answer can be stated almost as simply as doing right-face. Hear this:

If you like people, if you seek contact with them rather than hiding yourself in a corner, if you study your fellow men sympathetically, if you try consistently to contribute something to their success and happiness, if you are reasonably generous with your thoughts and your time, if you have a partial reserve with everyone but a seeming reserve with no one, if you work to be interesting rather than spend to be a good fellow, you will get along with your superiors, your subordinates, your orderly, your roommate and the human race.

It is easy enough to chart a course for the individual who is wise enough to make human relationships his main concern. But getting the knack of it is sufficiently more difficult that it is safe to say more talk has been devoted to this subject than to any other topic of conversation since Noah quit the Ark. From Confucius down to Emily Post, greater and lesser minds have worked at gentling the human race. By the scores of thousands, precepts and platitudes have been written for the guidance of personal conduct. The odd part of it is that despite all of this labor, most of the frictions in modern society arise from the individual's feeling of inferiority, his false pride, his vanity, his unwillingness to yield space to any other man, and his consequent urge to throw his own weight around. Goethe said that the quality which best enables a man to renew his own life, in his relation to others, is that he will become capable of renouncing particular things at the right moment in order warmly to embrace something new in the next.

That is earthy advice for any member of the officer corps. For who is regarded as the strong man in the service--the individual who fights with tooth and nail to hold to a particular post or privilege? Not at all! Full respect is given only to him who at all times is willing to yield his space to a worthy successor, because of an ingrained confidence that he can succeed as greatly in some other sphere.

For a fresh start in this study of getting along with people, we could not do better than quote what was published some time ago in the United States Coast Guard Magazine. Under the title "*Thirteen Mistakes*," the coast guardsmen raised their warning flares above the 13 pitfalls. It is a mistake:

1. To attempt to set up your own standard of right and wrong.
2. To try to measure the enjoyment of others by your own.
3. To expect uniformity of opinions in the world.
4. To fail to make allowance for inexperience.
5. To endeavor to mold all dispositions alike.
6. Not to yield on unimportant trifles.
7. To look for perfection in our own actions.
8. To worry ourselves and others about what can't be remedied.
9. Not to help everybody wherever, however, whenever we can.
10. To consider impossible what we cannot ourselves perform.
11. To believe only what our finite minds can grasp.
12. Not to make allowances for the weakness of others.
13. To estimate by some outside quality, when it is that within which makes the man.

The unobserving officer will no doubt dismiss this list as just so many clichés. The reflective man will accept it as a negative guide to positive conduct, for it engages practically every principle which is vital to the growth of a strong spiritual life in relation to one's fellow men.

Certain of these points stand out as prominently as pips on a radar screen to the military officer bent on keeping his own ship out of trouble. The morals contained in 4, 5, 12, and 13 all come to bear in the story told by Sgt. Fred Miller about Pvt. Fred Lang of Hospital No. 1 on Bataan. Miller had tried to do what he could for Lang, but no one else in the detachment was willing to give him a break. He was an unlettered hillbilly and, being ashamed of his own ignorance, he was shy toward other men. The rest of the story is best told in Miller's words.

"When the Japs made their first bombing run on Marivales, most of us, being new at war, huddled together under such cover as we could find. Some people were hit outside. We stayed where we were. But we looked out and saw Lang. He was trying to handle a stretcher by himself, dragging one end along the ground in an effort to bring in the wounded. I remember one member of our group remarking, 'Look at old Lang trying to do litter drill right in the middle of a war.' Lang was killed by an enemy bomb that night. I guess he had to die to make us understand that he was the best man."

There is hardly an American who has been in combat but can tell some other version of this same story, changing only the names and the surroundings. All too frequently it happens in the services--we look at a man, and because at a casual inspection we do not like the cut of his jib, or the manner of his response, or are over-persuaded by what someone else has said about him, we reach a permanent conclusion about his possibilities, and either mentally write him off, or impair our own capacity for giving him help.

It suffices to say that when any officer has the inexcusable fault that he takes snap judgment on his *own* men, he will not be any different in his relations with all other people, and will stand in his own light for the duration of his career. Which leads to one other observation. When any man, bearing a bad efficiency report, comes to a new organization, it is a fact to be noted with mild interest, but *without any prejudice whatever*. Every new assignment means a clean slate, and there should be no hangover from what has happened, including the possible mistaken judgments of others. The system was never intended to give a dog a bad name. To be perpetually supervised, questioned and shadowed is to be doubted, and doubt destroys confidence and creates fear, slyness and discontent in the other individual. Every man is entitled to a fresh hold on security with his new superior. Any wise and experienced senior commander will tell you this, and will cite examples of men who came to him with a spotty record, who started nervously, began to pick up after realizing that they were not going to get another kick, and went on to become altogether superior. For any right-minded commander, it is far more gratifying to be able to salvage human material than to take over an organization that is sound from bottom to top.

However, the truth in point 9 applies universally. The studied effort to be helpful in all of our relations with our fellow men, and to give help not grudgingly, but cheerfully, courteously and in greater measure than is expected, is the high road to wide influence and personal strength of character. More than all else, it is the little kindnesses in life which bind men together and help each wayfarer to start the day right. These tokens are like bread cast upon the water; they ultimately nourish the giver more than the direct beneficiary. One of our best-known corps commanders in the Pacific War made it a rule that if any man serving under him, or any man he knew in the service, however unimportant, was promoted or given any other recognition, he would write a letter to the man's wife or mother, saying how proud he felt. He was not a great tactician or strategist but, because of the little things he did, men loved him and would ride to hell for him, and their collective moral strength became the bastion of his professional success.

Of Maj. Gen. Henry T. Allen, who commanded our first Army of Occupation in Germany, a distinguished contemporary once said: "It surprised us that Allen did so well; in the old Army we regarded him as a swashbuckler." Maybe that was because he was a cavalryman and liked to strut, and he liked to see chestiness in his own people, right down to the last file. But General Allen was infinitely considerate of the dignity of all other men, and he disciplined himself to further their growth and give them some mark of his thoughtful regard so far as lay within his power. It was because of his rich understanding humanity, and not through any genial slackness, that he kept a tight hold on discipline. To the units he commanded he gave his own tone. He warmed men instead of chilling them with fear. Thousands returned to civil life better equipped for the passage because of what they had seen him do and heard him say.

So we can link points 1, 6, 7, and 8 from the Coast Guard's list into one binding truth not less essential to sound officership than to action anywhere which seeks the cooperation and goodwill of men: *It is not more blessed to be right than to be loved*, Henry Clay's remark that he would rather be right than president notwithstanding. The absolute perfectionist is the most tiresome of men, and a waster of time and of nerves. The stickler, the fly-speckler, the bully and the sadist serve only to encumber those parts of the establishment which they touch; their subordinates spend part of their own strength clearing away the wreckage which these misfits make.

Other than these comments, it is not necessary to say a great deal about the *inner qualities* which give an officer a free-wheeling adjustment with other persons in all walks of life. Once again, however, it might be well to speak of the importance of enthusiasm, kindness, courtesy, and justice, which are the safeguards of honor and the tokens of mutual respect between man and man. This last there must be if men are to go forward together, prosper in one another's company, find strength in the bonds of mutual service, and experience a common felicity in the relationship between the leader and the led.

But it is sadly the case that the reputation of any man, as to what he is inside, forms in large measure from what others see of him from the outside. That is what makes poignant the story of Pvt. Fred Lang; like a singed cat, he was better than he looked. In the military service, more than elsewhere in life, manner weighs heavily in the balance, if only for the reason that from the public point of view, the military officer is supposed to look the part. He is expected to be the embodiment of character, given to forthright but amiable speech, capable of expressing his ideas and purpose clearly, careful of customs and good usage, and carrying himself with poise and assurance. For if he does not have the aura of vitality, confidence and reflection which is expected in a leader of men, it will be suspected that he is incapable of playing the part. However unfairly discriminating that judgment may seem to be, in comparison with the attitude toward other professions, it has a perfectly logical basis. The people are willing to forgive preoccupation in all others, since how an engineer dresses has no relation to his skill as a mathematician, and when a doctor mumbles it doesn't suggest that he would be clumsy with a scalpel. But when they meet an uncivil or unkempt officer, or see an untidy soldier or bluejacket on the street, they worry that the national defense is going to pot. One reason for the great prestige of the Marine Corps is that the public seldom, if ever, sees a sloppy marine, though its members do sometimes look a little gruesome on the field of battle.

The officer corps does have its share of "characters." Some are men born in an uncommon mold, with a great deal of natural phlegm in their systems, a gift for salty speech and a tendency to drawl their words as if their thoughts were being raised from a deep well. Usually, they are men of extraordinary power, and are worth any dozen of that individual who scuttles about like a water bug, making an exhibition of great energy but, like the whirling dervish, keeping in such constant motion that he has no chance to observe what goes on under his nose. Here, as in all things, it is steadiness that does it. The blunt soldier, the old sea-dog type of naval officer, is endurable and even lovable in the eyes of most other people, when he has done his scrapping with fire rather than firewater, when his personal credentials are sound, and when his outward manner is bluff in both meanings of the word. But the fakers who affect the crusty manner, the glaring eye and the jutting jaw, simply because they are wearing military suits and think mistakenly that these things are in the tradition, will be recognized as counterfeit as quickly as a lead quarter.

There is nothing else that serves as well as the natural manner, with some polishing of the surfaces here and there, and a general tightening at the corners.

While a partial check list is not likely to reform the establishment overnight, if kept simple enough, it may afford help to an occasional individual, instead of giving him the fear that he is falling apart at the seams.

The smartest physical culturists are swinging around to the idea that correct posture alone is the great secret of physical fitness, that if a man sits well, stands erect and walks correctly all the time, he is doing more for his health and longevity than all of the setting-up exercises and sweat baths yet devised. At the same time he is making a favorable impression on all who see him. Clumsy one-sided postures, fidgeting on a chair, slouching while sitting or standing, moving along at a shambling gait and speaking with the chin down on the chest produce quite the opposite effect. Right or wrong, they are taken as a sign of indolence, fatigue, or inattention. There is always an hour for complete physical relaxation, for stretching and letting the muscles melt; Winston Churchill attributed a large part of his vigor and recuperative powers to the habit of taking a 30-minute cat nap in midday. That is a smart trick if one can master it. But trying most of all for *physical ease* when in conversation, or at conference, or in attending to any matter wherein one comes under the surveillance of those whose good opinion is worth cultivating is as certain a handicap as putting excess weight on an otherwise good horse.

In the services, as in any situation in life in which deference to higher opinion is compelled by the nature of an undertaking, the young will do well to consider the wisdom of the precept, "Be patient with your betters."

It is lamentably bad judgment to act by any other rules. Where differences of opinion exist, time and forbearance not infrequently will work the desired change, where stubbornness or rudeness would utterly fail. More than that, a junior owes this much consideration to any senior whose heart is in the right place. It is bad manners, but even worse from the standpoint of tactics, to attempt publicly to score a victory over a senior in any dispute, or to attempt by wit to gain the upperhand of him in the presence of others. Though the point may be gained for the moment, it is usually at the cost of one's personal hold on the confidence of the senior.

But there is also the other side of the case, that the superior should deal considerately with any earnest proposal from his subordinate, rather than dashing cold water in his face, just because he has not thought his proposition through. One of the best-loved editors of the United States, Grove Patterson, of Toledo, Ohio, was remembered by every young journalist who ever came under him because of the care with which he supported every man's pride. A youngster would go in to him, filled with enthusiasm for some idea, which he himself had not bothered to view in the round. Patterson would listen carefully, and would then say: "That's a corking idea. Take it and work it out carefully, going over every aspect of it. Then bring it back to me." On second thought, the youngster would begin having his own doubts, and would shortly begin hoping that the chief would forget all about the subject, which he invariably did. Many celebrated commanders in our military services have won the lasting affection of their subordinates by employing exactly this method.

Men like the direct glance. They feel flattered by it, particularly when they are talking, and in conversation they like to be heard through, not interrupted in mid-passage. That is true whatever their station. Nobody likes to be bored, but fully half of boredom comes from lack of the habit of careful listening. The man who will not listen never develops wits enough to distinguish between a bore and a sage and therefore cannot pick the best company. The vacant stare, the drifting of eyes from the speaker to a window, or a picture or a passing blonde, though greatly tempting in the midst of long discourse, are taken only as signs of inattention. Many a young officer called to the carpet for some trivial business has managed to square himself with his commander just by looking straight and talking straight in the few moments that decided his future.

Elsewhere in the book, a great deal has been said about the importance of the voice and of developing one's powers of conversation. Not a great deal more needs to be added here. But there is no excuse for the officer who talks so that others must strain to hear what he is saying--unless he is suffering from laryngitis. It is simple enough to keep the chin up and let the words roll out. Many persons have the bad habit of letting the voice drop at the end of a sentence; the effect on the other party is like watching a man run away from a fight. For clear understanding, and to create a good impression, there should be a cheerful lift upward at the end of a sentence.

Also, officers who look at lecturing simply as part of the routine tend to fall into either the singsong rhythm which one frequently hears in college professors and certain radio announcers, or go all out for the sonorous intonations which are beloved by many of the clergy. Many young officers get into these same cadences whenever they talk to men, and before they know it, they are trying the same thing in the family circle. They sound like alarm clocks running down, but instead of arousing the house, they are an invitation to slumber. Either on the lecture platform, or in man-to-man conversation, there is no valid reason why it is ever necessary to take the tone which suggests that the talk is one-sided. Words can be crisply uttered and still be personally directed, but not if the speaker is looking at the floor, the moon or the rafters. To discuss a question amicably is the best way to gain clear insight into it; when a man argues violently, his purpose usually is not to serve wisdom but to prevail despite his lack of it, thus stultifying both himself and his adversary.

Clothes are important. They have to be. One can't go very far without them, north of the Equator. But a fresh press counts more than a new suit by a Fifth Avenue tailor left unpressed, and neatness beats lavishness any day in the week.

Carefulness in the little things counts much. Men develop an aversion to the individual who cannot remember their names, their titles or their stations, but they will warm to the person who remembers, and they will overlook most of his other shortcomings. Likewise, they are won by any words of appreciation or of interest in what they are doing. Get a man talking about his business, his golf game or his family, and you are on the inside track toward his friendship. As for senior commanders, when the hours comes for them to bat the ball back and forth in friendly conversation, there is nothing they enjoy more than reminiscing about experiences on the battlefield. Other than inveterate surgical patients, no one can outdo them in talking about their operations.

It isn't lengthy advice which is needed on this subject, since a man commissioned is considered to have graduated from at least the kindergarten of good manners. What counts is simply caring about it, not to be ingratiating to other people, but for the sake of one's own dignity and self-respect.

None of the oracles on winning friends and influencing people have said it in those few words, and if they had, there would have been no books to sell.

CHAPTER NINE

LEADERS AND LEADERSHIP

In that gallery of Great Americans whose names are conspicuously identified with the prospering of the national arms in peace and war, there are almost as many types as there are men.

There were a certain few qualities that they had to possess in common or their names would never have become known beyond the county line.

But these were inner qualities, often deep buried, rather than outward marks of greatness which men recognized immediately upon beholding them.

Some almost missed the roll call, either because in early life their weaknesses were more apparent than their strengths, or because of an outward seeming of insignificance which at first fooled their contemporaries.

In the minority are the few who seemed marked for greatness almost from the cradle, and were acclaimed for leadership while still of tender years.

Winfield Scott, a Brigadier in the War of 1812 when Brigadiers were few, and Chief of Staff when the Civil War began, is a unique figure in the national history.

George Washington, Adjutant of the State of Virginia at 21, is one other military infant prodigy who never later belied his early fame.

The majority in the gallery are not like these. No two of them are strikingly alike in mien and manner. Their personalities are as different, for most part, as their names. Their characters also ran the range of the spectrum, or nearly, if we are talking of moral habit, rather than of conscientious performance of military duty. Some drank their whiskey neat and frequently; others loathed it and took a harsh line with any subordinate who used it.

One of the greatest generals in American history, celebrated for his fighting hardly more than for his tippling, would walk from the room if any man tried to tell an off-color story in his presence.

One of the most celebrated and successful of our Admirals endeared himself to millions of men in all ranks and services by his trick of gathering his chief subordinates together just prior to battle, issuing his orders sternly and surely, and then relaxing long enough to tell them his latest parlor story, knowing that finally it would trickle down through the whole command.

Among the warriors in this gallery are men who would bet a month's pay on a horse race. There are duellists and brawlers, athletes and aesthetes, men who lived almost sainted lives and scholars who lived more for learning than for fame.

Some tended to be so over-reclusive that they almost missed recognition; others were hail-fellow-well-met in any company.

Their methods of work reflected these extreme variations in personal type, as did the means they used to draw other men to them, thereby setting a foundation for real success.

Part of their number commanded mainly through the sheer force of ideas; others owed their fortune more to the magnetism of dynamic personality.

In a few there was the spark of genius. All things seemed to come right with them at all times. Fate was kind, the openings occurred, and they were prepared to take advantage of them.

But the greater number moved up the hill one slow step at a time, not always sure of their footing, buffeted by mischance, owning no exalted opinion of their own merits, reacting to discouragement much as other men would do, but finally accumulating power as they learned how to organize the work of other men.

While a young lieutenant, Admiral Sims became so incensed, when the United States would not take his word on a voucher, that he offered to resign.

General Grant signally failed to organize his life as an individual prior to the time when a turn of the wheel gave him his chance to organize the military power of the United States in war.

General Sherman, who commanded the Army for almost 15 years, was considered by many of his close friends to be a fit subject for confinement as a mental case just prior to the Civil War.

General Meade, one of the sweetest and most serene of men in his family relationships, lacked confidence in his own merits and was very abusive of his associates during battle.

Admiral Farragut, whose tenderness as an individual are marked by the 16 years in which he personally nursed an invalid wife, was so independent in his professional thought and action that both in and out of the Navy he was disqualified as a "climber." He got into wretched quarrels with his superiors mainly because he felt his assignments afforded him no distinction. The Civil War gave him his opportunity.

Admiral John Paul Jones, though an unusually modest man, was as redoubtable in the boudoir as at sea, and it would be hard to say which type of engagement most caught his fancy.

General Winfield Scott, as firm a commander as ever drew on a glove, plagued the service with his petty bickering over rank, seniority, and precedent.

They were all mortal. Being human, they had their points of personal weakness, just as any newly appointed ensign or second lieutenant also has weak spots in his armor, and sometimes views them in such false proportion that he doubts his own potential for high responsibility.

There is not one perfect life in the gallery of the great. All were moulded by the human influences which surrounded them. They reacted in their own feelings, and toward other men, according as their personal fortunes rose and fell. They sought help where it could be found. When disappointed, they chilled like anyone else. But along with their professional talents, they possessed, in common, a desire for substantial recognition, accompanied by the will to earn it fairly, or else the nation would never have heard their names.

All in all it is a multifarious gallery. If we were to pass it in review, and then inspect it carefully, it would still be impossible to say: "This is the composite of character. This is the prototype of military success. Model upon it and you have the pinnacle within reach."

The same thing would no doubt hold true of a majority of the better men who commanded ships, squadrons, regiments, and companies under these commanders, and at their own level were as superior in leadership as the relatively few who rose to national stature because of the achievements of the general body.

The same rule will apply tomorrow. Those who come forward to fill these same places, and to command them with equal or greater authority and competence, will not be plaster saints, laden with all human virtue, spotless in character and fit to be anointed with a superman legend by some future Parson Weems. They will be men with a human quality, and a strong belief in the United States and the goodness of a free society. They will have some of the average man's faults, and maybe a few of his vices. But certainly they will possess the qualities of courage, creative intelligence and physical fitness in more than average measure.

What we know of our great leaders in the current age should disparage the idea that only a superman may scale the heights. Trained observers have noted in their personalities and careers many of the plain characteristics which each man feels in himself and mistakenly believes is a bar to preferment.

Drew Middleton, the British correspondent, wrote of Gen. Carl "Tooey" Spaatz: "This man, who may be a heroic figure to our grand-children, is essentially an unheroic figure to his contemporaries. He is in fact such a friendly, human person that observers tend to minimize his stature as a war leader. He is not temperamental. He makes no rousing speeches, writes no inspirational orders. Spaatz, in issuing orders for a major operation involving 1,500 airplanes, is about as inspiring as a groceryman ordering another five cases of canned peas."

In the files of the Navy Department there is a picture of Admiral Marc A. Mitscher, the famed commander of Task Force 58, coming on board a flagship to take command of a force of carriers. Officers and men are lined up at spick-and-span attention. The Admiral himself appears as a little man in a rumpled khaki uniform, tieless and wearing an informal garrison cap. Under his arm is a book, and in the photograph the title can be read as "Send Another Coffin." Mitscher liked detective stories; he didn't like ceremonial pomp.

An interviewer who called on Gen. Ira C. Eaker when he was leading 8th Air Force against Germany found "a strikingly soft-spoken, sober, compact man who has the mild manner of a conservative minister and the judicial outlook of a member of the Supreme Court. But he is always about two steps ahead of everybody on the score, and there is a quiet, inexorable logic about everything he does." Of his own choice, Eaker would have separated from military service after World War I. He wanted to be a lawyer and he also toyed with the idea of running a country newspaper. In his off hours, he wrote books on aviation for junior readers. On the side, he studied civil law and found it "valuable mental training."

On the eve of the Guadalcanal landing, Gen. A. A. Vandegrift's final order to his command ended with the stirring and now celebrated phrase: "God favors the bold and strong of heart." Yet in the afterglow of later years, the Nation read a character sketch of him which included this: "He is so polite and so soft spoken that he is continually disappointing the people whom he meets. They find him lacking in the fire-eating traits they like to expect of all marines, and they find it difficult to believe that such a mild-mannered man could really have led and won the bloody fight." When another officer spoke warmly of Vandegrift's coolness under fire, his "grace under pressure," to quote Hemingway's phrase, he replied: "I shouldn't be given any credit. I'm built that way."

The point is beautifully taken. Too often the man with great inner strength holds in contempt those less well endowed by nature than himself.

While there are no perfect men, there are those who become relatively perfect leaders of men because something in their makeup brings out in strength the highest virtues of all who follow them. That is the way of human nature. Minor shortcomings do not impair the working loyalty, or growth, of the follower who has found someone whose strengths he deems worth emulating. On the other hand, to recognize merit, you must yourself have it. *The act of recognizing the worthwhile traits in another person is both the test and the making of character.* The man who scorns all others, and thinks no one else worth following, parades his own inferiority before the world. He puts his own character into bankruptcy just as surely as does that other sad camp follower of whom Thomas Carlyle wrote: "To recognize false merit, and crown it as true, because a long tail runs after it, is the saddest operation under the sun."

Sherman, Logan, Rawlins and the many others hitched their wagons to Grant's star because they saw in him a man who had a way with other men, and who commanded them not less by personal courage than by patient work in their interest. Had Grant spent time brooding over his civilian failures, he would have been stuck with a disorderly camp and would never have gotten out of Illinois.

The nobility of the private life and influence of Gen. Robert E. Lee and the grandeur of his military character are known to every American school boy. His peerless gifts as a battle leader have won the tribute of celebrated soldiers and historians throughout the English-speaking world. Likewise, the deep religiosity of his great lieutenant, Stonewall Jackson, the latter's fiery zeal and the almost evangelical power with which he lifted the hearts of all men who followed him, are hallmarks of character that are vividly remembered in whatever context his name happens to be mentioned.

If we turn for a somewhat closer look at Grant it is because he, more than any other American soldier, left us a full, clear narrative of his own growth, and of the inner thoughts and doubts pertaining to himself which attended his life experience. There was a great deal of the average man in Grant. He was beset by human failings. He could not look impressive. He had no sense of destiny. In his great hours, it was sweat, rather than inspiration, dogged perseverance, rather than the aura of power, which made the hour great.

Average though he was in many things, there was nothing average about the strong way in which he took hold, applying massive common sense to the complex problems of the field. That is why he is worth close regard. His virtues as a military leader were of the simpler sort which plain men may understand and hope to emulate. He was direct in manner. He never intrigued. His speech was homely. He was approachable. His mind never deviated from the object. Though a stubborn man, he was always willing to listen to his subordinates. He never adhered to a plan obstinately, but nothing could induce him to forsake the idea behind the plan.

History has left us a clear view of how he attained to greatness in leadership by holding steadfastly to a few main principles.

At Belmont, his first small action, he showed nothing to indicate that he was competent as a tactician and strategist. But the closing scene reveals him as the last man to leave the field of action, risking his life to see that none of his men had been left behind.

At Fort Donelson, where he had initiated an amphibious campaign of highly original daring, he was not on the battlefield when his army was suddenly attacked. He arrived to find his right wing crushed and his whole force on the verge of defeat. He blamed no one. Without more than a passing second's hesitation, he said quietly to his chief subordinates: "Gentlemen, the position on the right must be retaken." Then he mounted his horse, and galloped along the line shouting to his men: "Fill your cartridge cases quick; the enemy is trying to escape and he must not be permitted to do so." Control and order were immediately reestablished by his presence.

At Shiloh, the same thing happened, only this time it was worse; the whole Union Army was on the verge of rout. Grant, hobbling on crutches from a recent leg injury, met the mob of panic-stricken stragglers as he left the boat at Pittsburgh Landing. Calling on them to turn back, he mounted and rode toward the battle, shouting encouragement and giving orders to all he met. Confidence flowed from him back into an already beaten Army and in this way a field near lost was soon regained.

The last and best picture of Grant is on the evening after he had taken his first beating from General Lee in the campaign against Richmond. He was newly with the Army of the Potomac. His predecessors, after being whipped by Lee, had invariably retreated to safe distance. But this time as the defeated army took the road of retreat out of the Wilderness, its columns got only as far as the Chancellorsville House crossroad. There the soldiers saw a squat, bearded man, sitting horseback, and drawing on a cigar. As the head of each regiment came abreast him, he silently motioned it to take the right-hand fork--back toward Lee's flank and deeper than ever into the Wilderness. That night for the first time the Army sensed an electric change in the air over Virginia. It had a man.

"I intend to fight it out on this line" is more revealing of the one supreme quality which put the seal on all other of U. S. Grant's great gifts for military leading than everything else that the historians have written of him. He was the epitome of that spirit which moderns call "seeing the show through." He was sensitive to a fault in his early years, and carried to his tomb a dislike for military uniform, caused by his being made the butt of ridicule the first time he ever donned a soldier suit. As a junior lieutenant in the Mexican War, he sensed no particular aptitude in himself. But he had participated in every engagement possible to a member of his regiment, and had executed every small duty to the hilt, with particular attention to conserving the lives of his men. This was the school and the course which later enabled him to march to Richmond, when men's lives had to be spent for the good of the Nation. In more recent times, one of the great statesmen and soldiers of the United States, Henry L. Stimson, has added his witness to the value of this force in all enterprise: "I know the withering effect of limited commitments and I know the regenerative effect of full action." Though he was speaking particularly of the larger affairs of war and nation policy, his words apply with full weight to the personal life. The truth seen only halfway is missed wholly; the thing done only halfway had best not be attempted at all. Men can be fooled but they can't be fooled on this score. They will know every time when the bolt falls short for lack of a worthwhile effort. And when that happens, confidence in the leader is corroded, even among those who themselves were unwilling to try.

There have been great and distinguished leaders in our military services at all levels, who had no particular gifts for administration, and little for organizing the detail of decisive action either within battle or without. They excelled because of a superior ability to utilize the brains and command the loyalty of well-chosen subordinates. Their particular function was to judge the mark according to their resources and audacity, and then to hold the team steady until the mark was gained. So doing, they complemented the power of the faithful lieutenants who might have put them in the shade in any I. Q. test. Wrote Grant: "I never knew what to do with a paper except put it in a side pocket or pass it to a clerk who understood it better than I did." There was nothing unfair or irregular about this; it was as it should be. All military achievement develops out of unity of action. The laurel goes to the man whose powers can most surely be directed toward the end purposes of organization. *The winning of battles is the product of the winning of men.* That aptitude is not an endowment of formal education, though the man who has led a football team, a class, a fraternity or a debating society is the stronger for the experience which he has gained. It is not uncustomary in those who have excelled in scholarship to despise those who have excelled merely in sympathetic understanding of the human race. But in the military services, though there are niches for the pedant, character is at all times at least as vital as intellect, and the main rewards go to him who can make other men feel toughened as well as elevated.

> *Quiet resolution.*
> *The hardihood to take risks.*
> *The will to take full responsibility for decision.*
> *The readiness to share its rewards with subordinates.*
> *An equal readiness to take the blame when things go adversely.*
> *The nerve to survive storm and disappointment and to face toward each new day with the scoresheet wiped clean, neither dwelling on one's successes nor accepting discouragement from one's failures.*

In these things lie a great part of the essence of leadership, for they are the constituents of that kind of moral courage which has enabled one man to draw many others to him in any age.

It is good, also, to look the part, not only because of its effect on others, but because from out of the effort made to *look it*, one may in time come *to be it*. One of the kindliest and most penetrating philosophers of our age, Abbé Ernest Dimnet, has assured us that this is true. He says that by trying to look and act like a socially distinguished person, one may in fact attain to the inner disposition of a gentleman. That, almost needless to say, is the *real* mark of the officer who takes great pains about the manner of his dress and address, for as Walt Whitman has said: "All changes of appearances without a change in that which underlies appearance, are without avail." All depends upon the spirit in which one makes the effort. By his own account, U. S. Grant, as a West Point cadet, was more stirred by the commanding appearance of General Winfield Scott than by any man he had ever seen, including the President. He wrote that at that moment there flashed across his mind the thought that some day he would stand in Scott's place. Grant was unkempt of dress. His physical endowments were such that he could never achieve the commanding air of Scott, but he left us his witness that Scott's military bearing helped kindle his own desire for command, even though he knew that he could not be like Scott.

Much is said in favor of modesty as an asset in leadership. It is remarked that the man who wishes to hold the respect of others will mention himself not more frequently than a born aristocrat mentions his ancestor. However, the point can be labored too hard. Some of the ablest of the Nation's battlefield commanders have been anything but shrinking violets; we have had now and then a hero who could boast with such gusto that this very characteristic somehow endeared him to his men. But that would be a dangerous tack for all save the most exceptional individual. Instead of speaking of modesty as a charm that will win all hearts, thereby risking that through excessive modesty a man will become tiresome to others and rated as too timid for high responsibility, it would be better to dwell upon the importance of being natural, which means neither concealing nor making a vulgar display of one's ideals and motives, but acting directly according to their dictations.

This leads to another point. In several of the most celebrated commentaries written by higher commanders on the nature of generalship, the statement is made rather carelessly that to be capable of great military leadership a man must be something of an actor. If that were unqualifiedly true, then it would be a desirable technique likewise in any junior officer that he too should learn how to wear a false face, and play a part which cloaks his real self. The hollowness of the idea is proved by the lives of such men as Robert E. Lee, W. T. Sherman, George C. Marshall, Omar N. Bradley, Carl A. Spaatz, William H. Simpson, Chester A. Nimitz, and W. S. Sims. As commanders, they were all as natural as children, though some had great natural reserve, and others were warmer and more outgoing. They expressed themselves straightforwardly rather than by artful striving for effect. There was no studied attempt to appear only in a certain light. To use the common word for it, their people did not regard them as "characters." This naturalness had much to do with their hold on other men.

Such a result will always come. He who concentrates on the object at hand has little need to worry about the impression he is making on others. Even though they detect the chinks in the armor, they will know that the armor will hold.

On the other hand, a sense of the dramatic values, coupled with the intelligence to play upon them skillfully, is an invaluable quality in any military leader. Though there was nothing of the "actor" in Grant, he understood the value of pointing things up. *To put a bold or inspiring emphasis where it belongs is not stagecraft, but an integral part of the military fine art of communications.* System which is only system is injurious to the mind and spirit of any normal person. One can play a superior part well, and maintain prestige and dignity, without being under the compulsion to think, speak and act in a monotone. In fact, when any military commander becomes over-inhibited along these lines because of the illusion that this is the way to build a reputation for strength, he but doubles the necessity that his subordinates will act at all times like human beings rather than robots.

Coupled with self-control, recollection and thoughtfulness will carry a man far. Men will warm toward a leader when they come to believe that all the energy he stores up by living somewhat within himself is at their service. But when they feel that this is not the case, and that his reserve is simply the outward sign of a spiritual miserliness and concentration on purely personal goals, no amount of restraint will ever win their favor. This is as true of him who commands a whole service as of the leader of a picket squad.

To speak of the importance of a sense of humor would be unavailing if it were not that what cramps so many men isn't that they are by nature humorless but that they are hesitant to exercise what humor they possess. Within the military profession, it is as unwise as to let the muscles go soft and to spare the mind the strain of original thinking. Great humor has always been in the military tradition. The need of it is nowhere more delicately expressed than in Kipling's lines:

> My son was killed while laughing at some jest,
> I would I knew
> What it was, and it might serve me in a time
> When jests are few.

Marcus Aurelius, Rome's soldier philosopher, spoke of his love for the man who "could be humorous in an agreeable way." No reader of Grant's *Memoirs* (one of the few truly great autobiographies ever written by a soldier) could fail to be impressed by his light touch. A delicate sense of the incongruous seems to have pervaded him; he is at his whimsical best when he sees himself in a ridiculous light. Lord Kitchener, one of the grimmest warriors ever to serve the British Empire, warmed to the man who made him the butt of a practical joke. There is the unforgettable picture of Admiral Beatty at Jutland. The *Indefatigable* has disappeared beneath the waves. The *Queen Mary* had exploded. The *Lion* was in flames. Then word came that the *Princess Royal* was blown up. Said Beatty to his Flag Captain "Chatfield, there seems to be something wrong with our ... ships today. Turn two points nearer the enemy." Admiral Nimitz, surveying the terrible landscape of the Kwajalein battlefield for the first time, said gravely to his Staff: "It's the worst devastation I've ever seen except for that last Texas picnic in Honolulu." There is a characteristic anecdote of General Patton. He had just been worsted by higher headquarters in an argument over strategy. So he sat talking to his own Staff about it, his dog curled up beside him. Suddenly he said to the animal: "The trouble with you, too, Willy, is that you don't understand the big picture." General Eisenhower, probably more than any other American commander, had the art of winning with his humor. He would have qualified under Sydney Smith's definition: "The meaning of an extraordinary man is that he is eight men in one man; that he has as much wit as if he had no sense, and as much sense as if he had no wit; that his conduct is as judicious as if he were the dullest of human beings, and his imagination as brilliant as if he were irretrievably ruined."

There is hardly a soldier, marine, or bluejacket who has been long in battle but can tell some tale of an experience under fire when the pressure became almost unbearable, and then was suddenly relieved because somebody made a wisecrack or pulled something that was good for a laugh. At Bastogne the American headquarters was being shelled out of its position in the Belgian Barracks. The Commanding General called in his Chief Signal Officer and asked when it would be convenient to move. Said Lt. Col. Sid Davis, "Right now, while I've got one line left and you can still give the order." When the garrison was surrounded, and higher headquarters requested a description of the situation, the young G-3 of the operation, Col. H. W. O. Kinnard, radioed: "Think of a doughnut: we're the hole."

Who hasn't heard of the top kick who got his men forward by yelling: "Come on you ----! Do you want to live forever?" Both the Army and the Marine Corps claim him for their own, and it is possible that he was twins.

If the American fighting man did not have an instinctive feeling for the moral value of that kind of thing, the story would be long since buried, for it is as ancient as the other tale which ends: "That was no lady; that was my wife."

CHAPTER TEN

MAINSPRINGS OF LEADERSHIP

To what has been said, just a few things should be added so that the problem of generating greater powers of leadership within the officer corps may be seen in its true light.

The counselor says: "Be forthright! Be articulate! Be confident! Be positive! Possess a commanding appearance!" The young man replies: "All very good, so far as it goes. I will, if I can. But tell me, how do I get that way?" He sees rightly enough the main point, that these things are but derivatives of other inner qualities which must be possessed, if the leader is to travel the decisive mile between wavering capacity and resolute performance.

So the need is to get down to a few governing principles. Finding them, we may be able to resolve finally any argument as to whether leadership is a God-given power, or may be bestowed through earnest military teaching.

Two great American commanders have spoken their thoughts on this subject. The weight of their comment is enhanced by the conspicuous success of both men in the field of moral leading.

Said Admiral Forrest P. Sherman, Chief of Naval Operations: "I concur that we *can* take average good men and, by proper training, develop in them the essential initiative, confidence, and magnetism which are necessary in leadership. I believe that these qualities are present in the average man to a degree that he can be made a good leader if his native qualities are properly developed; whether or not he becomes a *great* leader depends upon whether or not he possesses that *extra* initiative, magnetism, moral courage, and force which makes the difference between the average man and the above-average man."

Said Gen. C. B. Cates, Commandant of the Marine Corps: "Leadership is intangible, hard to measure and difficult to describe. Its qualities would seem to stem from many factors. But certainly they must include a measure of inherent ability to control and direct, *self-confidence based on expert knowledge*, initiative, loyalty, pride, *and a sense of responsibility*. Inherent ability obviously cannot be instilled, but that which is latent or dormant can be developed. Other ingredients can be acquired. They are not easily taught or easily learned. *But leaders can be and are made.* The average good man in our service is and must be considered a potential leader."

There are common denominators in these two quotations which clearly point in one main direction. When we accent the importance of extra initiative, expert knowledge and a sense of responsibility, we are saying in other words that out of unusual application to duty comes the power to lead others in the doing of it.

The matter is as simple and as profound as that, and if we will consider for but a moment, we will see why it could hardly be otherwise.

No normal young man is likely to recognize in himself the qualities which will persuade others to follow him. On the other hand, any man who can carry out orders in a cheerful spirit, complete this work step by step, use imagination in improving it, and then when the job is done, can face toward his next duty with anticipation, need have no reason to doubt his own capacity for leadership.

The psychologists assure us that there is a sound scientific basis for what enlightened military trainers have long held to be true--that the first-class follower and the leader are one and the same. They say that this is literally true, and that their tests prove it so.

But it does not follow that every man can be taught to lead. In the majority of men, success or failure is caused more by mental attitude than by mental capacity. Many are unwilling to face the ordeal of thinking for themselves and of accepting responsibility for others. But the man determined to excel at his own work has already climbed the first rung of the ladder; in that process he perforce learns to think for himself while setting an example to those who are around him. Out of application to work comes capacity for original and creative progress. The personality characteristics, emotional balance, etc., which give him excellence in those things which he does with his own brain and hand will enable him to command the respect, and in turn, the service of other men.

To this extent, certainly leadership can be learned! It is a matter of mastering simple techniques which will give more effective expression to the character and natural talents of the individual.

Said one of this Nation's great political leaders: "There is no more valuable subordinate than the man to whom you can give a piece of work and then forget it, in the confident expectation that the next time it is brought to your attention it will come in the form of a report that the thing has been done. When this self-reliant quality is joined to executive power, loyalty and common sense, the result is a man whom you can trust."

Yes, indeed, and that is as it should be. For while no man can be sure of the possibilities of his influence over other men, every man knows by his own conscience when he is putting forth his best effort, and when he is slacking.

It is therefore not an arbitrary standard for measuring leadership capacity in men which puts the ability to excel in assigned work above everything else. The willingness and ability to strive, and to do, are best judged by what we see of men in action. If they are indifferent to assigned responsibilities, they are bad risks for larger ones, no matter how charming their personalities or what the record says about their prior experience and educational advantages. Either that proposition is both reasonable and sound, or Arnold Bennett was singing off key when he said: "I think fine this necessity for the tense bracing of the will before anything worth doing can be done. It is the chief thing that distinguishes me from the cat by the fire."

Love of work is the sheet-anchor of the man who truly aspires to command responsibilities; that means love of it, not for the reward, or for the skill exercised, but for the final and successful accomplishment of the work itself. For out of interest in the job comes thoroughness, and it is this quality above all which distinguishes the willing spirit. The willingness to learn, to study and to try harder are requisite to individual progress and the improvement of opportunity--the process that Thomas Carlyle described as the "unfolding of one's self." Thus it can be taken as an axiom that any man can lead who is determined to become master of that knowledge which an increased responsibility would require of him; and by the same token, that to achieve maximum efficiency at one's own working level, it is necessary to see it as if from the perspective of the next level up. To excel in the management of a squad, the leader must be knowledgeable of all that bears upon the command of a platoon. Otherwise the mechanism lacks something of unity.

Mark Twain said at one point that we should be thankful for the indolent, since but for them the rest of us could not get ahead. That's on the target, and it emphasizes that how fast and far each of us travels is largely a matter of free choice.

Personal advancement, within any worthwhile system, requires some sacrifice of leisure, and more careful attention to the better organization of one's working routine. But that does not entail heroic self-sacrifice or the forfeiting of any of life's truly enduring rewards. It means putting the completion of work ahead of golf and bridge. It means rejecting the convenient excuse for postponing solution of the problem until the next time. It means cultivating the mind during hours that would otherwise be spent in idleness. It means concentrating for longer periods on the work at hand without getting up from one's chair. But after all, these things do not require an extraordinary faculty. The ability of the normal man to concentrate his thought and effort are mainly the product of a personal conviction that concentration is necessary and desirable. Abbé Dimnet said: "Concentration is supposed to be exceptional only because people do not try and, in this, as in so many things, starve within an inch of plenty." And as to the mien and manner which will develop from firm commitments, another wise Frenchman, Honore Balzac, added this: "Conviction brings a silent, indefinable beauty into faces made of the commonest human clay." Here is a great part of the secret. It is in the exercise of the will that the men are separated from the boys, and that the officer who is merely anxious for advancement is put apart from the one who is truly ambitious to succeed in his life calling. Even a lazy-minded superior, in judging of his subordinates, will rarely mistake the one condition for the other.

When within the services we hear the highest praise reserved for the man "with character," that is what the term means--application to duty and thoroughness in all undertakings, along with that maturity of spirit and judgment which comes by precept, by kindness, by study, by watching, and above all, by example. The numerous American commanders from all services who have been accorded special honor because they rose from the ranks have invariably made their careers by the extra work, self-denial and rigor which the truly good man does not hesitate to endure. The question facing every young officer is whether he, too, is willing to walk that road for the rewards, material and spiritual, which will surely attend it.

There is of course that commonest of excuses for rejecting the difficult and taking life easy. "I haven't time!" But for the man who keeps his mind on the object, there is always time. Figure it out! About us in the services daily we see busy men who somehow manage to find time for whatever is worth doing, while at the adjoining desks are others with abundant leisure who can't find time for anything. When something important requires doing, it is usually the busy man who gets the call.

Of the many personal decisions which life puts upon a service officer, the main one is whether he chooses to swim upstream. If he says yes to that, and means it, all things then begin to fit into place. Then will develop gradually but surely that well-placed inner confidence which is the foundation of military character. From the knowing of *what to do* comes the knowing of *how to do*, which is likewise important. Much is conveyed in few words in Army Field Forces' "Brief on Practical Concepts of Leadership." It is stressed therein that the preeminent quality which all great commanders have owned in common is a *positiveness* of manner and of viewpoint, the power to concentrate on means to a given end to the exclusion of exaggerated fears of the obstacles which lie athwart the course. Every word of that should be underscored, and above all, what it says about the need for affirmative thinking, and concentrating on how the thing can be done. The service is no place for those who hang back and view through a glass darkly. The man who falls into the vice of thinking negatively must perforce in time become fearful of all action; he lacks the power of decision, because it has been destroyed by his habit of thought, and even when circumstances compel him to say yes he remains uncommitted in spirit.

But the shadow should not be mistaken for the substance. Positiveness of manner, and redoubtable inner conviction stem only from the mastery of superior knowledge, and this last is the fruit of application, preparation, thoroughness and the willingness to struggle to gain the desired end.

CHAPTER ELEVEN

HUMAN NATURE

In the history of American arms, the most revealing chapter as to the nature of the human animal does not come from any story of the battlefield but from the record of 23 white men and two Eskimos who, on August 26, 1881, set up in isolation a camp on the edge of Lady Franklin Bay to attempt a Farthest North record for the United States.

The Expedition under command of First Lt. A. W. Greeley, USA, expected to be picked up by a relief ship after 1 year, or 2 years at most. Its supply could be stretched to cover the maximum period. But the winters were so unduly harsh that the rescue mission could not break through the ice to keep the rendezvous. During the first year, two members of the party had set a new Far North mark. The party as a whole--3 officers, 19 enlisted men, 1 civilian surgeon and the 2 natives--had survived a winter closer to the Pole than civilized men had ever lived before. So doing, they had remained in reasonably good personal adjustment to each other, despite the Arctic monotony. The discipline of the camp had been strict. Rules of subordination, sanitation, work-sharing and religious observance had been maintained, without major friction occurring in the life of the group. Lectures were given regularly, and schools were organized. Though it is recorded that the men became melancholy, sleepless, and irritable because of the long Arctic night, temper was still in so good a state that an honor system within the camp meted out extra duty to any man using an oath.

The comradely feeling remained alive within the party throughout the first winter, though morale had its first blow when Greeley issued an unwise order forbidding enlisted men to go more than 500 yards from the base without permission. The strain was beginning to tell, but there was no fatal rift in the working harmony of the group while supply and hope remained reasonably full.

But June of the second year came and passed, and no relief ship arrived. In August, Greeley decided on a retreat, intending to fall back on bases which were supposed to hold food stores. Thereafter disaster was piled upon disaster, most of it having to do with the lack of food, and the varying animal and spiritual reactions of men to a situation of utmost desperation. When the Greeley Expedition was at last rescued at Cape

Sabine on June 22, 1884, by the third expedition--the *Revenue Cutter Bear* and the *Thetis* under Commander Winfield S. Schley, USN--only seven men remained alive. Even in these, the spark of life was so feeble that their tent was down over them and they had resigned themselves to death. Two died soon after the rescue, leaving five. Most of the other 20 had perished of slow starvation, but not all. Some had been shot. Others had met death with utmost bravery trying to save their failing comrades.

All that happened to Greeley's party during the months of its terrible ordeal is known because of a diary which records the main things--the fight of discipline against the primal instincts in men, the reversion of the so-called civilized man to his real type when he knows that death is at his elbow, the strength of unity which comes of comradeship, and also the weakness in some individuals which makes it impossible for them to measure up to honor's requirements.

Men are of all kinds. Some remain base, though given every opportunity to develop compassion. Others who may appear plodding and dull, and have been denied opportunity, still have in them an immortal spark of love for humanity which gives them an unbreakable bond with their fellows in the hours of crisis.

What the case history of the Greeley Expedition proves is that *in the determining number of men, the potential is sound.* Given a wise, understanding leadership, they will stand together, and they will either persuade the others to go along, or they will help break them if they resist. If that were not the truth of the matter, no military commander in our time would be able to make his forces keep going into battle.

Until the end, discipline was kept in Greeley's force. But this was not primarily due to Lieutenant Greeley, the aloof, strict disciplinarian who commanded by giving orders, instead of by trying to command the spirits and loyalties of men. That any survived was due to the personal force and example of Sgt. (later Brig. Gen.) David L. Brainard, who believed in discipline as did Greeley, and supported his chief steadfastly, but also supplied the human warmth and helping hand which rallied other men, where Greeley's strictures only made them want to fight back. Brainard was not physically the strongest man in the Expedition, nor necessarily the most self-sacrificing and courageous. But he had what counted most--mental and moral balance.

Among the most fractious and self-centered of the individuals was the camp surgeon, highly trained and educated, and chosen because he seemed to have a way among men. Greeley was several times at the point of having him shot; the surgeon's death by starvation saved Greeley that necessity.

Among the most decent, trustworthy, and helpful was Jens, the simple Eskimo, who died trying to carry out a rescue mission. He had never been to school a day in his life.

There were soldiers in the party whom no threat of punishment, or sense of pity, could deter from taking advantage of their comrades, rifling stores, cheating on duty and even stealing arms in the hope of doing away with other survivors. When repeated offense showed that they were unreformable, they were shot.

But in the greater number, the sense of pride and of honor was stronger even than the instinct for self-preservation, though these were *average* enlisted men, not especially chosen because their records proved they had unusual fortitude.

Private Schneider, a youngster who loved dogs and played the violin, succumbed to starvation after penning one of the most revealing deathbed statements ever written: "Although I stand accused of doing dishonest things here lately, I herewith, as a dying man, can say that the only dishonest thing I ever did was to eat my own sealskin boots and the part of my pants."

Private Fredericks, accused in the early and less-trying period of meanness and injustice to his comrades, became a rock of strength in the weeks when all of the others were in physical collapse or coma, and was made a sergeant because of the nobility of his conduct. Yet this man's ambition was to be a saloonkeeper in Minneapolis.

There is still an official report on file in the Department of the Army which describes Sergeant Rice as the "bravest and noblest" of the Expedition. He is identified with most of its greatest heroisms. The man was apparently absolutely indomitable and incorruptible. He died from freezing on a last forlorn mission into the Arctic storm to retrieve a cache of seal meat for his friends. Fredericks, who had accompanied him, was so grief-stricken at the tragedy that he contemplated dying at his side, then reacted in a way which signifies much in a few words, "Out of the sense of duty I owed my dead comrade, I stooped and kissed the remains and left them there for the wild winds of the Arctic to sweep over."

Such briefly were the extremes and the middle ground in this body of human material. At one end were the amoral characters whose excesses became steadily worse as the situation blackened. At the other were Brainard and Rice--good all the way through, absolute in integrity and adjusted perfectly to other men. In between these wholly contrasting elements was the group majority, trying to do duty, with varying degrees of success. That would include Greeley, strong in self-discipline but likewise brittle. It would include Lieutenant Lockwood, a lion among men for most of the distance, but totally downcast and beaten in the last dreadful stretch, Israel, the youngest of the party who won the love of other men by his frankness and generosity, Sergeant Gardiner who was always ready to share his scraps of food with whoever he thought needed them more, Private Whisler who died begging his comrades to forgive him for having stolen a few slices of bacon, and Private Bender who alternated between feats of heroism and acts of miscreancy.

Other than their common experience, there was probably nothing unusual about this group of men. They were an average slice of American manpower as found in the services of that day, and in the fundamentals, men have changed but little since. Those who had the chance to study American men under the terrible rigor of Japanese imprisonment during World War II give an analysis not unlike the chronicles of the Greeley party. In certain of the prisoners, character, and sanity with it, held fast against every circumstance. In others, some of whom had been well educated and came from gentle homes, the brute instinct was as uppermost as in an East African cannibal.

From such crucibles as these, even more than from the remittent stresses of combat in war, comes the clearest light on the inner nature of man, insofar as it needs to be understood by the officer who may some day lead a force into battle.

Snap judgment on the data might lead to the conclusion that every individual is exactly according to his own mould, that influence from without can not catalyze character, and that hence training has little to do with winning loyalty and instilling dutifulness. That would be as radically false as to believe that training, when properly conducted, can make all men alike and can infuse all ranks with the desire for a high standard. The vanity of that hope can be read out of what happened to the force at Cape Sabine. But the positive lesson glows even more strongly. The good Sergeant, Brainard, wrote of his Lieutenant, Lockwood, that he "loved him more than a brother." It was the service which taught him the worth of that attachment; Brainard's superb courage developed initially out of his unbounded admiration for Lockwood's dauntlessness, and in time the copyist outdistanced the model. Emotionally, Greeley and Brainard were quite unlike. One was a New England Puritan, the other a hard-boiled sergeant. But they became as one in the interests of the force; service training had made that possible.

Psychologists tell us that every sense impression leaves a trace or imprint of itself on the mind, or in other words, what we are, and what we may become, is influenced in some measure by everything touching the circumference of our daily lives. The imprints become memories and ideas, and in their turn build up the consciousness, the reason and finally the will, which translates into physical action the psychological purpose. In the process, moral character may be shaped and strengthened; but it will not be transformed if it is dross in the first place. That is something which every combat leader has learned in his tour under fire; the man of whom nobody speaks good, who is regarded as a social misfit, unliked and unliking, of his comrades, will usually desert them under pressure. There are others who have the right look but will be just as quick to quit, and look to themselves, in a crisis; underneath, they are made of the same shoddy stuff as the derelict, but have learned a little more of the modern art of getting by. Leadership, be it ever so inspired, can not make a silk purse from a sow's ear. But as shines forth in the record of Greeley and his men, it can reckon with the fact that the majority is more good than mean, and that from this may be developed the strength of the whole. In the clutch, the men at Cape Sabine who believed in the word "duty," and who understood spiritually that its first meaning was mutual responsibility, remained joined in an insoluble union. That was the inevitable outcome, leadership doing its part. The minority had no basis for organic solidarity, as each of its number was motivated only by self-interest. Goodwill and weakness may be combined in one man; bad will and strength in another. High moral leading can lift the first man to excel himself; it will not reform the other. But there is no other sensible rule than that all men will be approached with trust, and treated as trustworthy until proved otherwise beyond reasonable doubt.

To transfer this thought to even the largest element in war, it will be seen that *it is not primarily a cause which makes men loyal to each other, but the loyalty of men to each other which makes a cause.* The unity which develops from man's recognition of his dependence upon his fellows is the mainspring of every movement by which society, or any autonomy within it, moves forward.

It is a common practice to say "Men are thus-and-so." Nothing is more attractive than to make some glittering generalization about the human race, and from it draw a moral for the instruction of those who work with human material. But from all that we have learned from the experience of men under inordinate pressure, either in war or wherever else military forces have been sorely tested, it would be false to say either that the desire for economic security or the instinct for self-preservation is the driving force in every man's action. To those who possess the strength of the strong, honor is the main shaft; and they can carry a sufficient number of the company along with them to stamp their mark upon whatever is done by the group. No matter what their personal strength, however, they too are dependent on the others. There is no possibility of growth for any man except through the force, and by the works of those about him, though the manner of his growth is partly a matter of free choice. To most men, the setting of the good example is a challenge to pride and a stimulus to action. To nearly every member of the race, confidence and inspiration come mainly from the influence which living associates have upon them. That training is most perfect which takes greatest advantage of this truth, employing it in balance toward the development of a spirit of comradeship and the doing of work with a manifestly military purpose. Peace training is war training and nothing less. There is no other basis for the efficient operation of military forces even when the skies are clear. *But no commander or instructor can convince men of the decisive importance of the object if he himself regards it as only an intellectual exercise.*

The Army's "Brief on Practical Concepts of Leaderships," published 1 January 1950, well points out the desirability of leaders realizing it is vain to expect that training can bring men forward uniformly. The better men advance rapidly; the men of average attainments remain average; the below-average lose additional ground to the competition. In consequence, the chance for balance in the organizational structure depends upon the leader progressing in such close knowledge of his men that those who are strong in various aspects of the team's general requirements compensate for the weaknesses of others, irrespective of MOS numbers. It is not less essential that the followers know each other and prepare themselves to complement each other.

Obviously, this cannot be done when personnel changes are so frequent that those concerned have no chance to see deeper than the surface.

Even when to do any labor meant sapping the small store of energy deriving from a few ounces of food each day, Greeley's men kept alive the spark of morale and mutual support by maintaining a work schedule, until the day came when there was no longer a man who could stand. To fight off despondency, they held to a nightly schedule of lectures and discussions in their rude shelters, until speech became an agony because of throats poisoned by eating of caterpillars, lichens and saxifrage blossoms. In their worst extremity, Private Fredericks, unlettered but a man of great common sense and moral power, became the doctor, cook and forager for the party.

Men do not achieve a great solidarity, or preserve it, simply by *being* together. Their mutual bonds are forged only by *doing* together that which they have been made convinced is constructive. Their view of its importance is usually contingent upon what others tell them, and upon a continuing emphasis thereof. *Unity is all at one time a consequence of, and a cause and condition for great accomplishment.* Toward that end, it is neither vital nor desirable that all members of the group coincide in their motives, ideas and methods of expression. What is important is that each man should know, and to a reasonable extent incorporate into his own life the thoughts, desires and interests of the others. Such sentiments, fixed by repetition, remain as a habit during the life of the group, and provide the base for disciplined action. But when men are not thus drawn together and the cord of sympathy remains unstrung, there is no basis for control, nor any element of contact by which the group may identify itself with some larger entity and profit by transfusion of its moral strength.

The absence of a common purpose is the chief source of unhappiness in any collection of individuals. Lacking it, and the common standard of justice which is one of its chief agents, men become more and more separate units, each fighting for his own rights. Yet paradoxically, if an organic unity is to develop within any body of free men, drawn from a free society to serve its military institutions, and if the fairest use is to be made of their possibilities, the processes of the institution must embody respect for the dignity of the individual, for his rights, and not less, for his desire for worthwhile recognition. The profile of every man depends upon the space which others leave him. "Of himself," said Napoleon, "a man is nothing." But every man also contributes with his every act to the level of what his group may attain. One of the foremost leaders in the United States Navy in World War II said this about the integrity of personality: "Every person is unique. Human talents were never before assembled in exactly the same way that they have been put together in yourself. Nothing like you ever happened before. No one can predict with accuracy how you will grow in your particular combination of skills if allowed complete freedom of movement." If there is one word out of place in that statement, it is "complete;" no one has complete freedom but a buccaneer, and it is for the exercise of it that organized society swings him from a gibbet. It is only when personal freedom of action operates within an area limited by the rights and welfare of others that subordination, in its best sense, takes place. To direct a body of men toward the acceptance of this principle, so that thereby they may attain social coherence as a group and greater strength of personal character, is the most solid contribution that an officer can make to the arms of his country.

He can succeed in this without being godlike in wisdom or pluperfect in temper. But it is necessary at least that he be interesting, and that he know how to get out of his own tracks, lest he be over-run by his own organization. Whatever his rank, *it is impossible for any man to lead if he is himself running behind.* This bespeaks the need of constant study, the constant use of one's personal powers and the exercise of the imagination. As men advance, that which was good soon ceases to be good simply because something better is possible. Once men begin to acquire a sense of organization, they also come to take the measure of those who are over them. They will then move instinctively toward the one man who possesses the greatest measure of social energy. The accolade of leadership is not inherent in the individual but is conferred on him by the group. It does not always follow that a man can develop an influence with others which is proportionate to his talents and capacity for work. Leadership in work is a main requirement, but if the group does not warm toward the appointed leader, if its members can not feel any enthusiasm about him, they will be hypercritical of whatever he does.

History confirms, and a study of the workings of the human mind supports one proposition which many of the great captains of war have accepted as a truism. "There are no bad troops: there are only bad leaders." Taking on percentage what we already know of our average American raw material, as it had proved itself in every war, and as it has been studied in such a laboratory as the camp at Cape Sabine, no exception can be taken to that statement. On the other hand, we know equally well that leadership can be taught and it can be acquired. Much of our best material lies fallow, awaiting a hand on the shoulder, and the touch of other men's confidence, before it can step forward. This is not because men with a sound potential for leading must necessarily have an outward air of modesty among their major virtues, but because a man--particularly a young man--cannot gain a sense of his power among his fellows except as they give him their confidence, and vivify his natural desire to be something better than the average. There is no indication that at any stage of his career Gen. George S. Patton was an outwardly modest man. But in reviewing the milestones in his own making, he underscored the occasion when General Pershing, then commanding the Punitive Expedition into Mexico, supported Lieutenant Patton's judgment against that of a major. These are his words: "My act took high moral courage and built up my self-confidence." It would seem altogether clear, however, that Pershing had more than a little to do with it. Col. W. T. Sherman had to be kindled by the warm touch of Mr. Lincoln and steeled by the example and strong faith of Gen. U. S. Grant before he could believe in his own capacity for generalship. We all live by information and not by sight. We exist by faith in others, which is the source toward knowing greater faith in ourselves.

About the elements of human nature, it is good that an officer should know enough that he will be able to win friends and influence people. But it is folly to believe that he should pursue his studies in this subject until he habitually looks at men as would a scientist putting some specimen under a powerful microscope.

Self-consciousness is by no means a serious fault in anyone confronted by a new set of responsibilities, and working among new companions. There is scarcely an officer who has not felt it, particularly in the beginning, before he is assured in his own presence. But if the greater part of the officer corps were ever to become absorbed in the business of taking men apart to see what makes them tick, thereby superinducing self-consciousness all down the line, an irremediable blight would come upon the services. There is no need to look that deeply. What matters mainly is that an officer will know how men are won to accept authority, how they can be made to unify their own strength, how they can be helped to find satisfaction and success in their employment, how the stronger men can be chosen for preferment from among them, and finally, how they can be conditioned to face the realities of combat.

The chronicles of effective military leadership date back to Gideon and his Band. Therefore any notion that it is impossible for an officer to make the best use of his men unless he is armed with all available research data and can talk the language of the philosopher and modern social scientist is little more than a twentieth century conceit. To seek and use all pertinent information is commendable, but truth comes of seeing all things in their natural proportion. To know more than is necessary blunts one's own weapons. The application of common sense to the problem is more vital than the possession of an inexhaustible store of data which has no practical bearing upon the matter at hand. As was said by a philosopher three centuries ago: "It is remarkable in some that they could be so much better if they could but be better in some thing."

CHAPTER TWELVE

GROUP NATURE

In the same way that knowledge of individual nature becomes the key to building strength within the group, an understanding of crowd nature is essential to the preservation of the unique power within the group, particularly under conditions of extreme pressure.

Whereas the central object of a training discipline is to raise a safeguard against any military body reverting to crowd form under trial by fire, history shows that paralysis both of leadership and of the ranks, obliviousness to orders, forgetfulness of means of communication, disintegration and even panic are the not uncommon reactions of military forces when first entering into battle.

From Bunker Hill and Brandywine down to Pearl Harbor and the fight at Kasserine Pass, the American battle record shows that our own troops are by no means immune to these ill effects, and that our peace time training needs, therefore, always to be reappraised with a critical eye to the main issue.

Any of these unsteadying reactions can be prevented, or at least minimized, by training which anticipates the inevitable disorders of battle--including those who are of material sort as well as the disorders of the mind--and acclimates men to the realities of the field in war. All may be averted if leadership is braced to the shock and prepared to exercise strong control. Indeed, it is a truth worthy of the closest regard that the greater number of the disarrangements which take place during combat are due to leadership feeling a tightening of the throat, and a sticking of the palate, and failing to do that which the intellect says should be done.

To take any action, when even to think of action is itself difficult, is the essential step toward recovery and the surmounting of all difficulty. It is not because of a babel of mixed voices and commands that military bodies not infrequently relapse into helplessness and stagnation in the face of the enemy. From that cause there may occur an occasional minor dislocation. Their total effect is trivial compared to the failures which come of leadership, at varying levels, failing promptly to exercise authority when nothing else can resolve the situation. Among the commonest of experiences in war is to witness troops doing nothing, or worse, doing the wrong thing, without one commanding voice being raised to give them direction. In such circumstance, any man who has the nerve and presence to step forward and give them an intelligent order in a manner indicating that he expects to be obeyed, will be accepted as a leader and will be given their support.

For this reason, under the conditions of modern battle, the coherence of any military body comes not only of men being articulate all down the line but of building up the dynamic power in each individual. It is a thoroughly sound exercise in any unit to give every man a chance to take charge, and give orders in drill, or other limited exercises, once he had learned what the orders mean. By the same token, it is good practice for the junior leader to displace a file in a training exercise, and become commanded for a time, to sharpen his own perspective.

Progress comes of making the most of our strengths rather than looking for ways to repair weaknesses. This is true in things both large and small. The platoon leader who permits himself to be bedeviled by the file who won't or can't keep step cannot do justice to the ambitions of the 10 strongest men beneath him, upon whom the life of the formation would depend, come an emergency. To nourish and encourage the top rather than to concentrate effort and exhaust nerves in trying to correct the few least likely prospects is the healthy way of growth within military organization.

Not all men are fitted by nature for the precisions of life in a barracks. They may accept its discipline while not being able to adjust to its rhythm. The normal temptation to despair of them needs to be resisted if only for the reason experience has proved they sometimes make the best men in combat. There are many types which fit into this category--the foreigner but recently arrived in America, the miner who has spent most of his years underground, the boy from the sticks who has known only the plough and furrow, the woodsman, the reservation Indian, and the men of all races who have had hard taskmasters or other misfortune in their civilian sphere, and expect to be hurt again. It is not unusual for this kind of material to show badly in training because of an ingrained fear of other men. At the same time, they can face mortal danger. *To harass the man who is trying, but can't quite do it, therefore cuts double against the strength of organization. It may ruin the man; it may also give his comrades the feeling that he isn't getting a decent break.*

The military crowd requires, above all, maturity of judgment in its leaders. It cannot be patronized safely. Nor can it be treated in the classroom manner, as if wisdom were being dispensed to schoolboys. When it has been remiss, it expects to catch unshirted hell for its failings, and though it may smart under a just bawling out, it will feel let down if the commander quibbles. But any officer puts himself on a skid, and impairs the strength of his unit, if he takes to task all hands because of the wilful failings of a minority. Strength comes to men when they feel that they are grown up and as a body are in control and under control, since it amounts to the same thing; it is only when men unite toward a common purpose that control becomes possible. In this respect, the servant is in fact the master of the situation, fully realizes it, and is not unprepared to accept proportionate responsibility.

It is a sign of a good level of discipline in a command when orders are given and faithfully carried out. But it is a sign of a vastly superior condition when men are prepared to demand those orders which they know the situation requires, if it is to be helped. No competent subordinate sits around waiting for someone else to give impulse to movement if his senses tell him that things are going to pot. He either suggests a course of action to his superior, or asks authority to execute it on his own, or in the more desperate circumstances of the battlefield, gives orders on his own initiative. To counsel any lesser theory of individual responsibility than this would leave every chain of command at the complete mercy of its weakest link, and throughout the general establishment, would choke the fount of inspiration which comes of the upward thrust of energy and of ideas.

This latter characteristic in the masses of men composing any organization is the final statement of moral responsibility for success. Within military forces, an element of command is owned by every man who is doing his duty with intelligence and imagination. That puts him on the side of the angels, and the pressure which he exerts is felt not only by his subordinates but by those topside who are doing less. Many a lazy skipper has snapped out of it and at last begun to level with his organization because he felt the hot breath of a few earnest subordinates on his neck. Many a battle unit has held to ground which it had been ready to forsake because of the example of an aid man who stayed at his work and refused to forsake the wounded. Gen. Dwight D. Eisenhower was thinking on these things when he said during World War II: "There is among the mass of individuals who carry rifles in war a great amount of ingenuity and efficiency. If men can talk naturally to their officers, the product of their resourcefulness becomes available to all." But the art of open communication requires both receiving and sending, and the besetting problem is to get officers to talk naturally to men.

In the seventeenth century Marshal Maurice de Saxe rediscovered cadenced marching which, along with the hard-surfaced roads of France, had remained buried since the time of the Romans. He reinstituted precision marching and drill within military bodies, and by that action changed European armies from straggling mobs into disciplined troops. The effects of that reform have been felt right down to the present. Baron von Steuben, the great reorganizer of the forces in George Washington's Army, simply built upon the principles which de Saxe had set forth one century earlier. These two great architects of military organization founded their separate systems upon one controlling idea-- that *if men can be trained to think about moving together, they can then be led to move toward thinking together.* De Saxe wanted keen men, not automatons; in that, he was singular among the captains of his day. He started the numbering of regiments so that they would have a continuing history and thereby benefit from *esprit de corps.* He was the first to see the great importance of battle colors and to standardize their use. Of his own military opinions he wrote: "Experts should not be offended by the assurance with which I deliver my opinions. They should correct them; that is the fruit I expect from my work."

Now to take a look at von Steuben. He was the drillmaster of the American Revolution, but he was also its greatest student of the human mind and heart. He wrote the drill regulations of the Army, and as he wrote, committed them to memory. Of his labors he said: "I dictated my dispositions in the night; in the day I had them performed." But he learned the nature of the human material for which he thought these exercises were suited by visiting the huts of the half-clad soldiers of Valley Forge, personally inspecting their neglected weapons and hearing from their own lips of their sufferings. His main technic in installing his system was to depend upon the appeal of a powerful example; to allay all doubt of exactly what was wanted, he formed a model company and drilled it himself. He was a natural man; troops warmed to him because of an unabashed use of broken English and his violently explosive use, under stress, of "gottam!" which was his only quasi-English oath. In countenance he was strikingly like Gen. George S. Patton and there were other points of resemblance. A private soldier at Valley Forge was impressed with "the trappings of his pistols, the enormous holsters of his pistols, his large size, his strikingly martial aspect." But while he liked to dine with great men at his table, he chose to complete his list with officers of inferior rank. Once at Valley Forge he permitted his aides to give a dinner for junior officers on condition that none should be admitted that had on a whole pair of breeches. This was making the most of adversity. While wearing two stars and serving as Inspector General of the Army, he would still devote his whole day to the drilling of a squad of 10 or 12 men to get his system going. To a former Prussian associate he wrote this of Americans: "You say to your soldier, 'Do this!' and he doeth it; but I am obliged to say, 'This is the reason that you ought to do that,' and then he does it."

This was the key to the phenomenal success of his system. Within 6 weeks after he began work at Valley Forge, the Continental Army was on a new footing of self-confidence. His personal diligence in inquiring into the conduct of all officers toward their men, and his zeal in checking the accoutrement and carriage of every soldier established within the Army its first standard of inspection. Officers began to divide their scant rations with their men so that they would look better. But though he drilled the men of Valley Forge in marching and maneuver, Steuben paid no attention to the manual of arms, and let that wait until after he had gone into battle with these same forces. He explained why in these words: "Every colonel had introduced a system of his own and those who had taken the greatest pains were naturally the most attached to their work. Had I destroyed their productions, they would have detested me. I therefore preferred to pay no special attention to this subject until I had won their confidence." To take hold at the essential point and postpone action on the relatively unimportant, to respect a worthy pride and natural dignity in other men, and finally, to demonstrate that there is a better way in order to win men's loyalty and to use loyalty as the portal to more constructive collective thought--all of these morals shine in this one object lesson. The most revealing light upon the character of Steuben comes of the episode in which he had one Lieutenant Gibbons arrested for an offense, which he later learned another had committed. He then went before the Regiment. It was raining hard, but he bared his head and asked Gibbons to come forward. "Sir," he said, "the fault which was committed might, in the presence of an enemy, have been fatal. Your

Colonel tells me you are blameless. I ask your pardon. Return to your command."

Mistakes will occur. Tempers will go off half-cocked even among men of good habit. Action will be taken on impulse rather than full information, despite every warning as to its danger. But no officer who has ever done serious injustice to a subordinate can do less than Steuben did, if he wants to keep respect. Admiral Halsey wrote about how he had once relieved one of his Captains in battle, found months later that he had misjudged him, and then tried by every means within his power to make redress.

The main connecting link between the perfecting of group action in training and the end product of unity and economy of operations in battle has never been better than imperfectly expressed even by such masters as de Saxe and von Steuben, who felt it by profound instinct. The time-honored explanation is that when men accustom themselves to obeying orders, the time ultimately arrives when they will obey by habit, and that the habit will carry over into any set of circumstances requiring response to orders. This has the quality of relative truth; it is true so far as it goes, but it undersells the major values.

The heterogeneous crowd is swayed by the voices of instinct. Properly trained, any military unit, being a homogeneous body, should be swayed by the voice of training. Out of uniformity of environment comes uniformity of character and spirit. From moving and acting together men grow to depend upon, and to support, each other, and to subordinate their individual wills to the will of the leader. And if that were all that training profited them, they would rarely win a battle or a skirmish under modern conditions!

Today the supreme value of any training at arms which fixes habit is that, under conditions of absolute pressure, it enables men to take the primary steps essential to basic security without too great taxing of their mental faculties and moral powers; this leaves their senses relatively free to cope with the unexpected. The unforeseen contingency invari-ably happens in battle, and its incidence supplies the supreme test of the efficacy of any training method. Surprise has no regard for the impor-tance of rank; in combat any unit's fortune may pivot on the judgment and initiative of the file who has last joined it. Therefore the moral object in training is stated without any qualification in words once used by a wise Frenchman, Dr. Maurice Campeaux: "*It should be the subordination of the individual's will to the leader's, and not its surrender or destruction."* All training at all levels has a dual object--to develop us all as leaders of men and followers of leaders. Its technics are most perfect when they serve evenly these parallel purposes. In consequence, when any officer thinks only on: "What is policy?" rather than: "What should policy be for the good of the service?" he has trained his sights too low.

Even in modern warfare, however, there are exceptional circumstances in which success is altogether dependent upon the will and judgment of the leader, and undeviating response to his orders. The commander of a buttoned-up tank is the master of its fortunes, and what happens for better or worse is according to the strength of his personal control. Within a submerged submarine during action, the situation is still more remarkable. Only one man, the commander of the ship, can see what is occurring, and he only with one eye; the resolving of every situation depends on his judgment as to what should be done. Yet those who have the surest knowledge of this service have said that the main problem in submarine warfare is to find a sufficient body of officers who will rise superior to the intricacies of their complicated machines, and will make their own opportunities and take advantage of them. That is hardly unique. The same quality is the hallmark of greatness in any individual serving with a combat arm. The military crowd will double its effort for a leader when success rides on his coattails; but he needs first to capture their loyalty by keeping his contracts with them, sweetening the ties of organization, and convincing them that he is a man to be followed. His luck (which despite all platitudes to the contrary is an element in success) begins when his men start to believe that he was born under a lucky star. But they are not apt to be so persuaded unless he can make his outfit shine in comparison with all others. The best argument for establishing a low VD score and a high disciplinary and deportment record within any unit is that it convinces higher authority that the unit is well run and is trying, and is therefore entitled to any extra consideration that may be requested. All who have been closely identified with the inner working of any higher headquarters in the American establishment know that it works this way. On the other hand, the fundamental idea is almost as old as the hills. Turning back to Cicero, we will find these words: "Neither the physician nor the general can ever, however praiseworthy he may be in the theory of his art, perform anything highly worthwhile without experience in the rules laid down for the observation of all small duties."

The Old Roman added that between men nothing is so binding as a similarity of good dispositions.

Within the military crowd, and granting to each the same quality of human material, the problem of achieving organic unity in the face of the enemy is one thing on a ship, and quite another among land-fighting forces. Loyalty to the ship itself provides an extra and incisive bond among naval forces. Given steadiness in the command, men will fight the ship to the limit, if only for the reason that if they fail to do so, there is no place to go but down. The physical setting of duty is defined by material objects close at hand. The individual has only to fit himself into an already predetermined frame. He knows when he is derelict, and he knows further that his dereliction can hardly escape the eye of his comrades. The words: "Now Hear This!" have the particular significance that they bespeak the collected nature of naval forces, and the essential unifying force of complete communications.

If the situation were as concrete, and the integrating influences as pervading among field forces as in the Navy, land warfare would be relieved of a great part of its frictions. Except among troops defending a major fortress with all-around protection, there is no such possibility. Field movement is always diffusing. As fire builds up against the line, its members have less and less a sense of each other, and a feeling that as individuals they are getting support. Each man is at the mercy of the contact with some other file, and when the contact breaks, he sees only blackness in the enveloping situation. Men then have to turn physically back toward each other to regain the feeling of strength which comes of organization. That, in brief, is the mathematical and psychological reason why salients into an enemy line invariably take the form of a wedge; it comes of the movements of unnerved and aimless men huddling toward each other like sheep awaiting the voice of the shepherd. The natural instincts intervene ever in the absence of strong leadership. Said the French General de Maud'huy: "However perfectly trained a company may be it always tends to become once again the crowd when suddenly shocked."

But the priceless advantage which may be instilled in the military crowd by a proper training is that it also possesses the means of recovery. That possibility--the resolution of order out of chaos--reposes within every file who has gained within the service a confidence that he has some measure of influence among his fellows. The welfare of the unit machinery depends upon having the greatest possible number of human shock absorbers--men who in the worst hour are capable of stepping forward and saying: "This calls for something extra and that means me." The restoration of control upon the battlefield, and the process of checking fright and paralysis and turning men back to essential tactical duties, does not come simply of constituted authority again finding its voice and articulating its strength to the extremities of the unit boundary. Control is a man-to-man force under fire. No matter how lowly his rank, any man who controls himself contributes to the control of others. A private can steady a general as surely as a cat can look at a king. There is no better ramrod for the back of a senior, who is beginning to buckle, than the sight of a junior who has kept his nerve. Land battles, as to the fighting part, are won by the intrepidity of men in grade from private to captains mainly. Fear is contagious but courage is not less so. The courage of any one man reflects in some degree the courage of all those who are within his vision. To the man who is in terror and bordering on panic, no influence can be more steadying than that of seeing some other man near him who is retaining self-control and doing his duty.

The paralysis which comes of fear can be lifted only through the resumption of action which will again give individuals the feeling of organization. This does not mean ordering a bayonet charge, or the firing of a volley at such-and-such o'clock. It may mean only patting one man on the back, "talking it up" to a couple of others, sending someone out to find a flank, or turning one's self to dig-in, while passing the word to others to do likewise. This is action in the realest sense of the term. *Out of reinvigorating men toward the taking of many small actions develops the possibility of large and decisive action.* The unit must first find itself before doing an effective job of finding the enemy. Out of those acts which are incidental to the establishing of order, a leader reaffirms his own power of decision.

Such things are elementary, and of the very nature of the fire fight. While there is much more to be said about the play of moral forces in the trial and success of the group under combat conditions, most of it is to be learned from other sources, and it is the duty of every officer to study all that he can of this subject, and apply it to what he does in his daily rounds.

There is no rule pertaining to the moral unifying of military forces under the pressures of the battlefield which is not equally good in the training which conditions troops for this eventuality. For the group to feel a great spiritual solidarity, and for its members to be bound together by mutual confidence and the satisfactions of a rewarding comradeship, is the foundation of great enterprise. But it is not more than that. Unaccompanied by a strengthening of the military virtues and a rise in the martial spirit, a friendly unity will not of itself point men directly toward the main object in training, nor enable them to dispose themselves efficiently toward each other on entering battle.

It does not make the military man less an agent of peace and more a militarist that he relishes his membership within a fighting establishment and thinks those thoughts which would best put his arms to efficient use. The military establishment neither declares nor makes war; these are acts by the nation. But it is the duty of the military establishment primarily to succor the nation from any great jeopardy.

CHAPTER THIRTEEN

ENVIRONMENT

The saying of the Old Sergeant that, "It takes a war to knock the hell out of the Regular Army," applies as broadly to war's effects upon the general peacetime establishment.

In the rapid expansion of the armed service which comes of a national emergency, nothing seems to remain the same. Old units fill up, and change their character. By the time they have sent out three or four cadres of commissioned and enlisted leaders to form the base for entirely new organizations, little remains of the moral foundation of the parent unit except an honored name.

Promotion is rapid and moves are frequent among the higher commanders. No sooner does a man feel fairly settled under a new commander, and confident that he will get along, than he looks up to see someone else filling the space.

Installations grow like mushrooms. Schools multiply at a phenomenal rate. The best qualified men are taken away so that they will become better qualified, either by taking an officers' course or through specialist training. Their places are taken by men who may have an equal native ability, but haven't yet mastered the tricks of the trade. This piles high the load of work on those who command.

The intake and the pipelines in all services fill with men of a quite different fiber and outlook than those which commonly pass through the peacetime training establishment.

Particularly in the drafts which flow to the army there is a curious mixture of the good with the bad. The illiterates, the low IQs and the men who are physically a few notches below par are passed for service, though under normal conditions the recruiting standards shut them out. At the other end of the scale are the highly educated men from the colleges, and the robust individuals from the factory and farm. In natural quality they are as well suited to the service as any who seek it out in peacetime, but in disposition they are likely to be a little less tractable. On the whole, however, there is no radical difference between them, if we look at both groups simply as training problems for the study of the officer.

In the midst of war, when all else is in flux, at least one thing stands fast. The methods, the self-discipline, and the personality which will best enable the officer to command efficiently during peace are identical with the requirements which fit him to shape new material most perfectly under the conditions of war.

This is only another way of saying that for his own success, in addition to the solid qualities which win him the respect of other men, when war comes, he needs a vast adaptability and a confidence which will carry over from one situation to another, or he will have no peace of mind.

It is only to the man who is burdened with unnecessary and exaggerated fears, and who mistakes for a fancied security the privilege of sitting quietly in one place, that the uprooting which comes with war is demoralizing. The natural officer sees it as an hour of opportunity, and though he may not like anything else about war, he at least relishes the strong feeling of personal contention which always develops when there are many openings inviting many men. As one World War II commander expressed it: "During war the ball is always kicking around loose in the middle of the field and any man who has the will may pick it up and run with it."

Promotion, however, and the invitation to try one's hand at some greater venture, do not come automatically to an officer because of the onset of war. The man who had marked time on his job becomes relatively worse off, not only because the competition is keener, but because in lieu of anything which marks him for preferment, there is no good reason why he should get it. Years of service are not to a man's credit short of some positive proof that the years have been well used. The following are among the reasons why certain officers are marked for high places and find the door wide open, come an emergency:

-A consistently superior showing in the efficiency reports.
-A record showing that they have done well in service schools.
-The ability to attract the eye of some high-placed superior by exceptional performance on maneuvers, in committee work or any other testing problem.
-In addition to general dutifulness, the development to a conspicuous degree of the special talents such as writing, instructing, lecturing and staff administration.

-Fluency in other languages.

-Wide and resourceful study in the fields of military history, military geography, national military policy and logistics.

-The advancement of an original idea which has led to a general improvement in any one service.

Any and all of these are extra strings to one's bow. They are the means to greater satisfaction during peacetime employment and the source of great personal advantage during the shooting season. But they should not be mistaken for the main thing. *To excell in command, and to be recognized as deserving of it, is the rightful ambition of every service officer and his main hold on the probabilities of getting wider recognition.*

This holds true of the man who is so patently a specialist that it would be wrong to waste him in a command responsibility. If he understands the art of command, and his personality and moral fortitude fit him for the leading of men, he will be in better adjustment with his circumstances anywhere in the services, and will be given greater respect by his superiors. This rule is so absolute in its workings as to warrant saying that *every man who wears the insignia of an officer in the armed forces of the United States should aspire to the same bearing and the same inner confidence as to his power to meet other men and move them in the direction he desires that is to be marked in a superior company commander.*

The natural leader is the real specialist of the armed services. He is as prodigious, and as much a man apart, as the wizard who has mastered supersonic speeds. Here we speak not alone of the ability of an officer fully to control and develop his element under training conditions, but to take the same element into battle and conserve the total of its powers with complete efficiency. The man who resolves to develop within himself the prerequisite qualities which serve such an object is moved by the worthiest of all ambitions, for he has submitted himself to the most complex task within human reach.

The self-assurance that one has promise in the field of command is in part a derivative of growth and in part a matter of instinct. But to the normal young officer, it comes as something of a delightful surprise to learn that when he speaks other men will listen, when he reasons they will become convinced, and when he gives an order his authority is accepted. Far from being a bad quality, this ingenuousness is wholesome because it reflects warm appreciation of what has been given him. It does not lessen confidence if a commander feels this way about those who are within his charge throughout his service. The best results flow when the working loyalty of other men is accepted like manna from heaven, with gratitude rather than with gratification. *Simply to feel that it is one's rightful portion is the best proof that it is not, and leads to cockiness, windiness, and self-adulation, with attendant loss of the sympathy of other men.* The consequence to the individual whose dream of success is only that he will take on more and more authority is that he will suffer from a more and more one-sided development. The great philosopher, Albert Schweitzer, holds up to other self-reliant men the example of Defoe's hero, Robinson Crusoe, because he is continually reflecting on the subject of human conduct and he feels himself so responsible for this duty that when he gets in a fight he thinks about how he can win it with the smallest loss of human life. *The conservation of men's powers, not the spending thereof, is the object of main concern to the truly qualified military commander.*

At the same time, there should be no mistake about the manner in which command is exercised. To command is not simply to compel or to convince but a subtle mixture of both. Moral suasion and material compulsion are linked in its every act. *It involves not only saying that this is the best thing to do but inferring that the thing had best be done.* Force and reason are inseparably linked in its nature, and the force of reason is not more important than the reason of force, if the matter is to be brought to a successful issue. *The very touchstone of loyalty is that just demands will be put upon it.* It cannot endure and strengthen except through finding material means of expression. When men are given absolute freedom, with no compulsion upon them but to eat and sleep, as with a group of South Sea savages, there can be no strong, uniting bond between them. As for absolute security, outside of the walls of a penitentiary it is virtually nonexistent, though one would scarcely look inside the walls expecting to find loyalty. In brief, being an active force in the lives of humankind, *loyalty is developed through the unifying of action. The more decisive the action becomes, the greater becomes the vitality of the bond.* Service men look back with an esteem, amounting almost to the love that a son feels for his father, toward the captains who led them well on the battlefield. But the best skipper they ever had on a training detail gets hardly more than a kind word.

It has already been said that the man with a preeminent ability to organize and direct the action of the military group has an outstanding and greatly prized talent. The assumption that the holder of a commission in an armed service of the United States is possessed of this quality to a degree goes with the commission; lacking it, the warrant would have been withheld. But all men vary in their capacities to respond confidently to any particular situation. Some, no matter how hard they try, lack the keen edge.

To the officer who discovers that he is especially suited, by temperament and liking, to the leading of combat forces, it comes, therefore, almost as a personal charge that he will let nothing dissuade him from the conviction that his post of duty is with the line. Though he may seek other temporary duty to advance his own knowledge and interests, he should remain mentally wedded to that which he does best, and which most other men find difficult.

If it is a good rule for him, it applies just as well to all others within his charge. This means close attention to the careers of all junior leaders from the enlisted ranks, toward the end that the fighting strength of the establishment will be conserved. The personnel people will sometimes scuttle a fine natural leader of a tactical platoon, simply because they have discovered that in civilian life he ran a garage and there is a vacancy for a motor pool operator, or switch a gunner who is zealous for his new work back to a place in the rear, because the record book says that he is an erstwhile, though reluctant, keeper of books. From their point of view, this makes sense. But they are not always aware of how difficult and essential it is to find men who can lead at fighting. It is a point which all officers need ponder, for in our modern enthusiasm over the marvels that can be worked by a classification system, we tend to overlook that fighting power is the main thing, and that the best hands are not to be found behind every bush.

When war comes, there are vast changes in the tempo and pressure of life within the armed establishment. Faced with new and unmeasured responsibility, almost every man would be depressed by the feeling that he is out far beyond his depth, if he were not buoyed by the knowledge that every other man is in like case, and that all things are relative. Once these points are recognized, the experience becomes exalting. A relatively junior officer finds himself able confidently to administer a policy applying to an entire service; a bureau, which might have been laboring to save money in the purchase of carpet tacks and pins, becomes suddenly confronted with the task of spending billions, and of getting action whatever the cost.

But despite the radical change in the scale of operations, the lines laid down for the conduct of business remain the same. The regulations under which the armed services proceed are written for peace and war, and cover all contingencies in either situation. The course of conduct which is set forth for an officer under training conditions is the standard he is expected to follow when war comes. Administration is carried out according to the same rules, though it is probably true that there is less "paper doll cutting"--meaning that the tide of paper work, though larger in volume, is more to the point. To the young officer, it must oftentime seem that, under peacetime training conditions, he is being called on constantly to read reports which should never have been written in the first place and is required to write memoranda which no one should be forced to read in the second place. For that matter, the same thought occurs not infrequently to many of his seniors. But there is this main point in rebuttal--it is all a part of the practice and conditioning for a game which is in deadly earnest when war comes. If the armed services in peace were to limit correspondence up and down the line to those things which were either routine or altogether vital, few men would develop a facility at staff procedures.

In one sense, the same generalization applies to the workings of the security system. There is the common criticism that the services always tend to over-classify papers, and make work for themselves by their careful safeguarding of "secrets" in which no one is interested. The idea is not without warrant; part of the trouble stems from the fact that the line between what can safely be made of public knowledge and what can not is impossible of clear definition. Hence the only safe rule-of-thumb is, "When in doubt, classify." There is, however, the other point that it is only through officers learning how to safeguard security, handle papers according to the regulations, and keep a tightly buttoned lip on all things which are essentially the business of the service during peacetime that they acquire the disciplined habit of which matures not only their personal success but the national safety when war comes.

Oftentimes the rules seem superfluous. A man scans a paper and sees that the contents are innocuous, and ignoring the stamp, he leaves the document on his desk, because he is too lazy to unlock the file. *But the rules mean exactly what they say, and because their purpose is of final importance to the nation, they will be enforced.* There is no surer way for an officer to blight an otherwise promising career than to become careless about security matters. The superior who looks lightly on such an offense is but seeking trouble for himself.

Even so, it is to be observed that regulations are a general guide to conduct, and though they mean what they say they are not utterly inflexible. One must not be like the half-wit described by Col. George F. Baltzell to his trainees during World War I. Joe had attached himself to the Confederate command of the Colonel's father, whose last chore before turning in was to post the boy. One night in a Virginia Tidewater operation, Joe was told to stay by a stump until morning. At dawn the unit was moving out in a fog when the elder Baltzell bethought himself of Joe. Down by the riverside his cries finally brought a faint answer through the mist, "Here I is." "What are you doing there, boy?" barked the officer, "I told you not to move." "I hain't moved, sir," replied the invisible Joe, up to his neck in water, "the river done riz." An occasional unforeseen circumstance arises in which it is nonsensical, or even impossible, to adhere to the letter of regulations, as of orders. It is then essential that an officer use plain common sense, acting according to the spirit of the regulation, so that it is clearly manifest he did the best possible thing within the determining set of conditions. For example, in the European Theater, the Historian had charge of 32 tons of documents, all classified "Confidential," "Secret" or "Top Secret." There were not enough safes or secured files in the whole of France to hold this material, which meant that established procedures could not be followed. A permanent guard and watch was put on the archive. Wooden cases were made from scrap lumber. Ample fire-fighting equipment was brought in. Personnel was drilled in evacuating the material in its order of importance, should fire occur. The setup was inspected twice daily by the commander or his executive. Though these arrangements still fell short of the letter of regulations, they perforce had to satisfy any inspector because there was no sounder alternative.

When circumstances require any officer to take a course which, while appearing in his view to be in the best interests of the service, runs counter to the lines of action laid down by constituted authority, he has the protection that he may always ask for a court to pass judgment on what he had done. We are all prone to associate the court martial process only with the fact of punishment, but it is also a shield covering official integrity. The privilege of appealing to the judgment and sense of fair play in a group of one's fellow officers is a very comforting thing in any emergency situation, requiring a desperate decision, and engaging conflicting interests. It gives one a feeling of backing even when circumstances are such that one is making a lonely decision. Almost needless to say, cases of this sort are far more likely to occur in war than during peace.

Inspection takes on a somewhat different hue during war. It becomes more frequent but, on the whole, less zealous with respect to spit-and-polish and less captious about the many little things which promote good order and appearance throughout the general establishment. This condition is accentuated as organizations move closer to the zone of fire. Higher authority becomes more engrossed in the larger affairs of operation. At all levels more and more time is taken in dealing with the next level above, which means that less and less can be given to looking at the structure down below.

What then is the key to over-all soundness in the services in any hour of great national peril? This, that in all services, at all times and at all levels, each officer is vigilant to see that his own unit, section or office is inspection-proof by every test which higher authority might apply.

It should not require the visit of an inspector to any installation to apprise those who are in charge as to what is being badly done.

The standards are neither complex nor arbitrary. They can be easily learned. Thereafter, all that is needed are the eyes to see and the will to insist firmly that correction be made.

In officership, there is simply no substitute for personal reconnaissance, nor any other technique that in the long run will have half its value. Gen. Carl A. Spaatz, the first leader of our independent Air Force, was so renowned for this disciplined habit of getting everywhere and seeing everything that, even when he was a relatively young major, a story about his ubiquitousness gained service-wide fame. An ailing recruit was being examined by a doctor at March Field. "Do you see spots before your eyes?" the doctor asked. "Heavens," groaned the recruit. "Do I have to see him in here, too?"

Once formed, the habit of getting down to the roots of organization, of seeing with one's own eyes what is taking place, of measuring it against one's own scale of values, of ordering such changes as are needed, and of following-through to make certain that the changes are made, becomes the mainspring of all efficient command action.

In battle, there is no other way to be sure. In training, there is no better way to move toward self-assurance.

CHAPTER FOURTEEN

THE MISSION

There is a main reason why the word "mission" has an especial appropriateness to the military services and implies something beyond the call of duty. The arms of the United States do not advance simply through the process of correct orders being given and then executed with promptness, vigor, and intelligence.

That is the greater part of the task, but it is by no means all. Military systems reflect the limitations and imperfections of their human material. Whatever his station, and experience, no man is wise enough and all-seeing enough that he can encompass every factor in a given problem, take correct judgment on every area of weakness, foresee all of that which has not yet happened, and then write the perfect analysis and solution for the guidance of his subordinates.

The perfecting of operations, and the elimination of grit from the machinery, therefore become the concern of *all*, directing their thought and purpose to the doing of whatever needs to be done to further the harmony and efficiency of the establishment, taking personal action where it is within their province, or calling the matter to the attention of higher authority when it is not. In this direct sense, every ensign and second lieutenant has a personal responsibility for the general well-being of the security structure of the United States. This is fact, and not theory. In World War II, many of the practical ideas which were made of universal application in the services were initiated by men of very junior rank. But the extent to which any man's influence may be felt beyond his immediate circle depends first of all upon the thoroughness with which he executes his assigned duties, since nothing else will give his superiors confidence in his judgments. It is only when he is exacting in small things, and is careful to "close the circuit" on every minor assignment, that he qualifies himself to think and act constructively in larger matters, through book study and imaginative observation of the situation which surrounds him. At this stage, an officer is well on the road to the accomplishment of his general mission.

When an order is given, what are the responsibilities of the man who receives it? In sequence, these:

To be certain that he understands what is required.

To examine and organize his resources as promptly as possible.

Fully to inform his subordinates on these points.

To execute the order without waste of time or means.

To call for support if events prove that his means are inadequate.

To fill up the spaces in the orders if there are developments which had not been anticipated.

When the detail is complete, to prepare to go on to something else.

Lt. Gen. Sir Frederick Morgan, who planned the invasion of Normandy, put the matter this way: "When setting out on any enterprise, it is as well to ask oneself three questions. To whom is one responsible? For precisely what is one responsible? What are the means at one's disposal for discharging this responsibility?"

Nothing so warms the heart of a superior as that, on giving an order, he sees his subordinate salute, say "Yes sir," then about face and proceed to carry it out to the hilt, without faltering or looking back. This is the kind of man that a commander will choose to have with him every time, and that he will recommend first for advancement.

On the other hand, clarification of the object is not only a right but a duty, and it cuts both ways. Orders are not always clear, and no superior is on firm ground when he is impatient of questions which are to the point, or resentful of the man who asks them. But it is natural that he will be doubtful of the man whose words show either that he hasn't heard or is concerned mainly with irrelevencies. The cultivation of the habit of careful, concentrated listening, and of collected thought in reading into any problem, is a principal portal to successful officership.

To say that promptness and positiveness in the execution of a mission are at all times major virtues does not imply that the good man, like an old fire horse, moves out instantly at the clang of a bell. Soundness of action involves a sense of timing. Thoroughness is the way of duty, rather than a speed which goes off half-cocked. There is frequently a time for waiting; there is always time for acute reflection. The brain which works "like a steel trap" exists only in fiction. Even such men as General Eisenhower, or Admiral Nimitz, or for that matter, Gen. U. S. Grant, have at times deferred decision temporarily while waiting for a change in tide or circumstance to help them make up their minds. This is normal in the rational individual; it is not a sign of weakness. Rather than to cultivate a belief in one's own infallibility, the mature outlook for the military man is best expressed in the injunction of the Apostle Paul: "*Let all things be done decently and in order.*" Grant, wrote of the early stage of his advance on Richmond: "At this time I was not entirely decided as to how I should move my Army." From the pen of General Eisenhower come these words: "The commander's success will be measured more by his ability to lead than by his adherence to fixed notions." Thus, in the conduct of operations not less than in the execution of orders, it is necessary that the mind remain plastic and impressionable.

Within military organization, to refuse an order is unthinkable, though to muster a case showing why some other order would serve in its place is not undutiful in an individual subordinate, any more than in a staff. By the same rule, insistence that an order be carried out undeviatingly, simply because it has been given, does not of itself win respect for the authority uttering it. Its modification, however, should never be in consequence of untempered pressure from below. To change or rescind is justified only when reestimate of all of the available facts indicates that some other order will serve the general purpose more efficiently.

Taking counsel of subordinates in any enterprise or situation is therefore a matter of giving them full advantage of one's own information and reasoning, weighing with the intellect whatever thought or argument they may contribute to the sum of considerations, and then making, without compromise, a clean decision as to the line of greatest advantage. To know how to command obedience is a very different thing from making men obey. Obedience is not the product of fear, but of understanding, and understanding is based on knowledge.

On D-day in Normandy, Lt. Turner B. Turnbull undertook to do with his platoon of 42 men a task which had been intended for a battalion; he was to block the main road to enemy forces pressing south from the Cherbourg area against the American right flank. In early morning he engaged a counterattacking enemy battalion, supported by mortars and a self-propelled gun at the village of Neuville au Plain. The platoon held its ground throughout the day. By dusk the enemy had closed wide around both its flanks and was about to cut the escape route. Turnbull had 23 men left. He said to the others, "There's one thing left to do; we can charge them." Pfc. Joseph Sebastian, who had just returned from reconnoitering to the rear, said, "I think there's a chance we can still get out; that's what we ought to do." Turnbull asked of his men, "What's your judgment?" They supported Sebastian as having the sounder idea. In a twinkling Turnbull made his decision. He told the others to get set for the run; he was losing men even while he talked; he ordered that the 12 wounded were to be left behind. Corp. James Kelly, first aid man, said he would stay with the wounded. Pfc Sebastian, who had argued Turnbull into a withdrawal, volunteered to stand his ground and cover the others with a BAR. Corp. Raymond Smitson said he would stay by Sebastian and support him with hand grenades. Sgt. Robert Niland started for one of the machine guns, to help Smitson and Sebastian in covering the withdrawal, but was shot dead by a German closing in with a machine pistol before he could reach it. The 16 remaining survivors took off like so many shots fired from a pistol, at full speed but at intervals, to minimize the target. All got back to their Battalion, though Turnbull was killed in action a few days later. Their 1-day fight had preserved the flank of an Army. For economy of effort, and power of decision, there is not a brighter example in the whole book of war.

To encourage subordinates to present their views, and to weigh them in the light of reason, is at the same time the surest way to win their confidence and to refine one's own information and judgments. However, to leave final decision to them in matters which are clearly in the area of one's own responsibility, is fatal to the character of self and to the integrity of the force.

Any officer is one among many. Behind the smallest unit is the total power of the combined services. In the main, effectiveness develops out of unity of effort. To commit one's force to desperate, unhelped enterprises, when there is support at hand which may be had for the asking, may be one road to glory, but it is certainly not the path to success in War. The Charge of the Light Brigade at Balaklava was made immortal by Tennyson's poem, but it was as foolhardy as asking a troop of Boy Scouts to capture Gibraltar. In battle, a main obligation of those who lead is to make constant resurvey of the full horizon of their resources and means of possible support. This entails in time of peace the acquisition of a great body of knowledge seemingly unrelated to the administration of one's immediate affairs. It entails, also, facing forthrightly toward every task, or assignment, giving it a full try, sweating out every obstacle, but not being ashamed to ask for help or counsel if it proves to be beyond one's powers. *To give it everything, though not quite making the grade personally, is merely an exercise in character building. But to have the mission fail because of false pride is inexcusable.*

The prayer that Sir Francis Drake wrote down for his men as he led them forth to a great adventure might well be repeated by any leader in the hour when he begins to despair because in spite of his striving he has not gained all he sought: "O Lord God, when Thou givest to thy servants to endeavour any great matter, grant us also to know that it is not the beginning, but the continuing of the same until it is thoroughly finished, which yieldeth the true glory."

The courage to start will carry a man far. Under the conditions of either war or peace, it is astonishing how many times all things come in balance for the man who is less fearful of rebuff than of being counted a cypher. One of Britain's great armored leaders, Lt. Gen. Sir Giffard Martel, digested the lesson of his whole life experience into this sentence: "If you take a chance, it usually succeeds, presupposing good judgment." Finally, it comes to that, for the willingness to accept calculated risks is of the essence of effective personal performance within the military profession. There must be careful collection of data. There must be weighty consideration of all known and knowable factors in the given situation. But beyond these things, what?

To convey the idea that an officer must by ingrained habit dispose himself to take action only after he has arrived at an exact formula, pointing exclusively in one direction, would mean only that under the conditions of war he could never get off his trousers-seat. For such fullness of information and confidence of situation are not given to combat commanders once in a lifetime.

It is customary to treat "estimate of situation" as if it were pure mathematical process, pointing almost infallibly to a definite result. But this is contrary to nature. The mind of man does not work that way, nor is it consistent with operational realities. Senior commanders are as prone as even the newest junior lieutenant to labor in perplexity between two opposing courses of action during times of crisis, and then make their decisions almost with the abruptness of an explosion. *It is post-decision steadiness more than pre-decision certitude which carries the day.* A large part of decision is intuitive; it is the byproduct of the subconscious. In war, much of what is most pertinent lies behind a drawn curtain. The officer is therefore badly advised who would believe that a hunch is without value, or that there is something unmilitary about the simple decision to take some positive action, even though he is working in the dark.

The youthful Col. Julian Ewell of the 501st Parachute Infantry Regiment, reaching Bastogne, Belgium, on the night of December 18, 1944, with only his lead battalion at hand, insisted that he be given orders, even though higher headquarters could tell him almost nothing about the friendly or enemy situations. He got his orders, and with the one battalion moved out through the dark to counter-attack. So doing, he stopped cold the German XXXXVII Panzer Corps, and compelled Hitler to alter his Ardennes plan.

To grasp the spirit of orders is not less important than to accept them cheerfully and keep faith with the contract. But the letter of an instruction does not relieve him who receives it from the obligation to exercise common sense. In the Carolina maneuvers of 1941, a soldier stood at a road intersection for 3 days and nights directing civilian traffic, simply because the man who put him there had forgotten all about it. Though he was praised at the time, he was hardly a shining example to hold up to troops. Diligence and dullness are mutually exclusive traits. The model who is well worth pondering by all services is Chief Boatswain L. M. Jahnsen who on the morning of Pearl Harbor was in command of the yard garbage scow YG-17. She was collecting refuse from the fleet when the first Japanese planes came over. As the West Virginia began to burn, Jahnsen headed his scow into the heat and smoke and ordered his men to man their single fire hose. The old assignment forgotten, with overheated ammunition exploding all around him, he stood there directing his men in all that could be done to lessen the ruin of the fleet.

Within the services, a special glory attends those whose heroism or service is "above and beyond the call of duty." But they owe their fundamental character to the millions of men who have followed the path of duty above and beyond the call of orders.

Whatever the nature of an officer's assignment, there are compensations. The conventional attitude is to speak disparagingly of staff duty, sniff at service with a higher administrative headquarters as if it were somehow lacking in true masculine appeal, and express a preference for duty "at sea," "with troops" or "in the field." Although most of this is flapdoodle, it probably does no more harm than Admiral William F. Halsey's grimace over the fact that he once "commanded an LSD--Large

Steel Desk." He is a poor stick of a military man who has no natural desire to try his hand at the direct management of men, if for no better reason than to test his own mettle. Even the avowed specialist is better equipped for his own groove if he has proved himself at the other game.

Staff work, however, has its own peculiar rewards. Chief among them are the broadening of perspective, a more intimate contact with the views, working methods and personality characteristics of higher commanders and the chance to become acquainted with administrative responsibility from the viewpoint of policy. Although it sounds mysterious and even forbidding, until one has done it, the procedures are not more complex nor less instructive than in any other type of assignment.

There are no inside secrets about what goes here that is different, or will not work equally well elsewhere. The staff is simply the servant of the general force; it exists but to further the welfare of the fighting establishment. Those within it are remiss if they fail to keep this rule uppermost. Consequently, no special attitude is called for, other than an acute receptiveness. The same military bearing, the same naturalness of manner which enable an officer to win the confidence and working loyalty of his men will serve just as well when he is dealing with higher authority.

CHAPTER FIFTEEN

DISCIPLINE

Though many of the aspects of discipline can be discussed more appropriately in other sections of this book, an officer must understand its particular nature within American military forces if he is to win from his men obedience coupled with activity at will.

It frequently happens that the root meaning of a word more nearly explains the whole context of ideas with which it is legitimately associated than the public's mistaken use of the same word. Coming from the Latin, "to discipline" means "to teach." Insofar as the military establishment of the United States is concerned, nothing need be added to that definition. Its discipline is that standard of personal deportment, work requirement, courtesy, appearance and ethical conduct which, inculcated in men, will enable them singly or collectively to perform their mission with an optimum efficiency.

Military discipline, in this respect, is no different than the discipline of the university, a baseball league or a labor union. It makes specific requirements of the individual; so do they. It has a system of punishments; so do they. These things are but incidental to the end result. Their main object is to preserve the interests and further the opportunity of the cooperative majority. But the essential difference between discipline in the military establishment and in any other free institution is this, that if the man objects, he still does not have the privilege of quitting tomorrow, and if he resists or becomes indifferent and is not corrected, his bad example will be felt to the far end of the line.

Though the failure to stop looting by our forces during World War II, and the redeployment riots which followed it, are both unpleasant memories, they underscored a lesson already affirmed by every American experience at arms. The most contagious of all moral diseases is insubordination, and it has no more respect for rank than the plague. When higher authority winks at its existence among the rank and file, it will contaminate upward as well as down. Once a man condones remissness, his own belief in discipline begins to wither. The officer who tolerates slackness in the dress of his men soon ceases to tend his own appearance, and if he is not called to account, his sloppy habits will shortly begin to infect his superior. There is only one correct way to wear the uniform. When any deviations in dress are condoned within the services, the way is open to the destruction of all uniformity and unity. This continuing problem of stimulating all ranks to toe-up to that straight line of bearing and deportment which will build inner confidence and win public respect is the main reason why, as George Washington put it: "To bring men to a proper degree of subordination is not the work of a day, a month, or a year." It calls not simply for a high-minded attitude toward the profession of arms but for infinitely patient attention to a great variety of detail. An officer has a disciplined hold upon his own job only when, like the air pilot preparing to take off, he makes personal check of every point where the machinery might fail. The stronger his example of diligence, the more earnestly will it be followed by the ablest of his subordinates, and they in turn will carry other men along. No leader ever fails his men--nor will they fail him--who leads them in respect for the disciplined life. Between these two things--discipline in itself and a personal faith in the military value of discipline--lies all the difference between military maturity and mediocrity. A salute from an unwilling man is as meaningless as the moving of a leaf on a tree; it is a sign only that the subject has been caught by a gust of wind. But a salute from the man who takes pride in the gesture because he feels privileged to wear the uniform of the United States, having found the service good, is the epitome of military virtue. Of those units which were most effective, and were capable of the greatest measure of self-help during World War II combat, it was invariably remarked that they observed the salute and the other rules of courtesy better than the others, even when engaged.

The level of discipline is in large part what the officers in any unit choose to make it. The general aim of regulations is to set an over-all standard of conduct and work requirement for all concerned. Training schedules, operational directives and other work programs serve the same end. *But there is still a broad area in which the influence of every officer is brought to bear. To state what is required is only the beginning; to require what has been stated is the positive end.* The rule of courtesy may be laid down by the book; it remains for the officer to rule by work rather than working by rules, and by setting the good example for his men, stimulate their acceptance of orderly military habits. A training schedule may stipulate that certain tasks be carried out but only the officer in charge can assure that the work will be accomplished with fidelity.

The level of discipline should at all times be according to what is needed to get the best results from the majority of dutiful individuals. There is no practical reason for any sterner requirement than that. There is no moral justification for countenancing anything less. *Discipline destroys the spirit and working loyalty of the general force when it is pitched to the minority of malcontented, undutiful men within the organization, whether to punish or to appease them.* When this common sense precept is ignored, the results invariably are unhappy.

However, it is not here inferred that what has to be done to build strong discipline in forces will at all times be welcomed by the first-class men within a unit, or that their reaction will always be approval. Rather, it is to say that they will accept what is ordered, even though they may gripe about it, and that ultimately their own reason will convince them of the value of what is being done.

Until men are severely tried, there is no conclusive test of their discipline, nor proof that their training at arms is satisfying a legitimate military end. The old game of follow-the-leader has no point if the leader himself, like the little girl in a Thomas Hardy novel, is balked by insuperable obstacles one-quarter inch high. *All military forces remain relatively undisciplined until physically toughened and mentally conditioned to unusual exertion.* Consider the road march! No body of men could possibly enjoy the dust, the heat, the blistered foot and the aching back. But hard road marching is necessary if a sound foundation is to be built under the discipline of fighting forces, particularly those whose labors are in the field. And the gain comes quickly. The rise in spirits within any organization which is always to be observed after they rebound from a hard march does not come essentially from the feeling of relief that the strain is past, but rather from satisfaction that a goal has been crossed. *Every normal man needs to have some sense of a contest, some feeling of resistance overcome, before he can make the best use of his faculties. Whatever experience serves to give him confidence that he can compete with other men helps to increase his solidarity with other men.*

It must be accepted that discipline does not break down under the strain of placing a testing demand upon the individual. It is sloth and not activity that destroys discipline. Troops can endure hard going when it serves an understandable end. This is what they will boast about mainly when the fatigue is ended. A large part of training is necessarily directed toward conditioning them for unusual hardship and privation.

They can take this in stride. But no power on earth can reconcile them to what common sense tells them is unnecessary hardship which might have been avoided by greater intelligence in their superiors. When they are overloaded, they know it. When they are required to form for a parade two hours ahead of time because their commander got over-anxious, or didn't know how to write an order, again they know it! *And they are perfectly right if they go sour because this kind of thing happens a little too often within the command.*

Within our system, that discipline is nearest perfect which assures to the individual the greatest freedom of thought and action while at all times promoting his feeling of responsibility toward the group. *These twin ends are convergent and interdependent for the exact converse of the reason that it is impossible for any man to feel happy and successful if he is in the middle of a failing institution.* War, and all training operations in preparation for it, have become more than ever a problem of creating diversity of action out of unity of thought. Its modern technological aspects not only require a much keener intelligence in the average file but a higher degree of initiative and courageous confidence in his own judgments. If the man is cramped by monotonous routine, or made to feel that he cannot move unless an order is barked, he cannot develop these qualities, and he will never come forward as a junior leader. *On the other hand, the increased utilization of the machine in military operations, far from lessening the need of mutual support and unified action, has increased it.* One of the hazards of high velocity warfare is that reverse and disaster can occur much more swiftly than under former systems. Thus the need for greater spiritual integration within forces, and increased emphasis upon the values of more perfect communication in all forms, at the same time that each individual is trained to initiate action for the common good. Only so can the new discipline promote a higher efficiency based on a more steadfast loyalty of man to man. In the words of Du Picq, who saw so deeply into the hearts of fighting men: "If one does not wish bonds broken, one should make them elastic and thereby strengthen them."

The separate nature of military service is the key to the character of the discipline of its several forces. In the United States, we have fallen into the sloppy habit of saying that a soldier, bluejacket, airman, coast guardsman or marine is only an American civilian in uniform. The corollary of this quaint notion is that all military organization is best run according to the principles of business management. The truth of either of these ideas is to be disputed on two grounds: both are contrary to truth and contrary to human nature. An officer is not only an administrator but a magistrate, and it is this dual role which makes his function so radically different than anything encountered in civil life--to say nothing of the singleness of purpose by which the service moves forward. Moreover, the armed service officer deals with the most plastic human material within the society--men who, in the majority, the moment they step into uniform, are ready to seek his guidance toward a new way of life.

However, these fancies are but tangential aspects of a much larger illusion--that the Armed Services of the United States, since they serve a democracy, can better perfect themselves according to the measure that they become more and more democratic. Authority is questioned in democratic countries today, not only in government, but in industry, the school, the church and the home. But to the extent that military men lose their faith in its virtue and become amenable to ill-considered reforms simply to appease the public, they relinquish the power to protect and nurture that growth of free men, free thought and free institutions which began among a handful of soldiers in Cromwell's Army and was carried by them after the Restoration to the North American mainland. The relation of the military establishment to American democracy is as a shield covering the body. But no wit of man can make it a wholly "democratic" institution as to its own processes without vitiating its strength, since it progresses through the exercise of unquestioned authority at various levels.

One of these levels is the plane on which an ensign or second lieutenant conducts his daily dealings with his men. George Washington left behind these words, which are as good today as when he uttered them from his command post: "Whilst men treat an officer as an equal, regard him no more than a broomstick, being mixed together as one common herd, no order nor discipline can prevail." Out of his experience in the handling of deck divisions during World War II, Edmund A. Gibson, Boatswain's Mate, First Class, also said something which, put alongside Washington's words, brings the whole subject of officer-man relationships into clear focus: "Speaking for Navy men, I am certain that they are entirely without any feeling of inferiority, social or otherwise, to their officers. If superiority or inferiority of any kind enters into their contemplation at all, it is in the shape of a conviction, doubtless a wrong one, that every serviceman, as a professional warrior, is above the narrow interests which obsess the civilian."

Those who have served both as officer and under-officer well understand the appropriateness of these two ideas, each to the other, that the superior position of the officer must be preserved for the good of the service, but that this engages recognition of the individual equality of the enlisted man. They know, if they have observed well and truly during their service in the ranks, that the highest type enlisted man wants his officer to act the part, maintain dignity and support the ideals which are consonant with the authority vested in him by the Nation. But this same man at the same time expects his officers to concede him his right to a separate position and to respect his privacy. It is a pitiable eminence that is not well founded upon sure feeling for the value of its own prestige and the importance of this factor at all levels.

In the military service of the United States, there is always room for firm and forthright friendship between officer and man. There is room for a close, uniting comradeship. There is room for frank intellectual discussion and the exchange of warm humor; no man goes far if he is all salt and no savor. There is room for that kind of intimacy which enables each to see the other as a human being, know something of the other's emotions and help clear the atmosphere for honest counsel on personal and organizational problems.

But there is no room for familiarity, since as in any other sphere, it breeds contempt. When it occurs, respect flies out the window, the officer loses part of his command authority and discipline breaks down. Familiarity cannot obtain between the superior and the subordinate without the vice of favoritism entering into the conduct of organizational matters, even though the former is guilty only of an over-zealous goodwill and the latter is otherwise sensible to the interests of the unit. The chief damage comes from the effect upon all others. It is when all the bars are let down that men communicate those inner failings which a greater reserve would keep under cover. Familiarity toward a superior is a positive danger; toward a subordinate, it is unbecoming and does not increase his trust. In excess, it can have no other effect than a breach of confidence on both sides.

Changes in the environmental situation do not alter the natural proprieties of this relationship between any two men, the one having higher authority and the other having the obligation of obedience. Under the conditions of modern war, the two not infrequently may be required to work together as a unit, almost apart from the influence of organizational discipline. Hardship and necessity may compel them to extend the limit of personal accommodation to each other. They may go into battle together. They may sleep in the same bed or foxhole. They may drink from a common bottle and draw upon each other for the means to keep going. But in adapting one's course according to the rigors of any unconventional situation, authority is maintained only through the exercise of a higher sense of responsibility. However, the rule is applied according to the circumstance, the rule itself remains inflexible.

Officers and men working together as a compact team, in any type of military operation where success, and coordinated action in the face of danger, depend mainly upon the moral resources within one small group, develop a closer camaraderie and become less formal than is normal elsewhere throughout the services. The close confinement in which tank forces, airplane crews and submarine crews must operate would stifle morale and torture nerves otherwise. Whatever the patience of men under such conditions, sooner or later they get on each other's nerves. Therefore that system of relationships is best which is least artificial and most relaxing to the spirit of the natural man. But to construe this as a deviation from the standards of discipline is to mistake the shadow for the substance.

CHAPTER SIXTEEN

MORALE

To grow in knowledge of how to win a loyal and willing response from military forces, there must first be understanding of the springs of human action, what they are, and how they may be directed toward constructive ends. This done, the course which makes for the perfecting of forces during peacetime training need only be extended to harden them for the risk and stress of war.

The mainspring is morale. The meaning of the word is already known in a general way to every man who has qualified for officership, so it is hardly necessary to redefine it. A World War II bluejacket said it this way: "Morale is when your hands and feet keep working when your head says it can't be done." That says it just as well as anything written by du Picq or Baron von Steuben. Nothing new need be added.

The handiest beginning is to consider morale in conjunction with discipline, since in military service they are opposite sides of the same coin. When one is present, the other will be also. But the instilling of these things in military forces depends upon leadership understanding the nature of the relationship.

As to discipline, until recent years, military forces tended to stress the pattern rather than the ideal. The elder Moltke, one of the great masters of the military art, taught his troops that it was of supreme importance that they form accurately in training, since the perfection of their formations would determine their efficiency in battle. Yet in the Franco-Prussian War, these formations proved utterly unsuited to the heavily-wooded terrain of the theater, and new ones had to be devised on the spur of the moment.

This is the familiar story. It was repeated by United States forces in World War II during the Normandy hedgerow fighting and the invasions of the Central Pacific atolls. Troops had to learn the hard way how to hit, and how to survive, in moving through jungle or across the mountains and desert. When that happened, the only disciplinary residue which mattered was obedience to orders. The movements they had learned by rote were of less value than the spiritual bond between one man and another. The most valuable lesson was that of mutual support. And unless this lesson was supported by confidence in the judgment of those in authority, it is to be doubted that they were helped at all.

Finally, that confidence is the *sine qua non* of all useful military power. The moral strength of an organic unity comes from the faith in ranks that they are being wisely directed and from faith up top that orders will be obeyed. When forces are tempered by this spirit, there is no limit to their enterprise. They become invincible. Lacking it, however, any military body, even though it has been compelled to toe the mark in training, will deteriorate into a rabble under conditions of extraordinary stress in the field, as McDowell's Army did at Bull Run in the American Civil War, and as Hitler's Armies did in 1945 after the Rhine had been crossed at Remagen.

In its essentials, discipline is not measured according to how a man keeps step in a drill yard, or whether he salutes at just the right angle. The test is how well and willingly he responds to his superiors in all *vital* matters, and finally, whether he stands or runs when his life is at stake. History makes this clear. There are countless examples of successful military forces which had almost no discipline when measured by the usual yardsticks, yet had a high battle morale productive of the kind of discipline which beats the enemy in battle. The French at Valmy, the Boers in the South African War, and even the men of Capt. John Parker, responding to his order on the Lexington Common, "Don't fire unless fired upon, but if they mean to have a war, let it begin here," instance that men who lack training and have not been regimented still may express themselves as a cohesive force on the field of fire, provided that they are well led.

If we will accept the basic premise that discipline, even within the military establishment of the United States, is not a ritual or a form, but is simply that course of conduct which is most likely to lead to the efficient performance of an assigned responsibility, it will be seen that morale does not come of discipline, but discipline of morale.

True enough, our recruits are given a discipline almost from the moment that they take the oath. Their first lesson is the necessity for obedience. They are required immediately to conform to a new pattern of conduct. They respond to disciplinary treatment even before they learn to think as a group and before the attitude of the group has any influence upon them. Discipline bears down before morale can lift up. Momentarily, they become timid before they have felt any pain. These

131

first reactions help condition the man to his new environment. They are in part demoralizing, but on the upswing he begins to realize that half the fun in life comes of seeing what one can do in a new situation. The foundation of his morale is laid when he begins to think of himself as a member of the fighting establishment, rather than as a civilian. Thereafter all that is done to nourish his military spirit and to arouse his thirst for professional knowledge helps to build his moral power.

But follow the man a little longer. The time quickly comes when he knows his way around in the service. His earlier fears and hesitations are largely gone. He acquires strength and wisdom from the group. He becomes able to judge his own situation against an attainable standard within the service. He is critically conscious of the merits of his superiors from what he has himself experienced and what others tell him. He knows what is boondoggling and what is not.

From that point on, discipline has little part in alerting the man or in furthering the building of his moral power. That which moves him mainly is the knowledge that he is a personal success, and that he belongs to an efficient unit which is in capable hands. Certain of the outer signs of discipline, such as the cadence of the march or snap in the execution of the manual, he may subconsciously reenforce his impression of these things. But if he feels either that he is an outsider or that the club isn't worth joining, no amount of spit and polish will alter his opinion.

He is able to recognize a right and reasonable discipline as such, even though it causes him personal inconvenience, because he has acquired a sense of military values. But if it is either unduly harsh or unnecessarily lax, he likewise knows it and wears it as a hairshirt,[1] to the undoing of his morale. Though the man, like the group, can be hurt by being pushed beyond sensible limits, his spirit will suffer even more sorely if no real test is put upon his abilities and moral powers. The greater his intelligence, the stronger will be his resentment. That is a law of nature. The enlightened mind has always the greatest measure of self-discipline but it also has a higher sense of what constitutes justice, fairplay and a reasonable requirement in the performance of duty. If denied these things, he will come to hold his chief, his job, and himself in contempt. The greater part of man's satisfactions comes of activity and only a very small remnant comes of passive enjoyment. Forgetting this rather obvious fact in human nature, social reformers aim at securing

---

1. A shirt woven of hair cloth, worn by those who practice self-denial.

more leisure, rather than at making work itself more satisfactory. But it need not be forgotten in the military service.

Even to those who best understand the reasons for the regimenting of military forces, a discipline wrongfully applied is seen only as indiscipline. Invariably it will be countered in its own terms. No average rank-and-file will become insubordinate as quickly, or react as violently, as a group of senior noncommissioned officers, brought together in a body, and then mishandled by officers who are ignorant of the customs of the service and the limits of their own authority. Not only are they conscious of their rights, but they have greater respect for the state of decency and order which is the mark of a proper military establishment than for the insignia of rank. It is this firm feeling of the fitness of things, and his unbounded allegiance to an authority when it is based on character which makes the NCO and the petty officer the backbone of discipline within the United States fighting establishment. Sergeant Evans of "Command Decision" was an archtype of the best ball carriers among them. In a sense, they remain independent workmen, rather than a tool of authority, until the hour comes when they fall in completely with someone their own nature tells them is good. In the past, we have not always made the wisest use of this latent strength. The normal desire of the veteran who has won his stripes by hard service is to support his officers and reduce the friction down below. Whatever is done to lessen his dignity and prestige damages morale and creates new stresses in the relations between the officer corps and the ranks. When he is rebuffed, either because those above him are indifferent to his pride or are unaware that he is their chief advocate among the men, the military machinery loses its cushion and becomes subject to increasing shock. Said a newly arrived lieutenant to an old sergeant of the 12th Cavalry: "You've been here a long time, haven't you?" "Yes sir," replied the sergeant. "The troop commanders, they come and they go, but it don't hurt the troop."

To comment on these things, however, is to emphasize once again the supreme importance of the judgment of the officer in dealing with all of his military associates in such way that he will support that native pride, without which a man cannot remain whole, and at the same time direct it toward the betterment of the organization. To lecture troops about the importance of morale and discipline serves no earthly purpose, if the words are at odds with the general conditions which have been imposed on the command. They impose their values only as reflection of the leader's entire thought concerning his men. At the same time, there is this to be remembered, that even when things are going wrong at every other level, men will remain loyal and dutiful if they see in the one junior officer who is nearest them the embodiment of the ideals which they believe should apply throughout the service. That is the main object lesson in that remarkable novel written around a World War II Navy auxiliary, "Mister Roberts." But it holds just as true in our ground and air forces as for those afloat.

Morale comes of the mind and of the spirit. The question is how it is to be developed. Admiral Ben Moreell has stated a formula in understanding terms by his explanation of what made the Seabees notable for competence and devotion to duty during World War II. This is what he said: "We used artisans to do the work for which they had been trained in civil life. They were well led by officers who 'spoke their language.' We made them feel that they were playing an important part in the great adventure. And thus they achieved a high standard of morale." The elements underscored by Admiral Moreell deserve special note.

-Satisfaction in a work program.
-Mutual confidence between leaders and ranks.
-Conviction that all together were striving for something more important than themselves.

True, that was wartime, and the challenge was apparent to all concerned. But the principles hold good under any and all conditions, and can be applied to any organization by the officer who approaches his task with enthusiasm and imagination. The mission of keeping the world at peace, through a moral strengthening of the security structure of the United States, is a more difficult objective than that which confronted fighting forces after Pearl Harbor. In his book, "World War: Its Cause and Cure," Lionel Curtis stated our problem in its broadest and most challenging terms: "Civilization began with a war between freedom and despotism: we are now fighting its latest campaign, and our task is to make it the last."

Under training conditions or in combat, the mental ills and the resulting moral and physical deterioration which sometimes beset military forces cannot be cured simply by the intensification of disciplinary methods. It is true that the signs of a recovery will sometimes attend the installation of a more rigid, or less rigid, discipline. This onset is in fact usually due to the collateral influence of an increased confidence in the command, whereby men are made to feel that their own fortunes are on the mend. Then discipline and morale are together revitalized almost as if by the throwing of an electric switch.

In Army history, there is no better example of the working of this principle than the work of Brig. Gen. Paul B. Malone of St. Aignan-sur-Cher, France, in 1919. He took over a command where slackness and indiscipline were general. The men were suffering terrible privation and too many of their officers were indifferent to their needs. Many of the men had been battle casualties. Some had been discharged from hospitals before their wounds were healed. The mess was abominable. The camp was short of firewood and other supply. In freezing weather, men were sleeping on the ground with only a pair of blankets apiece. The death toll from influenza, pneumonia, and the aggravation of battle wounds rose daily. Despair and resentment over these conditions began to express itself in semiviolent form. Every fresh breach of discipline was countered with harassing punishments until an air of wretched stagnation hung over the whole camp. General Pershing visited the base. The men refused to form for him. When he tried to address them at a mass meeting, they wouldn't hear him out. Instead of taking any action against the men, he sent for General Malone.

The new commander arrived without any instructions except to determine what was wrong and correct it. With soldierly instinct, he recognized that the indiscipline of the camp was an effect and not a cause. But even as he gave orders for relieving the physical distress of the men, he demanded that they return to orderly habits.

He walked around the areas. Already, on his order, duck-boards were being laid through the mud, and the whole physical setup was in process of reorganization. The men, grown listless from weeks of mistreatment, paid no heed. "Get on your feet! I'm your general. I respect you but I want your respect," were his words. They restored the situation. The first impact of this one man on that camp was never forgotten by anyone who saw it. It is a point to remember: *A firm hold at the beginning pays tenfold the dividend of a timid approach, followed by a show of firmness later on.* Within 48 hours the physical condition of the camp was showing improvement and 60,000 men were again doing their duty and bearing themselves in a military manner. The lessons from this one incident stand out like beams from a searchlight battery.

One man is able to accomplish a miracle by an act of will accompanied by good works.

The morale of the force flows from the self-discipline of the commander, and in turn, the discipline of the force is reestablished by the upsurge of its moral power.

The inculcation of military habits and thoughts is the only means by which these forces may be made to work together toward more perfect ends, so that control can be exercised promptly.

When the redeployment period which followed World War II threatened a complete collapse to the morale of the general military establishment, the remedy attempted by some unit leaders was to relax discipline and the work requirement all around. Other officers met this crisis by improving the conditions of work, setting an example which proved to the men that they believed in its importance and paying sedulous attention to the personal problems of those within the unit. They found that they could still get superior performance in the midst of chaos. Organic strength materializes in the same way on the field of war. *However adverse the general situation, men will stick to the one man who knows what he wants to do and welcomes them to a full share in the enterprise.*

The rule applies in matters great and small. No man who leads a squad or a squadron, a group of men or a group of armies, can develop within his force a well-placed confidence in its own powers, if he is uncertain of himself or doubtful of his object. The moral level of his men is mainly according to the manner in which he expresses his personal force working with, and for, them. If he is timid or aloof, uncommunicative and unenthusiastic, prone to stand on his dignity and devoid of interest in the human stuff of those who are within his charge, they will not respond to him, and he will have raised a main barrier to his own success. If, given a course or taking one of his own choice, he worries so greatly about the obstacles in his way that he cannot make penetrating search for the clear channel, he will waste the powers of his men even though he may have won their sympathy.

It would be futile to make these comments on the nature of moral leading if it were not fully within the power of the average young officer to cut his cloth according to the suggested pattern. The commonplace that human nature cannot be changed is untrue. The characters of each of us, and of all of our acquaintances, are greatly affected by circumstances. No man's impulses are fixed from the beginning by his native disposition; they remain plastic until the hour of his death, and whatever touches his circumference, influences them for better or worse. *The power of decision develops only out of practice. There is nothing mystic about it. It comes of a clear-eyed willingness to accept life's risks, recognizing that only the enfeebled are comforted by thoughts of an existence devoid of struggle.*

Nothing more radical is being suggested here than that the officer who would make certain that the morale of his men will prove equal to every change cannot do better than concentrate his best efforts upon his primary military obligation--his duty to them. They dupe only themselves who believe that there is a brand of military efficiency which consists in moving smartly, expediting papers and achieving perfection in formations, while at the same time slighting or ignoring the human nature of those whom they command. The art of leadership, the art of command, whether the forces be large or small, is the art of dealing with humanity. Only the officer who dedicates his thought and energy to his men can convert into coherent military force their desire to be of service to the country. Such were the fundamental values which Napoleon had in mind when he said that those who would learn the art of war should study the Great Captains. He was not speaking of tactics and strategy. He was pointing to the success of Alexander, Caesar, and Hannibal in moulding raw human nature, and to their understanding of the thinking of their men and of how to direct it toward military advantage. These are the grand objects.

Diligence in the care of men, administration of all organizational affairs according to a standard of resolute justice, military bearing in one's self, and finally, an understanding of the simple facts that men in a fighting establishment wish to think of themselves in that light and that all military information is nourishing to their spirits and their lives, are the four fundamentals by which the commander builds an all-sufficing morale in those within his charge.

There are other motor forces and mechanisms, most of which come under the heading of management principles, and are therefore discussed in other portions of this volume. The exception is the greatest force of all--patriotism. It may be deemed beyond argument that belief in the social order and political doctrine of their country is the foundation of a loyal, willing spirit in military forces. Yet this alone cannot assure efficiency in training or a battle *elan* which is the result of proper training methods. There is nothing more soulless than a religion without good works unless it be a patriotism which does not concern itself with the welfare and dignity of the individual. This is a simple idea though wise men in all ages have recognized it as one of the most profound truths. From Aristotle on down the philosophers have said that the main force in shaping the characters of men is not teaching and preaching, though these too are important, but the social framework in which a man lives. In an age when there is widespread presumption that practical problems can be solved by phrases, the military body needs more than ever to hold steadfastly to first principles. It does no good for an officer to talk patriotism to his men unless he stands four-square with them, and they see in him a symbol of what is right with the country. Under those circumstances, he can always talk to them about the cause, and what he says will be a tonic to morale.

In the Normandy invasion, a young commander of paratroops, Lt. Col. Edward C. Krause, was given the task of capturing a main enemy communications center. Three hours before the take-off he assembled his Battalion, held a small American flag in front of them and said these words; "This is the first flag raised over the city of Naples. You put it there. I want it to be the first flag raised over a liberated town in France. The mission is that we will put it up in Ste. Mere Eglise before dawn. You have only one order--to come and fight with me wherever you land. When you get to Ste. Mere Eglise, I will be there."

The assignment was kept. Next morning, Krause and his men raised the flag together, even before they had completed capture of the town. As Americans go, they were extremely rugged individualists. But they were proud of every line of that story.

CHAPTER SEVENTEEN

ESPRIT

To proceed toward a better understanding of *esprit* and its part in the building of military forces, it is necessary to look beyond the organization and consider the man.

The life of any socially upright individual is organized around only a few basic loyalties and the degree of satisfaction which he derives from existence can usually be measured in terms of his service to them. He is loyal first to himself, for failing that, he fails in loyalty to all else. If he cannot acquit himself ably for his own sake, he cannot do honor to anything less personal. Along with loyalty to self come loyalty to our beliefs, loyalty to family, loyalty to country, loyalty to friends, and loyalty to humanity in general.

Stated as a factual and not as an ideal matter, the interesting and important thing that happens to a man when he enters military service is that, the moment he takes the oath, loyalty to the arms he bears ranks first on the list, above all other loyalties. To get ahead, to serve himself well, he must persevere in ways that are most useful to the organization. If the circumstances of his family are reduced because of this new loyalty, his means of compensating them is to strive for such honor as may come to him through service to the United States. In his life, service to country is no longer a beautiful abstraction; it is the sternly concrete and unremitting obligation of service to the regiment, the group or the ship's company. He parts with old friends and finds new ones.

In this radical reorientation of the individual life and the arbitrary imposition of a commanding loyalty is to be found the key to the esprit of any military organization. Too long esprit has been regarded as something bequeathed to the unit by the dead hand of tradition. There is nothing moribund about it. It is a dynamic and vital substance conducted to the living by the living. We can banish from our minds the idea that esprit is what the regiment, the ship or the company gives the man because of some spark which its past deeds and the legends thereof have lighted in him. Esprit, at all times, is what the unit gives the man, in terms of spiritual force translated into constructive good. Considering what the unit has taken from him initially, its obligation is great indeed.

To see this clearly, we need to look once again at what happens to the individual when he puts on the uniform. The basis of his life changes in broad and fundamental ways. His legal status is changed; the extent and intensity of his obligations are magnified. He puts aside the banner of individualism for that of obedience. Yet in the words of Chester Barnard: "Scarcely a man, I think, who has felt the annihilation of his personality in some organized system, has not also felt that the same system belonged to him because of his own free will he chose to make it so."

To that must be added the further thought that while the military service is antecedent to the individual who enters it, that individual is also in a sense antecedent to the service. He becomes a factor in the equation which expresses the achievement or the failure of the service in its particular mission. The thoughtful commander will give careful regard to that relationship. One man cannot make or break an Army or a Navy, but he can help break it, since each service at all times derives its nature from the quality and wills of its men. General Harbord, in *The American Army in France*, expressed it this way: "Discipline and morale influence the inarticulate vote that is constantly taken by masses of men when the order comes to move forward--a variant of the crowd psychology that inclines it to follow a leader. But the Army does not move forward until the motion has carried. 'Unanimous consent' only follows cooperation between the individual men in ranks."

But we can go one step beyond General Harbord's suggestion that the multiplied individual acceptance of a command alone gives that command authority. It is not less true that the multiplied rejection of a command nullifies it. In other words, authority is the creature rather than the creator of discipline and obedience. In the more recent experiences of our arms, under the stresses of battle, there are many instances of troops being given orders, and refusing to obey. In every case, the root cause was lack of confidence in the wisdom and ability of those who led. When a determining number of men in ranks have lost the will to obey, their erstwhile leader has *ipso facto* lost the capacity to command. *In the final analysis, authority is contingent upon respect far more truly than respect is founded upon authority.* In the words of Col. G. F. R. Henderson: "It is the leader who reckons with the human nature of his troops, and of the enemy, rather than with their mere physical attributes, numbers, armament and the like, who can hope to follow in Napoleon's footsteps."

Esprit then is the product of a thriving mutual confidence between the leader and the led, founded on the faith that together they possess a superior quality and capability. The failure of the spirit of any military organization is less frequently due to what men have forgotten than to what they can't forget. No "imperishable record" of past greatness can make men serve with any greater vigor if they are being served badly. Nor can it sustain the fighting will of the organization so much as one mil beyond the radius within which living associations enable men to think great thoughts and act with nobility toward their fellows. Unless the organization's past conveys to its officers a sense of having been especially chosen, and unless they respond to this trust by developing a complete sense of duty toward their men, the old battle records might as well be poured down the drain, since they will not rally a single man in the hour of danger. Said Col. LeRoy P. Hunt in a mimeographed notice to his troops just prior to the Guadalcanal landing: "We are meeting a tough and wily opponent but he is not sufficiently tough and wily to overcome us because We Are Marines." (The capitals are Hunt's.)

Personality plays a part in the ability to command, both under training conditions and under fire. But though a man be a veritable John Paul Jones or Mad Anthony Wayne in the time of action, his hardihood will never wholly undo any prior neglect of his men. While men may be rallied for a short space by someone setting an example of great courage, they can be kept in line under conditions of increasing stress and mounting hardship only when loyalty is based upon a respect which the commander has won by consistently thoughtful regard for the welfare and rights of his men, and a correct measuring of his responsibility to them.

There are a few governing principles, and before considering their application in detail we should think first about the file. He is a Man; he expects to be treated as an adult, not as a schoolboy. He has rights; they must be made known to him and thereafter respected. He has ambition; it must be stirred. He has a belief in fair play; it must be honored. He has the need of comradeship; it must be supplied. He has imagination; it must be stimulated. He has a sense of personal dignity; it must not be broken down. He has pride; it can be satisfied and made the bedrock of his character once he gains assurance that he is playing a useful and respected part in a superior and successful organization. To give men working as a group the feeling of great accomplishment together is the acme of inspired leadership.

In the degree that the disciplinary method and the training procedure of the military service, and the common sense of his superiors, combine to nourish these satisfactions in the individual, *esprit de corps* comes into being and furthers his advance in the practice of arms and his potential usefulness as a fighting man. He becomes loyal because loyalty has been given to him. He learns to serve an ideal because an ideal has served him. For it is to be remembered that it is always the Army, the Navy or the nation that disengages the man from his old moorings, but it is the regiment or the ship's company which gives him a fresh anchor and enables him to feel secure again. The service cancels out the man's old life; the unit gives him a fresh start in a new environment, which may prove salutary or utterly damnable, as the man and the unit together make it. Where there is enlightened leading, neither can fail the other. *The majority of men, so long as they are treated fairly and feel that good use is being made of their powers, will rejoice in a new sense of unity with new companions even more than they will mind the increased separation from their old associations.* The ability to adjust is itself a landmark of success in the life of a normal individual.

This is the primary gift of the organization to the man and the primary advantage of its relationship to him. Once it has given the file a sense of belonging, it restores his balance. It is this feeling of possession which is the beginning of true esprit. Without it, the man becomes a derelict. Indeed, we may go so far as to say that the man who lacks it, and does not aspire to it, will almost invariably be unsuited for combat or any military responsibility of consequence, not because he is disrespectful of tradition, but because he is a social outcast with no sense of duty to his fellows.

Referring once again to the list of satisfactions due the man, it will be noted that they differ little, if at all, from the demands of his spirit before he has put on the uniform. But there should be marked also the vital difference that whereas a complex of social and economic forces and of totally disconnected influences contribute to his outlook so long as he is a civilian, the measure of his satisfactions is almost wholly in the hands of the organization once he has raised his right hand and taken the oath of military service to country. The condition of his health, the amount of his pay, the organization of his leisure time, his diet, his sleeping habits, his sex problems, even the manner in which he shaves and wears his hair, are matters of organizational concern. Within the new company, he may either attain greatly, or miserably fail. It should speak to him with the voice of Stentor, the bronze voice of 10,000 men--meaning the thousand or so who are still with the ship, the group or the regiment, and the thousands who are in the shadows but who once served it well, thereby inspiring those who follow to give an extra portion of service to their fellows. Unless tradition has that effect upon the living, it will not produce esprit, but military "mossbackism."[1]

What does this imply in terms of practical application? Simply that the custodianship of esprit must ever be in the hands of the officer corps. When the heart of the organization is sound, officership is able to see its own reflection in the eyes of the enlisted man. For this simple reason: insofar as his ability to mould the character of troops is concerned, the qualifying test of the leader is the judgment placed upon his military abilities by those who serve under him. If they do not deem him fit to command, he cannot train them to obey. But if they see in one man directly over them a steady example, the strongest of their number will model after him, instead of sagging because of weakness elsewhere in the command structure.

This point is irreducible. Though an officer have absolute confidence in himself, and though he have an instinct amounting to genius for the material things of war, these otherwise considerable gifts will avail him little or nothing if his *manner* is such that his troops remain unconvinced of his capacity and doubtful of his power to maintain command in periods of extreme trial. He will fail because he has not sufficiently regarded the LAW OF PERSONALITY--LOOKS, ACTIONS, WORDS.

Among military men, there has been much mistaken praise for the virtue of "mechanical obedience." There is no such thing. Men think in their smallest actions; if this were not so, it would not be possible to lead them. What has been blindly termed "mechanical response" requires perhaps a higher concentration of will than any other type of action, and hence of thought itself, since the two are inseparable. The forces in which this characteristic was outstanding have been those which were led with

---

1. The Oxford English Dictionary's best definition for this intriguing word is: "One behind the times; one attached to antiquated notions; an extreme conservative."

the highest degree of intelligence and of understanding of human nature. For unity of spirit and of action, which is the essence of *esprit de corps*, is of all military miracles the most difficult to achieve.

Yet its abiding principle is simple. It comes of integrity and clarification of purpose. The able officer is not a Saul waiting for the light to strike him on the Damascus road, but a Paul having a clear understanding that unless the trumpet give forth a certain sound at all times, none shall prepare himself for the battle.

Given such officers, the organization comes to possess a sense of unity and of fraternity in its routine existence which expresses itself as the force of cohesion in the hour when all ranks are confronted by a common danger. It is not because of mutual enthusiasm for an honored name but because of mutual confidence in one another that the ranks of old regiments or the bluejackets serving a ship with a great tradition are able to convert their esprit into battle discipline. Under stress they move and act together because they have imbibed the great lesson, and experience has made its application almost instinctive, that only in unity is there safety. They believe that they can trust their comrades and commanders as they would trust their next of kin. They have learned the necessity of mutual support and a common danger serves but to bind the ranks closer.

But the race is not always to the swift nor the battle to the strong. The newest unit--one born only yesterday--is as susceptible to a vaulting esprit as any which traces its founding to the beginnings of the Republic. Led by those who themselves are capable of great endeavour, who are quick to encourage and slow to disparage, and are ever ready to make due acknowledgment of worthy effort and to let men know wherein they are forging ahead, any military organization serving our flag will come to count this among its strengths.

There are no tricks to the building of esprit. Its techniques are those which come naturally in the course of stimulating the interest of ranks in all of the great fundamentals of the military profession, rather than selling short their intelligence, and taking it for granted that they want nothing beyond the routine of work, liberty, mess call, and payday.

But there is one pitfall. Toward the growth of esprit, the attitude, "My organization first, and the rest nowhere," never pays off. It begins with the idea, *"The service first, and my unit the best in the service."* In all human enterprise, the whole is greater than the sum of the parts.

The citizen who thinks most deeply about his country will be the first to share the burdens of his community and neighborhood. The man who feels the greatest affection for the service in which he bears arms will work most loyally to make his own unit know a rightful pride in its own worth. Among all of the military services from out of the present and past, none has been more faithful to this principle than the United States Marine Corps. Among its members, being a Marine is the thing that counts mainly; after that comes service to the Regiment or Battalion. Even the other services marvel at the result. Though they take due pride in their own virtues and accomplishments, they still regard the esprit of the Marine with admiration, and more than a little envy. What is the secret? Perhaps it is this, that the Corps emphasizes the rugged outlet for men's energies, and never permits its members to forget that the example of courage is their most precious heritage.

Six years after his defeat at Wake Island, the things that remained uppermost in the mind of Col. James P. S. Devereux, as he put together the story of the most tragic hours of his life, were the heroisms of the individuals who had been trained in a tradition to which he had fully committed his own purpose. One incident of that day, typical of many, is best related in Devereux's own words.

"Master Sergeant J. Paszkiewicz, a Marine for 20 years, was caught in the first blast at the airfield. Bombs shattered his right leg. He started crawling off, dragging his smashed leg limply behind him. The second wave of bombers came in. Paszkiewicz reached a little pile of wreckage and found what he wanted, a piece of wood. With a little fixing it could serve as a crutch. The bombs were dropping again. Paszkiewicz started hobbling off. He seemed to be going the wrong way. Somebody tried to help him, but he wasn't having any. Lieutenant David D. Kliewer saw him stumbling along on his makeshift crutch, giving first aid to the wounded or trying to make a dying man a little easier."

Could a man give that much, and could his superior, Devereux, have remembered it so vividly from amid his own personal trials, unless both had been inspired by the traditions of the Corps?

CHAPTER EIGHTEEN

KNOWING YOUR JOB

In one of his little-known passages, Robert Louis Stevenson did the perfect portrait of the man who finally failed at everything, because he just never learned how to take hold of his work.

It goes like this: "His career was one of unbroken shame. He did not drink. He was exactly honest. He was never rude to his employers. Yet he was everywhere discharged. Bringing no interest to his duties, he brought no attention. His day was a tissue of things neglected and things done amiss. And from place to place and from town to town he carried the character of one thoroughly incompetent."

No one would say that the picture is overdrawn or that the poor devil got other than his just deserts. In the summing up, the final judgment that is put on a man by other men depends on his value as a working hand. If he has other serious personality faults, they will be overlooked as somewhat beside the point, provided that he levels with his job. But if he embodies all of the surface virtues, and is shiftless, any superior with sense will mark him for the discard, and his coworkers will breathe a sigh of relief when he has gone on his way.

Within the armed services, the tone of grudging admiration is never missing from such altogether familiar comments as:

"He's a queer duck but he has what it takes."

"We can't get along with him but we can't get along without him."

By such words, we unconsciously yield the palm to the man who, whatever his other shortcomings, excels us in application to duty. One of the worst rascals ever raised in Britain said that while he wouldn't give a farthing for virtue, he would pay 10,000 pounds for character, because, possessing it, he would be able to sell it for much more.

Is it possible then that men of thoroughly good intentions will neglect the one value which a knave says is worth prizing? Not only is it possible; it happens every day! We see officers of the armed establishment who, thinking themselves employed all day, would still, if they had to make an honest reckoning of the score after tattoo sounded, be compelled to say that they had done exactly nothing. Lacking some compelling duty, they may have read several hours mechanically, neither studying what was said, making notes, nor reflecting on the value and accuracy of it. Such papers as they signed, they had glanced over perfunc-torily. If any subordinate approached them with some small matter, they reacted by trying to get rid of him as quickly as possible. When they entered the company of their fellow officers, they partook of it as little as they could, not bothering to enter vigorous conversation, failing to make any note of the character and manner of their associates, and learning not at all from the words that were said.

It is all good enough, and yet strangely it is neither good nor is it enough. That idea of what life in the officer corps is meant to be simply cannot stand up under the pressures of modern operations. True enough, assignments do not all have the same level of work requirement, and one is sometimes handed a wide open opportunity to goldbrick. But taking advantage of it is like the dope habit; the more that it is sniffed, the greater becomes the craving of the nervous system. It is harder to throw off sloth than to keep it from climbing onto one's back in the first place. And finally, the truth of the matter is this, that there is never any assignment given an armed service officer which entitles him to waste any of the working hours of his day. Though he be marking time in a casual depot or replacement center, there still awaits his attention the entire range of military studies, through which he can advance his own abilities. And if he is not of a mind for tactics, map-reading, military law, and training doctrine, it still follows that the study of applied psychol-ogy, English composition, economic geography and foreign languages will further his career. Just as a rough approximation, any officer's work week should comprise about 50 percent execution and the other half study, if he is to make the best use of his force. The woods are loaded with go-getters who claim they are men of action and therefore have no need of books; that they are "the flat-bottoms who can ride over the dew." Though they are a little breezier, they are of the same bone and marrow as the drone who is always counseling halfspeed. "Don't sweat; just get by; extra work means short life; you're better off if they don't notice you." This chant can be heard by anyone who cares to listen; it's the old American invitation to mediocrity. But while mediocre, as commonly used, means "indifferent, ordinary," it also has in old English the odd meaning "a young monk who was excused from performing part of a monk's duties." And that, too, fits. It is always worthwhile to ask a few very senior officers what they think of these jokers who refuse to study. They will say that the higher up you go, the more study you have to make up, because of what you missed somewhere along the line. They will say also that when they got to flag or star rank, things didn't ease off a bit.

But not all wisdom is to be found in books, and at no time is this more true than when one is breaking in. What is expected of the novice in any field is that he will ask questions, *smart ones if possible*, but if not, then questions of all kinds until he learns that there is no such item as reveille oil and that skirmish line doesn't come on spools. For on one point there should be no mistake: the newly appointed officer is a novice. Though many things go with the commission, the assumption that he is all wise to all ways of the service, and will automatically fit into his element as neatly as a loaded ship settles down to its Plimsoll's mark, just isn't among them. Within the services, seniors are rarely, if ever, either patronizing or intolerant of the greenness of a new officer; they just stand ready to help him. And if he doesn't permit them to have that chance, because he would rather pretend that he knows it all, they will gradually become bored with him because of the manifest proof that he knows so very little.

Wisdom begins at the point of understanding that there is nothing shameful about ignorance; it is shameful only when a man would rather remain in that state than cultivate other men's knowledge. There is never any reason why he should hesitate, for it is better to be embarrassed from seeking counsel than to be found short for not having sought it.

In one of the toughest trades in the world of affairs--that of the foreign correspondent--initial dependence upon one's professional colleagues is the only certain stepping stone to success. A man arrives in strange country feeling very much alone. His credentials lack the weight they had at home. The prestige of his newspaper counts for almost nothing. Even the name of his home city stirs little respect. The people, their ways, their approaches and their taboos are foreign to him. This sweeping environmental change is crushing to the spirit; it would impose an almost insuperable moral handicap if the newcomer could not go to other Americans who have already worked the ground, ask them how the thing is done, seek their advice about dealing with the main personalities, learn from them about the facilities for processing copy, and soak up everything they have to say about private and professional procedures. Then as the ropes grow gradually familiar in the grasp, confidence and nervous energy come flooding back.

Surely there is a close parallel between this experience and that of the journeyman moving from the familiar soil of civilianism to the *terra incognita* of military life. But there is also the marked difference that everyone he meets can tell him something that he needs to know. More particularly, if he has the ambition to excel as a commander of men, rather than as a technician, then the study of human nature and of individual characteristics within the military crowd become a major part of his training. That is the prime reason why the life of any tactical leader becomes so very interesting, provided he possesses some imagination. Everything is grist for his mill. Moreover, despite the wholesale transformation in the scientific and industrial aspects of war, there has been no revolution in the one thing that counts most. Ardant du Picq's words, "The heart of man does not change," are as good now as when he said them in an earlier period of war. Whatever one learns for certain about the nature of man as a fighting animal can be filed for ready reference; the hour will come when it will be useful.

We have emphasized the value of becoming curious, and of asking questions about what one doesn't know, and have said that even when the questions are a little on the dumb side, it does no harm. But the ice gets very thin at one point. The same question asked over and again, like the same error made more than once, will grate the nerves of any superior. It is the mark of inattention, and the beginning of that "tissue of things neglected and things done amiss" which put Stevenson's oddball character in the ditch. When an officer lets words go in one ear and out the other like water off a duck's back, to quote the Dutch janitor, he is chasing rainbows by rubbing fur in the wrong direction.

Ideally, an officer should be able to do the work of any man serving under him. There are even some command situations in which the ideal becomes altogether attainable, and a wholly practicable objective. For it may be said without qualification, that if he not only has this capability, but demonstrates it, so that his men begin to understand that he is thoroughly versed in the work problems which concern them, *he can command them in any situation*. This is the real bedrock of command capacity, and nothing else so well serves to give an officer an absolutely firm position with all who serve under him. As said elsewhere in this book, within the armed establishment, administration is not of itself a separate art, or a dependable prop to authority. When administrators talk airily of things that they clearly do not understand, they are simply using the whip on the team without having control of the reins.

However, the greater part of military operation in present days is noteworthy for the extreme diversity and complexity of its parts, and instead of becoming more simplified, the trend is toward greater elaboration. It is obviously absurd to expect that any officer could know more about radio repair than his repairman, more about mapping than his cartographical section, more about moving parts than a gunsmith, more about radar than a specialist in electronics and more about cypher than a cryptographer. If the services were to set any such unreasonable standard for the commissioned body, all would shortly move over into the lunatic fringe. Science has worked a few wonders for the military establishment but it hasn't told us how to produce that kind of man.

Plainly, there must be a somewhat different approach to the question of what kind of knowledge an officer is expected to possess, or the requirement would be unreasonable and unworkable.

The distinction lies in the difference between the power to do a thing well and that of being able to judge when it is well done. A man can say that a book is bad, though not knowing how to write one himself, provided he is a student of literature. Though he has never laid an egg, he can pass fair judgment on an omelette, if he knows a little about cookery, and has sampled many good eggs, and detected a few that were overripe.

"He who lives in a house," said Aristotle, "is a better judge of it being good or bad than the builder of it. He can say not only these things, but wherein its defects consist. Yet he might be quite unable to cure the chimney, or to draw out a plan for his rooms which would suit him better. Sometimes he can even see where the fault is which caused the mischief, and yet he may not know practically how to remedy it."

Adjustment to a job, and finally, mastery of it, by a service officer, comes of persistent pursuit of this principle. The main technique is study and constant reexamination of criteria. To take the correct measure of standards of performance, as to the value of the work itself, and as to the abilities of personnel, one must become immersed in knowledge of the nature, *and purpose*, of all operations. There is no shortcut to this grasp of affairs. The sack is filled bean by bean. Patient application to one thing at one time is the first rule of success; getting on one's horse and riding off in all directions is the prelude to failure. All specialists like to talk about their work; the interest of any other man is flattering; all men grow in knowledge chiefly by picking other men's brains. Book study of the subject, specialized courses in the service schools, the instructive comments of one's superiors, the informed criticism of hands further down the line and the weighing of human experience, at every source and by every recourse, are the means of an informed judgment. It was the scientist, Thomas Huxley who reminded us that science is only "organized common sense."

Other things being equal, the prospect for any man's progress is largely determined by his attitude. It is the receptive mind, rather than the oracle, which inspires confidence. General Eisenhower said at one point that, after 40 years, he still thought of himself as a student on all military questions, and that he consciously mistrusted any man who believed he had the full and final answer to problems which by their nature were ever-changing.

But priggishness about knowledge is not more hurtful than is the arbitrary use of it to limit action. *To rule by work rather than to work by rules* must be the abiding principle in military operations, for finally, when war comes, nothing else will suffice. In peacetime, absolute accountability is required, because dollar economy in operations is a main object. This entails adherence to rigid forms, time-consuming, but still necessary. In many of war's exigencies, these forms frequently have to be swept aside, to bring victory as quickly as possible and to save human life. In the book, "General Kenney Reports," that great air commander spoke at one point of a difficulty in one of his combat groups. "It was a lot of hard-working earnest kids, officers and enlisted men, who were doing the best they could under poor living and eating conditions. But their hands were tied by the colonel in command whose passion for paper work effactually stopped the issuing of supplies and the functioning of the place as an air depot should. He told me that he thought 'it was about time these combat units learned how to do their paper work properly.' I decided that it would be a waste of time to fool with him so I told him to pack up to go home on the next plane."

Though this is a tragic example of wrong-headedness, it is by no means unique. The profession moves ahead, and national security advances with it, because of men who have the confidence and courage to toss the rule book out the window when it doesn't fit the situation, and who dare to trust their own decisions and improvise swiftly.

151

But in all walks of life, this willingness to take hold of the reins firmly is by no means common among men in relatively subordinate positions who can play it safe by falling back on "SOP."

But there is also a far wider vista than that which is to be viewed only within the services themselves, and its horizons are almost infinite. The American way in warfare utilizes everything within the national system which may be applied to a military purpose toward the increase of training and fighting efficiency. Much of our potential strength lies in our industrial structure, our progress in science, our inventiveness and our educational resources. Toward the end that all of these assets will be given maximum use, and every good idea which can be converted to a military purpose will be in readiness to serve the nation when war comes, there must be a continuing meeting of minds between military leadership and the leaders and experts in these various fields during peace.

That union cannot be perfected, however, unless there is a sufficient number of men on both sides of the table who can think halfway into the field of the man opposite. Just as the civilian expert in electronics, airplane manufacture or motion picture production needs to know more about the military establishment's problem and requirements if he is to do his part, the service officer with whom he is dealing needs to be informed on industry's resources, possibilities and limitations if he is to enable the civilian side to do its part well. The same for science. The same for education, and all other backers of the fighting force.

An enlightened Englishman, D. W. Brogan, in a book written during World War II, "The American Character," gave us this thought: "The American officer must think in terms of material resources, existing but not organized in peacetime and taking much time and thought and experiment by trial and error to make available in wartime. He finds that his best peacetime plans are inadequate for one basic reason: that any plan which in peacetime really tried to draw adequately on American resources would cause its author to be written off as a madman; and in wartime, it would prove to have been inadequate, pessimistic, not allowing enough for the practically limitless resources of the American people--limitless once the American people get ready to let them be used. And only war can get them ready for that. The American officer can draw then, but not before, on an experience in economic improvization and in technical adaptation which no other country can equal."

This is true to the last syllable, and it means in essence that unless the American officer can think of the whole nation as his workshop, and along with his other duties, will apply himself as a student, seeking to understand more and more about the richness and the adaptability of our tremendous resources, neither he nor the country will be relatively ready when war comes.

There is a last point to be made on the matter of attitude. The most resolute opposition to changes in any system usually comes from those who control them. That is universally true, and not peculiar to military systems; but the services are foremost in recognizing that, as a consequence, the encouragement of original thought at the lower levels is essential to over-all progress.

All depends upon the manner. We can ponder the words of William Hazlitt, "A man who shrinks from a collision with his equals or superiors will soon sink below himself; we improve by trying our strength with others, not by showing it off." They are good so far as they go, but something new should be added. There is a vast difference between contending firmly for ideas that seem progressive when one is reasonably sure of one's data, and the habit of throwing one's weight around through a mistaken belief that this of itself manifests an independence of spirit which inspires respect.

Truculence can never win the day. Restraint, tolerance, a sense of humor and of proportion and the force of logic are the marks of the man qualified for intellectual leading. Within the services, even though he has no great rank, there is practically nothing he cannot carry through, if his proposals have the color of reason and propriety, and if he will keep his head, keep his temper, and keep his word.

CHAPTER NINETEEN

KNOWLEDGE OF YOUR MEN

An admiring contemporary spoke of Paul G. Hoffman, the director of the European Recovery Program, as "the kind of man who if tossed through the air would always pick out the right trapeze."

Within any military organization, there is always a number of such men, enlisted and commissioned. They know how and where to take hold, even in the face of a totally unexpected and unnerving situation, and they have what amounts to an instinct for doing the right thing in a decisive moment.

If it were not so, no captain of the line would ever be able to manage a company in battle, and no submarine commander would be able to cope with an otherwise overwhelming danger. These men are the foundation of unit integrity. The successful life of organization depends upon husbanding, and helping them to cultivate, their own powers, which means that their initiative and vigor must never be chilled by supercilious advice and thoughtless correction.

They will go ahead and act responsibly on their own when given the confidence, and if they want it, the friendship, of their commander. But they cannot be treated like little children. The lash will ruin them and the curb will merely subdue that which needs to be brought forward. As in handling a horse with a good temper and a good mouth, nothing more is needed than that gentle touch of the rein which signals that things are under control.

From where the executive sits, the main secret of building strength within organization comes of identifying such men, and of associating one's authority with theirs, so it is unmistakable in whose name they are speaking and acting. One of the acid tests of qualification in officership is the ability properly to delegate authority, to put it in the best hands, and thereafter to uphold them. If an officer cannot do that, and if he is mistrustful of all power save his own, he cannot command in peace, and when he goes into battle, his unit strength will fragment like an exploding bomb, and the parts will not be rewelded until some stronger character takes hold.

Command is not a prerogative, but rather a responsibility to be shared with all who are capable of filling up the spaces in orders and of carrying out that which is not openly expressed though it may be understood. Admittedly, it is not easy for a young officer, who by reason of his youth is not infrequently lacking in self-assurance and in the confidence that he can command respect, to understand that as a commander he can grow in strength in the measure that he succeeds in developing the latent strength of his subordinates. But if he stubbornly resists this premise as he goes along in the service, his personal resources will never become equal to the strain which will be imposed upon him, come a war emergency. The power to command resides largely in the ability to see when a proper initiative is being exercised and in giving it moral encouragement. When an officer feels that way about his job and his men, he will not be ready to question any action by a junior which might be narrowly construed as an encroachment upon his own authority. Of this last evil come the restraints which reduce men to automatons, giving only that which is asked, or less, according to the pressing of a button.

There are other men who have as sound a potential as these already-made leaders, but lack the initial confidence because they were not constructively handled in earlier years. They require somewhat more personal attention, for the simple reason that more frequent contact with their superiors, words of approval and advice as needed, will do more than all else to put bottom under them. They must be encouraged to think for themselves as well as to obey orders, to organize as well as to respond, if they are to become part of the solution, rather than remaining part of the problem, of command. If left wholly to their own devices, or to the ministrations of less thoughtful subordinates, they will remain in that majority which moves only when told. It takes no more work, though it does require imagination, to awaken the energies of such men by appealing to their intelligence and their self-interest, than to nauseate them with dull theory, and to cramp them by depriving them of responsibility.

Careful missionary work among these "sleepers" is as productive as spading the ground, and sprinkling a garden patch. When an officer takes hold in a new unit, his main chance of making it better than it was comes of looking for the overlooked men. He uses his hand to give them a firm lift upward, but it will not be available for that purpose if he spends any of his time tugging at men who are already on their feet and moving in the right general direction.

In the words of a distinguished armored commander in our forces: "To the military leader, men are tools. He is successful to the extent that he can get the men to work for him. Ordinarily, and on their own initiative, people run on only 35 percent capacity. The success of a leader comes of tapping the other 65 percent." This is a pretty seasoned judgment on men in the mass, taking them as they come, the mobile men, the slow starters, the indifferent and the shiftless. Almost every man wants to do what is expected of him. When he does not do so, it is usually because his instructions have been so doubtful as to befog him or give him a reasonable excuse for noncompliance. This view of things is the only tenable attitude an officer or enlisted leader can take toward his subordinates. He will recognize the exceptions, and if he does not then take appropriate action, it is only because he is himself shiftless and is compassionate toward others of his own fraternity.

It is the military habit to "plow deep in broken drums and shoot crap for old crowns," as the poet, Carl Sandburg, put it. As much as any other profession, and even possibly a little more, we take pride in the pat solution, and in proof that long-applied processes amply meet the test of newly unfolding experience. But despite all the jests about the Gettysburg Map, we wouldn't know where we're going if we couldn't be reasonably sure of where we've been.

Therefore, it is as well to say now that from all of the careful searching made by the armed services as to the fighting characteristics of Americans during World War II, not a great deal was learned in addition to what was already well known, or surmised. The criteria that had been used in the prior system of selection proved to be substantially correct; at least, if it had faults, they were innate in the complex problem of weighing human material, and were beyond correction by any rule of thumb or judgment. Men were chosen to lead because of personality, intelligence at their work, response to orders, ability to lead in fatigues or in the social affairs of organization, and disciplinary record. In combat these same men carried 95 percent of the load of responsibility and provided the dynamic for the attack. But in every unit, there was almost invariably a small sprinkling of individuals, who having shown no prior ability when measured by the customary yardsticks of courtesy, discipline and work, became strong and vital in any situation calling for heroic action. They could fight, they could lead, they knew what should be done, they could persuade other men to rally around, and by these things, they could command instantly the previously withheld respect of their superiors.

Neither the scientific nor the military mind has yet been able to provide the answer as to how men of this type--so indispensable to the fighting establishment in the thing that matters most, though lacking in strong surface characteristics--can be detected beforehand, and conserved, instead of being wasted possibly in a labor or housekeeping organization.

All concerned recognize the extreme importance of the problem, and would like to do something about it. What is as yet not even vaguely seen is the large possibility that the problem might be self-liquidating if all junior officers became more concerned with learning all they could about the private character and personal nature of their subordinates. This does not mean invading their privacy; but it implies giving every man a fair chance to open up and to talk freely, without fear of contempt. It means studying the background of a man even more carefully than one would read a map, looking for the key to command of the terrain. These are usually repressed men; many of the foreign-born are to be found among them; they cover up because of pride, but they are not afraid of physical danger. Once any man, and particularly a superior, gets through the outer shell, he may have the effect of a catalyst on what is happening inside. If such men did not have basic loyalty, they would never fight. When at last they give their loyalty to an individual, they are usually his to command and will go through hell for him.

There was an Oklahoma miner named Alvin Wimberley in 90th Division during World War I. On the drill field, he could do nothing correctly. He couldn't step off on the left foot; he would frequently drop his piece while trying to do right shoulder. Solely because his case was unfathomable, his platoon leader asked that he be taken to France with the unit instead of separated with the culls. At the front, Wimberley immediately took the lead in every detail of a dangerous sort, such as exploding a mine field, or hunting for traps and snares. His nerve was inexhaustible; his judgment sure. There was, after all, a simple key to the mystery. Wimberley had led a solitary life as a dynamiter, deep under ground. He was frightened of men, but danger was his element. When he saw other men recoil at the thing which bothered him not at all, he realized that he was the big man, though he only stood 5 feet 3 inches in issue socks.

To know men, it is not necessary to wet-nurse them, and no officer can make a sorrier mistake than to take the overly nice, worrying attitude toward them. This, after all, is simply the rule of the well-bred man, rather than an item peculiar to the code of the military officer. But it is a little less becoming in a service officer than in anyone else, because, when a man puts on fighting clothes in the name of his country, it is an insult to treat him as if he were a juvenile.

In any situation where men need to know one another better, someone has to break the ice. Where does the main responsibility lie within a military unit? True enough, the junior has to salute first, and in some services is supposed to say, "Good morning!" first, though beating a man to the draw with a greeting is one way to win him.

However, the main point is this: unless an officer has himself been an enlisted man, it is almost impossible for him to know how formidable, and even forbidding, rank at first seems to the eyes of the man down under, even though he would be loath to say so.

Many recruits have such a mistaken hearsay impression of the United States military system, that it is for them a cause for astonishment that any officer enjoys free discussion with them. They feel at first that there is a barrier there which only the officer is entitled to cross; it takes them a little while to learn better.

But in the continuing relationship, it is the habit of the average well-disciplined enlisted man to remain reticent, and talk only on official matters, unless the officer takes the lead in such way as to invite general conversation. For that matter, the burden is the same anywhere in the service in relations between a senior officer and his subordinates, and the former must take the lead if he expects to really know his men.

Many newly joined officers believe, altogether mistakenly, that there is some strange taboo against talking to men except in line of duty, and that if caught at it, it will be considered *infra dig*. There is always the hope that they will remain around long enough to learn better.

CHAPTER TWENTY

WRITING AND SPEAKING

Other things being equal, a superior rating will invariably be given to the officer who has persevered in his studies of the art of self-expression, while his colleague, who attaches little importance to what may be achieved through working with the language, will be marked for mediocrity.

A moment's reflection will show why this has to be the case and why mastery of the written and spoken word is indispensable to successful officership.

As the British statesman, Disraeli, put it, "Men govern with words." Within the military establishment, command is exercised through what is said which commands attention and understanding and through what is written which directs, explains, interprets or informs.

Battles are won through the ability of men to express concrete ideas in clear and unmistakable language. All administration is carried forward along the chain of command by the power of men to make their thoughts articulate and available to others.

There is no way under the sun that this basic condition can be altered. Once the point is granted, any officer should be ready to accept its corollary--that superior qualification in the use of the language, both as to the written and the spoken word, is more essential to military leadership than knowledge of the whole technique of weapons handling.

It then becomes strictly a matter of personal decision whether he will seek to advance himself along the line of main chance or will take refuge in the excuse offered by the great majority: "I'm just a simple fighting file with no gift for writing or speaking."

How often these or similar words are heard in the armed services! And the pity of it is that they are usually uttered in a tone indicating that the speaker believes some special virtue attaches to his kind of ignorance. There is the unmistakable innuendo that the man who pays serious attention to the fundamentals of the business of communication is somehow less possessed of sturdy military character than himself. There could hardly be a more absurd or disadvantageous professional conceit than this. It is the mark only of an officer who has no ambition to properly qualify himself, and is seeking to justify his own laziness.

Not all American military leaders have been experts at polishing a phrase or giving clear expression and continuity to the thoughts which made them useful in command. But of those who have excelled in the conduct of great operations, at least four out of five made some mark in the field of letters. A long list would include such names as U. S. Grant, W. T. Sherman, Robert E. Lee, John J. Pershing, James G. Harbord, Henry T. Allen, Dwight D. Eisenhower, George S. Patton, Jr., H. H. Arnold, Douglas MacArthur, William F. Halsey, W. B. Smith, Joseph W. Stilwell, Holland M. Smith, and Robert L. Eichelberger among many others.

Of them all, it can be said without exception that they acquired their skill at self-expression by sustained practice which was part of a self-imposed training in the interests of furthering their military efficiency. No one of them was a born writer. There is no such thing. Nor did any one of them owe his abilities as a writer to any other person. Writers are self-made. But it is a reasonable speculation that history might never have heard of the greater number of these men had they not worked sedulously to become proficient with the pen as well as with the sword. Granting that they had other sound military qualities in the beginning, an acquired ability to express themselves lucidly and with force became a touchstone to preferment. The same thing holds true of their celebrated military contemporaries almost without exception. Even those who had no public reputation for authorship, and would have been ill at ease if called upon to speak to an average audience, knew how to use the language in presenting their thoughts to their staffs and their troops, whether the occasion called for a succinct operational order, a doctrinal exposition or an inspirational message on the eve of battle.

Wherever one looks, the same precept may be noted. It was not coincidence merely, but related cause and effect, that Ferdinand Foch was one of the ablest military writers of the twentieth century before he won immortality on the field of war, that the elder von Moltke was as skilled with ink as with powder, and that we still marvel at the picture of the great von Steuben dictating drill manuals far into the night so that there would be greater perfection in his formations on the following day. The command of language was one of the main sources of their power over the multitude.

As it was with these commanders, so it is with leadership at every level: *Men who can command words to serve their thoughts and feelings are well on their way to commanding men to serve their purposes.*

All senior commanders respect the junior who has a facility for thinking an idea through and then expressing it comprehensively in clear, unvarnished phrases. Moreover, even when they are stilted in their own manner of expression, they will warm to the man whose style achieves strength through its ease and naturalness. They will quickly make note of any young officer who is making progress in this direction and will want to have him around. He is a rare bird in the services, and for that reason his opportunities are far above the average. Staff work could not be carried forward at any of its levels if it were not for this particular talent, and command would lose a great part of its magnetism.

Toward the building of a career, the best break that can come to any young man is to have three or four places bidding simultaneously for his services. There are possibly better arguments than that as to why perfection in writing should be a main pursuit of the service officer, such as the sense of personal attainment which comes of it.

Any man who has the brain to qualify for commission can make of himself a competent writer. Because of natural limitations, he may never come to excel in this art. But if he has had average schooling, knows how to open a dictionary, can find his way to a library, is willing to commit himself to long study and practice, particularly in nonduty hours, and will finally free himself of the superstition that writing is a game only for specialists, he can acquire all the skill that is necessary to further his advance within the military profession.

That is the great difference between writing ability and specialized knowledge in such fields as electronics and atomic research.

But where should work begin? How about a little practical advice?

The only way to learn to write is to write. That is it--there is no other secret than hard, unremitting practice. Most writers at the start are mentally muscle-bound, and poorly coordinated. They have thoughts in their heads. They think they can develop them clearly. But when they try to apply a largely dormant vocabulary to the expression of these thoughts, the result is stiff and selfconscious.

The only cure for this is constant mental exercise, with one's pen, or over one's typewriter. After a man has written perhaps a half million relatively useless words there comes, sometimes almost in a flash, and at other times gradually, a mastery not only of words, but of phrases, sentences and the composition of ideas. It is a kind of rhythmic process, like learning to swim, or to row a boat, or navigate an airplane. When a writer has at last conquered his element, his personality and his character can be transmitted to paper. What is said will reflect the force, adaptability, reason and musing of the writer. In fact, the discipline through which one learns to write adds substance to thought, whereby one's ideas are given body and connection. Such common faults as wordiness, overstatement, faulty sentence structure and weak use of words are gradually corrected. With their passing, confidence grows. This does not mean, however, that the task then becomes easy. Though its rewards will increase, good writing continues to be a strain even to the man who does it well. Many celebrated men of letters never get beyond the "sweating" stage, but have to fight their way through a jungle of words, and rewrite almost endlessly, before finding satisfaction in their product.

This description makes it all seem more than a little formidable. But what was promised in the first place was that any service officer, who will accept the necessary discipline, can make himself reasonably proficient as a writer, and thereby further his professional progress. What he writes about during the conditioning period makes very little difference. It might be an operational order one night, a treatise on discipline the next, a lecture to his men on the elements of combat the third. Fortunately, the list of topics within the services and directly applicable to their operations, is practically inexhaustible. That is a main reason why the military establishment is a better school for writing than perhaps any other place in our society.

Winston Churchill, whose gift of forceful expression is the envy of all other writing men, won his literary spurs in his early twenties as a soldier with the Malakand Field Force. He saw the essential idea--that to learn English, he had literally to learn, just as though he had been acquiring Latin or French. As a writer, his main strength is his employment of Anglo-Saxon, the words of our common speech.

But simply to take regular exercise in composition is not quite enough. Of it would come the shadow but not the substance. To progress as a writer, one must become a student of the best things which have been written by men who understand their craft. A military officer can do that without going beyond the field of military studies, if that should be his disposition, such is the richness and variation of available works in this realm of literature. The purpose at hand is not only to seek great ideas for their own sake but to make careful note of the manner in which they are expressed. So doing, one unconsciously invigorates his own powers and adopts techniques which the masters have used to great advantage.

To paraphrase what a distinguished journalist once said on this subject in a speech to young writers: "For an officer it is in the first place a shame to be ignorant--ignorant, as not a few are, of history and geography: and in the second place, it is a pity that any officer should lack a vigor in writing which can be produced through imitation of vigorous writers."

As to what is best worth seeking, a man can not go wrong by "falling in love" with the works of a relatively limited number of authors who kindle him personally. It is all right to widen the field occasionally, for diversion, for contrast, for sharpening style, and for balancing of ideas, but strength comes of finding a main line and holding to it. No man can read a book with sympathetic understanding without taking from it something that makes him more complex and more potent.

The main test is in this: if you read a book and feel stirred by it, even though alternately you strongly agree with certain of its passages and warmly contend against others, something new has been added. The writer is making you see things. Your own powers of observation are being made more acute. All good writers are in a sense hitch-hikers. While going along for the ride, and enjoying the essence of some highly developed mind, they are not loath to study the technique by which some other man develops his driving power, and to make note of his strong words and best phrases for possible future use.

It is a good habit to underscore passages in books which have contributed something vital to one's own thought--always provided that the books have not been borrowed.

Without mentioning names, we can take a cue from a man who some years ago entered one of the services while still a youth. He had had little formal education, but he began an earnest study of military litera-ture, and the search for knowledge whetted his thirst to join the company of those who could speak to the world because they had something to say. He read such books as were at hand, and clipped pieces from magazines and newspapers which had particularly appealed to him, for one reason or another. Whenever he saw a new word, he wrote it down and sought the meaning in the dictionary, considering whether it had a shade of meaning which added anything important to his vocabulary. This done, he wrote sentences, many sentences, employing his new words in various ways, until their use became instinctive. On this foundation alone, he built his career as a national writer. There was nothing extraordinary about this start and the ultimate result. Literally thousands of Americans have qualified themselves for one branch or another of the writing profession by what they learned to do in military service. Too, an ability to "organize a good paper" has been a large element in the success of most of the men who have moved from the military circle into top posts in the diplomatic service, in education or in industrial administration. Had they been capable only of delegating this kind of work, their powers would never have been recognized.

As a practical matter, it is better to concentrate on a few elementary rules-of-thumb, such as are contained in the following list, than to bog down attempting to heed everything that the pedants have said about how to become a writer.

The more simply a thing is said the more powerfully it influences those who read. Plain words make strong writing.

There is always one best word to convey a thought or a feeling. To accept a weaker substitute, rather than to Search for the right word, will deprive any writing of force.

Economy of words invigorates composition.

To quote Carl Sandburg: "Think twice before you use an adjective."

It is better to use the adverb because an adverb enhances the verb and is active, whereas the adjective simply loads down the noun.

On the other hand, it is the verb that makes language live. Nine times out of ten the verb is the operative word giving motion to the sentence. Hence, placing the verb is of first importance in giving strength to sentence structure.

In all writing, but in military writing particularly, there is no excuse for vague terminology or phrases which do not convey an exact impression of what was done or what is intended. The military vocabulary is laden with words and expressions which sound professional but do not have definite meaning. They vitiate speech and the establishment would gladly rid itself of them if a way could be found. Men fall into the habit of saying "performed," "functioned" or "executed" and forget that "did" is in the dictionary. A captain along the MLR (main line of resistance) notifies his battalion commander that he has "advanced his left flank" when all that has actually occurred is that six riflemen from the left have crawled forward to new, and possibly, untenable ground.

It is better at all times to rein in. The strength of military writing, like the soundness of military operations, does not gain through overstatement and artificial coloring. The bigger the subject, the less it needs embroidery.

For lucidity and sincerity, the important thing is to say what you have to say in whatever words most accurately express your own thoughts. That done, it is pointless to worry about the effect on the audience.

The list of suggestions could be extended indefinitely. But enough has already been said to stake out a main line for those who have already decided that this subject deserves their interest.

A majority of the world's most gifted writers would in all probability be struck dumb if put before an audience; though dealing confidently with ideas, they lack confidence when dealing with people. The military officer has need of both talents, and as to where the accent should be placed, it is probably more important that he should speak well than that his writing prose should be polished. A unit commander may permit a clerk or a subordinate to do the greater part of his paper work, either because his own time is taken with other duties or because he is awkward at it, but if he permits any other voice to dominate the councils of the organization, he soon ceases to exercise moral authority over it.

Of this there is no question. The judgment men take of their superior is formed as much by what he says and how he says it as by his action.

The matter of nerve is a main element in speaking. When an officer is ill at ease, fidgety and not to the point, the vote of his command for the time being is "no confidence," and so long as he remains that way, they will not change, no matter though his good will shines forth through other acts.

On the other hand, the military crowd is an extremely sympathetic audience. It has to be; it is drawing pay for so being. But even if that were not true, the ranks have a generous spirit and are ever disposed to give the newcomer an even break. If he meets them confidently and calmly, measures his words, smiles at his own mistakes and breaks it off when he has covered his subject, they'll pay no attention to his little fumbles, and they'll approve him. There is no better way to pick up prestige than through instruction or discourse which commands attention, for despite all that is said in favor of the "strong, silent man," troops like an officer who is outgiving, and who has an intelligence that they can respect because they have seen it at work.

As for *how* an officer should talk to men, his manner and tone should be no different than if he were addressing his fellow officers, or for that matter, a group of his intellectual and political peers from any walk of life. If he is stuffy, he will not succeed anywhere. If he affects a superior manner, that is a mark of his inferiority. If he is patronizing, and talks to grown men as a teacher might talk to a class of adolescents, the rug, figuratively, will be pulled from under him. His audience will put him down as a chump.

It is curiously the case that the junior officer who can't get the right pitch when he talks to the ranks will also be out of tune when he talks to his superiors. This failing is a sign mainly that he needs practice in the school of human nature. By listening a little more carefully to other men, he may himself in time attain maturity.

Concerning subject matter, it is better always to aim high than to take the risk of shooting too low. It is too often the practice to spell out everything in words of one syllable so that the more witless files in the organization will be able to understand it. When that is done, it insults the intelligence of the keenest men, and nothing is added to their progress. The target should be the intellect of the upper 25 or 30 percent. When they are stimulated and informed, they will bring the others along, and even those who do not fully understand all that was under discussion will have heard something to which to aspire. *The habit of talking down to troops is one of the worst vices that can afflict an officer.*

There are no dull lecture topics; there are only dull lecturers. A little eager research will enliven any subject under the sun. Good lecturing causes men's imaginations to be stirred by vivid images. Real good is accomplished only when they talk to each other of what they have heard and sharpen their impressions. Schopenauer somewhere observes that "people in general have eyes and ears, but not much else--little judgment and even little memory," which isn't far wrong. Consequently, competent lecturing entails the employment of every technique which can be used to hammer a point home. In this way, a truth or a lesson has a better chance of adhering because it is identified with some definite image. Simply to illuminate this point, it is noted that the jests which best stick in the memory are those which are associated with some incongruous situation. To relate a pertinent anecdote, to provide an apt quotation from some well-known authority and to draw upon our own rich battle history for illustrative materials are but a few of the means of freshening any discussion and sharpening its purpose. Men are always ready to listen to the story of other men's experience provided that it is told with vigor. And insofar as combat is concerned, such teaching is in point, for what has happened once will happen again.

For his way as an instructor of young infantry officers of the A. E. F. in 1918, Lt. Col. H. M. Hutchinson of the British Army was awarded our D. S. M. Officers who sat at his feet at Gondrecourt were unlikely ever to forget the point of such an anecdote as:

"There will be no 'Stack arms' in my army. It is a thing one sees on a brewer's calendar--The Soldier's Dream--showing a brave private sleeping under a stack of rifles which it will take him a good half-hour to untangle when the call comes to stand to. No, a soldier had better carry the rifle with him to his meals, have it beside him always, lavish his care upon it, and in short treat it more like a wife than a weapon.

"I am reminded of the times in South Africa when we would come to a country inn where a chap could stop for beer. Well, a soldier would walk into the place, and immediately he would stand his rifle in a corner--like an umbrella, you know--'We've arrived!'--and he'd get well into his beer and a song, say, and suddenly firing would break out on the inn from four sides.

"It seemed that a Boer had slipped into the entry and picked up all the rifles and passed them around to his mates in the bushes, and--well--there you are!"

As a cadet and later as an instructor at Sandhurst, Colonel Hutchinson well knew the usefulness of the anecdote in catching and holding the attention of the young. Who could forget the lesson in this, related at Gondrecourt:

"In my youth I was a dashing ignoramus with clearer ideas than I now have on the line of demarcation between the officer and his men. They sent me out to South Africa during the trouble and I brought a detachment into a country village. It seemed quite unpromising but I was told of a sort of place 3 miles in the country that you would call a chateau in France. So I cantered out and spent the night, turning my men over to a sergeant-major. After a refreshing breakfast along in the middle of the morning--the late middle of the morning--I rode back into town, but try as I might I could not locate a single one of my men.

"Now nothing, you know, is as ineffective in a war as an officer without his men. Well, I spent the day in agony and it was not until along at dusk that the first of the blighters straggled in--quite drunk, all of them, and swearing to a man that they had engaged in five ferocious battles. It seems that about 2 miles away, in a barn, they had come on a hogshead of ginger brandy, and had stayed with it to the bitter end. Need I say that it was a great lesson to me, and that from then on I was never billeted farther than 15 rods from my men.

"As a matter of fact, I love ginger brandy."

Or this, in which the whole lesson of exactitude in the written communication is implicit:

"Now on the subject of messages, it might be well to say immediately that as far as I know no one ever received a written message during a battle. They may be written, but that I think is as far as it goes. However, they are occasionally received before and after battles, and in this connection let me say that it is no earthly good writing generalities to signify times and places.

"I mean to say, suppose you are writing a message and you write 'Report after breakfast.' Well, to Sergeant Ramrod it might mean stand-to at 3 in the morning; while to Captain Brighteyes it would mean, say, 8 o'clock. But to Colonel Blue-fish it would signify some time after 11, depending quite a bit on how the old fellow felt.

"So it is better to say 7 o'clock in the morning, if that is what you mean, for after all there is only one 7 o'clock in the morning. And, by the way, I must warn you chaps against the champagne on sale in the Cafe de l'Univers down here in the square. It is made in the basement--of potatoes."

On as simple and basic a thing as continuing liaison between small units, the Colonel's listeners never forgot his elementary parable:

"One rule is about all a chap can handle in a battle, and as good a one as any to remember is to keep in some sort of touch with the chaps to your right and left. If you do this--and I dare say you Americans will have as much trouble as ourselves in remembering to--then a great deal of distress to yourselves and all hands will be obviated.

"Now here we have a triangular wood. There is to be an attack, and the objective is this line beyond the wood. So on this side of the wood at the hour of attack the Welsh Guards go forward--and on this side, here, the Inniskilling Fusiliers, and a tremendous battle ensues. Well, after an hour or two, with not much progress, it is discovered that the Welsh Guards have been firing into the Inniskilling Fusiliers, and the Fusiliers have been firing into the Welsh. This is thought a bit thick, you know, even in the confusion of battle. So eventually it is stopped."

Some of the experts warn the lecturer who is only a beginner against the use of humor, commenting that if a joke is unlaughed at, it is disconcerting to all concerned. The only intelligent answer to that is: "Well, what of it?" The speaker who is going to cringe every time one of his passages falls a little flat had best not start. This happens at times to every lecturer; there are good days and bad days, live audiences and sour ones. If a man takes his work seriously, it is hardly within nature for him to harden his emotions against an unexpectedly dull reaction. But he can keep from ever showing that he is upset if as a speaker he consciously forms the habit of rapidly driving on from one point to another.

Thus as to the use of humor in public address, it is not only an asset but almost a necessity. It is better to try with it, and to fall flat occasionally, thereby sharpening one's own wit through better under-standing of what goes and what does not, than to attempt to go along humorlessly. Said William Pitt: "Don't tell me of a man's being able to talk sense. Everyone can talk sense. Can he talk a little nonsense?" Even more to the point is the remark of Thomas Hardy that men thin away to insignificance quite as often by not making the most of good spirits when they have them as by lacking good spirits when they are indispens-able. Fighting is much too serious a trade to have a large place for men who are dry as dust.

One of the spellbinders of ancient Greece, we are told, orated on the sands with his mouth filled with pebbles. In World War I, it was the custom of many higher commanders to take their officers out for voice exercises and have them talk through 150 feet of thicket; they were not satisfied unless the words came through distinctly on the far side. If, under average acoustical conditions, a military officer cannot get across to five hundred men, he needs to improve his voice placement. It is remarkable what miracles can be worked by consistent exercise of the vocal cords.

The final thought is that it is all a matter of buildup. An officer can cut his audience to his own size, and strengthen his powers and his confidence as he goes along. That is his supreme advantage. He can start with a short talk to a minor working detail and move from that to a more formal address before a slightly larger group. By taking it gradually, and increasing his store of knowledge in the interim period, he will see the time come when he can hold any audience in the hollow of his hand. This is precisely the routine which was followed by most of the military leaders who have been celebrated for their command of speech.

CHAPTER TWENTY-ONE

THE ART OF INSTRUCTION

Keep it simple.

Have but one main object.

Stay on the course.

Remain cheerful.

Be enthusiastic.

Put it out as if the ideas were as interesting and novel to you, as to your audience.

By abiding by these few simple rules you will keep cool, preserve continuity and hold your audience.

Instruction is just about the begin-all and end-all of every military officer's job. He spends the greater part of his professional life either pitching it or catching it, and the game doesn't stop until he is at last retired. Should he become a Supreme Commander, even, this is one thing that does not change; it remains a give-and-take proposition. Part of his time is taken instructing his staff as to what he wants done and just as much of it is spent in being instructed by his staff as to the means available for the doing of it.

Instruction is the generator of unified action. It is the transmission belt by which the lessons of experience are passed to untrained men. Left uninstructed, men may progress only by trial-and-error and the hard bumps which come of not knowing the way.

Need more than that be said to suggest that the officer who builds a competent skill in this field, so that it becomes a part of his reputation, has at the same time built the most solid kind of a foundation under his service career?

The services do not discard that kind of man when the economy pinch comes and the establishment has to contract. The Reservist, who is known as a good instructor, is always on the preferred list. In any period of emergency, such officers move rapidly to the top; there are always more good jobs than there are good men. Look back over the lineup of distinguished commanders from World War II! It will be found that the high percentage of them first attracted notice by *being good school men.*

Within the services, in all functions related to the passing on of information, the accent is on "knowing your stuff." The point is substantial, but not conclusive. It is upon the way that instruction is delivered rather than upon its contents as such that its moral worth rests. The pay-off is not in what is said, but in what sinks in. *A competent instructor will not only teach his men but will increase his prestige in the act.* There are many inexpressibly dull bores who know what they're talking about, but still haven't learned how to say it, because they are contemptuous of the truth that it is the dynamic flow of knowledge, rather than the static possession of it, which is the means to power and influence. As technicians, they have their place. As instructors, they would be better off if they knew only half as much about their subject, and twice as much about people.

To know where truth lies is not more important than knowing how to pitch it. Take the average American military audience: what can be said fairly of its main characteristics? Perhaps this--that it is moderately reflective; that it is ready to give the untried speaker a break; that it does not like windiness, bombast or prolonged moralizing; that it refuses to be bullied; and that it can usually be won by the light touch and a little appeal to its sporting instinct. It is the little leavening in the bread which makes all the difference in its savor and digestibility.

In World War I an American major, name now long forgotten, was given the task of making the rounds of the cantonments, talking to all combat formations, and convincing them that the future was bright--no Boy Scout errand. But wherever he went, morale was lifted by his words. In substance, what he said was this:

"None of us cares about living with any individual who wants every break his own way. But when the odds are even, the gamble is worth any good man's time. So let's look at the proposition. You now have one chance in two; you may go overseas, you may not. Suppose you do. You still have one chance in two. You may go to the front, or you may not. If you don't, you'll see a foreign country at Uncle Sam's expense; if you do, you'll find out about war, which is the toughest chance of them all. But up there, you still have one chance in two: you may get hit, or you may not. If you breeze through it, you'll be a better man for all the rest of your life. And if you get hit, you still have one chance in two. You may get a small wound, and become a hero to your family and friends. Or there is always the last chance that it may take you out altogether. And while that is a little rugged, it is at least worth remembering that very few people seem to get out of this life alive."

There was as simple an idea as any military instructor ever unloaded, and yet troops cheered this man wherever he went.

Lt. Col. H. M. Hutchinson, of the British Army, already described in this book as an instructor who made a powerful impression on the American Army in World War I because of his droll wit, was a master hand at taking the oblique approach to teach a lesson. Old officers still remember the manner and the moral of passages such as this one:

"On the march back from Mons--and I may say that a very good army sometimes must retreat, though no doubt it wounds the sensibilities to consider it--we did rather well. But I noticed often the confusion caused by marching slowly up one side of a hill and dashing down the other. It is a tendency of all columns on foot.

"A captain is sitting out in front on a horse, with a hell of a great pipe in his mouth and thinking of some girl in a cafe, and of course he moves slowly up the hill. He comes to the top and his pace quickens. Well, then, what happens? The taller men are at the top of the column, and they lengthen their stride--but what becomes of Nipper and Sandy down in the twentieth squad? Half the time, you see, they are running to catch up. So the effect is to jam the troops together on an upgrade and to stretch them out going down--you know--like a concertina."

Where then is the beginning of efficiency in the art of instruction? It resides in becoming diligent and disciplined about self-instruction. No man can develop great power as an instructor, or learn to talk interestingly and convincingly, until he has begun to think deeply. And depth of thought does not come of vigorous research on an assignment immediately at hand, but from intensive collateral study throughout the course of a career. We are all somewhat familiar with the type of commander who, when asked: "What are your officers doing about special studies, so that they may better their reading habits and further their powers of self-expression?" will puff himself up by replying, "They are kept so busily employed that they have no time for any such exercise." This is one way of saying that his subordinates are kept too busy to get essential work done.

Research, on the spot and at the time, is vital and necessary so that the presentation of any subject will be factually freshened and

173

documented. But its nature and object should not be overrated. The real values can be compared to what happens to a pitcher when he warms up before a game. This is merely an act of suppling the muscles; the real conditioning process has already taken place, and it has been long and arduous.

Even so is it with immediate research, in its relation to continuing military study, in the perfecting of instructorship. That which gives an officer power, and conviction, on the platform, or before a group, is not the thing which he learned only yesterday, having been compelled to read it in a manual or other source, but the whole body of this thought and philosophy, as it may be directed toward the invigorating of any presentation of any subject. If he forms the habit of careful reflection, then almost everything that he reads and hears other people say that arouses his own interest becomes grist for his mill.

Like 10 years in the penitentiary, it's easy to say but hard to do. So much time, seemingly, has to be wasted in profitless study to find a few kernels amid much chaff. Napoleon said at one point that the trouble with books is that one must read so many bad ones to find something really good. True enough but, even so, there are perfectly practical ways to advance rapidly without undue waste motion. Consider this: Among one's superiors there are always discriminating men who have "adopted" a few good books after reading many bad ones. When they say that a text is worthwhile, it deserves reading and careful study.

The junior who starts building a working library for his professional use cannot do better than to consult those older men who are scholars as well as leaders, and ask them to name five or six texts which have most stimulated their thought. It comes as a surprising discovery that some of the titles which are recommended with the greatest enthusiasm are not among the so-called classics on war. The well-read man need not have more than a dozen books in his home, provided that they all count with him, and he continues to pore over them and to ponder the weight of what is said. On the other hand, the ignorant man is frequently marked by his bookshelf stocked with titles, not one of which suggests that he has any professional discernment.

The notebook habit is invaluable, nay, indispensable, to any young officer who is ambitious to perfect himself as an instructor. Most men who are distinguished for their thinking ability are inveterate keepers of scrapbooks and of reference files where they have put clippings and notes which jogged their own thoughts. This is not a cheap device leading to the parroting of other men; the truth is that the departure line toward original thinking by any man is established by the mental energy which he acquires by imaginative observation of other men's ideas.

To get back to the notebook, it should be loose-leaf and well-bound, else it is not likely to be given permanent use. Whether it is kept at home or the office is immaterial. What matters is that it be made a receptacle for everything that one hears, reads or sees which may be of possible future value in the preparation of classroom work. Books can't be clipped; but short, decisive passages can be copied, and longer ones can be made the subject of a reference item. Copying is one way of fixing an idea in the memory. While on the subject of books, it is all right to quote the classics and to be able to refer to the great authorities on the science of war. But it is more effective by far to read deeply into such writers as Clausewitz, Mahan and Fuller, and to find some of their strongest but least-known passages for one's self, than to rely on the more popular but shop-worn quotations which are in general circulation. Such old chestnuts as, "The moral is to the material as three to one," do not refresh discourse.

Even so, the classics are only one small field worth cultivating. Nearly every major speech by current military leadership contains a passage or two well worth salting away. The writings of the philosophers, the publications of the industrial world, the daily press and the scientific journals are goldmines containing rich nuggets of information and of choice expression worth study and preservation.

In fact, the military instructor has the whole world as his workshop. His notebook should be as ready to receive some especially apt saying by a new recruit as the more ponderous words uttered by the sages. And it should contain, not less, comments on techniques and methods used by other speakers and instructors, which were visibly unusually effective.

Above all, the consistent use of obvious and stereotyped devices and methods of presentation should be avoided. For the fact is that *no one has yet discovered the one best way.* In our service thinking, we tend to get into a rut, and to use none but the well-tried way. For example, we overwork the twin principles of thought-surprise and thought-concentration, and in the effort to produce dramatic effect, we sometimes achieve only an anticlimax. Using the techniques of the advertising

175

world, the military instructor puts his exhibits behind a screen, in order to buildup anticipation, and at the appropriate moment he yanks the cover off. This is perfectly effective, in some instances. But it becomes a *reductio ad absurdum*[1] when he is working with only one chart, or a pair or so of objects. Let's say that he is talking about one machine gun, and he has one chart highlighting its characteristics. How much more impressive it would be if they were in the open at the beginning and he were to start by saying: "Gentlemen, I am talking about this one gun and what keeps it going. It is more important that you see and know this gun from this moment than that you be persuaded by what I am about to say!"

It is a very simple but inviolable rule that where there is an obvious straining to produce an effect by the use of any training aid, then the effect of the training aid is lost and the speaker is proportionately enfeebled. A famous World War II commander said of all operations: "It is the chaps, not the charts, that get the job done."

What needs to be kept in mind is the psychological object in their use. The scientists tell us, and we can partly take their word for it, that people learn about 75 percent of what they know through their sight, 13 percent through their hearing, and 12 percent through their other senses. But this is a relative and qualitative, rather than an absolute, truth. It has to be so. Otherwise, book study, which employs sight exclusively, would be the only efficient method of teaching, and oral instruction, which depends primarily on sound impact, would be a wasteful process.

The more fundamental truth is that when oral instruction is properly done, the mind becomes peculiarly receptive because it is being bombarded by both sight and sound impressions. Nor is this small miracle wrought primarily by what we call training aids. The thoughts and ideas which remain most vivid in the memory get their adhesive power because some particular person said them in a graphic way in a pregnant moment. Our working thoughts are more often the product of an association with some other individual than not. We remember words largely because we remember an occasion. We believe in ideas because first we were impressed by the source whence they came.

The total impression of a speaker--his sincerity, his knowledge, his enthusiasm, his mien, and his gestures--is what carries conviction

---

1. A type of argument attempting to prove a statement by demonstrating the denial of the statement results in the absurd.

and puts an indelible imprint on the memory. Man not only thinks, but he moves, and he is impressed most of all by animate objects. Vigorous words mean little or nothing to him when they issue from a lack-luster personality.

Artificiality is one of the more serious faults, and it is unfortunately the case that though an instructor may be solid to the core, he will seem out of his element, unless he is careful to avoid stilted words and vague or catch-all phrases and connectives. Strength in discourse comes of simplicity.

But it has become almost an American disease of late that we painfully avoid saying it straight. "We made contact, and upon testing my reaction to him, found it distinctly adverse" is substituted for "I met him and didn't like him." But what is equally painful is to hear public remarks interlarded with such phrases as "It would seem," "As I was saying," "And so, in closing," "Permit me to call your attention to the fact" and "Let us reflect briefly"--which is often the prelude to a 2-hour harangue.

Not less out of place in public address is the apologetic note. The man who starts by explaining that he's unaccustomed to public speaking, or badly prepared, is simply asking for the hook. "To explain what I mean" or "to make myself clear" makes the audience wonder only why he didn't say it that way in the first place. But the really low man on this totem pole is the one who says, "Perhaps you're not getting anything out of this."

A man does not have to go off like a gatling gun merely because he is facing the crowd. Mr. Churchill, one of the great orators of the century, made good use of deliberate and frequent pauses. It is a trick worth any young speaker's cultivation, enabling the collection of thought and the avoiding of tiresome "and ah-h-h's."

Likewise, because a man is in military uniform does not require that his speech be terse, cold, given to the biting of words and the overemployment of professional jargon. Training instruction is not drill. Its efficiency does not come of its incisiveness but of the bond of sympathy which comes to prevail between the instructor and his followers.

Another main point: It is disconcerting to talk about the ABCs, if the group already knows the alphabet. To devote any great part of a presentation to matters which the majority present already well understand is to assure that the main object will receive very little serious attention. Thus in talking about the school of the rifle, only a fool would start by explaining what part of it was the trigger and from which end the bullet emerged, though it might be profitable to devote a full hour to the discussion of caliber. Likewise, in such a field as tactical discussion, the minds of men are more likely to be won, and their imagination stirred, through giving them the reasoning behind a technique or method than by telling them simply how a thing is done.

In talk, as in tactics, at the beginning the policy of the limited objective is a boon to confidence. It scares any green man to think about talking for an hour. But if he starts with a subject of his own choice and to his liking, and works up to 15-minute talk for a group of platoon size, he will quickly develop his powers over the short course; the switch from sprinting to distance running can be made gradually and without strain. But it's easy that does it, and one step at a time.

Excessive modesty is unbecoming. No matter how firm his sources, or complex the subject, any instructor should form the habit of adding a few thoughts of his own to any presentation. It is not a mark of precocity but of interest when an instructor knows his material, and its application to the human element, sufficiently well to express an occasional personal opinion. Since he is not a phonograph record, he has a right to say, "I think" or "I believe." Indeed, if he does not have his subject sufficiently in hand that it has stirred his own imagination, he is no better than a machine.

That leads to a discussion of outlines. They are necessary, if any subject is to be covered comprehensively. But if they are overelaborated, the whole performance becomes automatic and dull. A little spontaneity is always needed. Even when working from a manuscript, a speaker should be ever-ready to depart from his text if a sudden idea pops into his mind. It is better to try this and to stumble now and then than to permit the mind to be commanded by words written on paper.

Likewise, revision of outline between talks is the way of the alert mind. A man cannot do this work without seeing, in the midst of discussion, points which need strengthening, and bets which have been missed. Notes should be revised as soon as the period is completed.

There are many methods of instruction, among them being the seminar, critique, group discussion and conference. They are not described here for the reason that every young officer quickly learns about them in the schools, and gets to know the circumstances under which one form or another can be used to greatest advantage.

It suffices to say that their common denominator, insofar as personal success and ease of participation are concerned, is the ability to think quickly and accurately on one's feet; the one best school for the sharpening of this faculty is the lecture platform. Keenness is a derivative of pressure.

Use of a wire recorder or a platter, so that one can get a playback after talking, is an aid to self-criticism. But it is not enough. A man will often miss his own worst faults, because they came of ignorance in the first place; too, voice reproduction proves nothing about the effectiveness of one's presence, expression and gesture. It is common-sense professional procedure to ask the views of one or two of the more experienced members of the audience as to how the show went over, and what were its weak points.

There is one hidden danger in becoming too good at this business. Too frequently, polished speakers fall in love with the sound of their own voices, and want to be heard to the exclusion of everyone else. In the military establishment, where the ideal object is to get 100 percent participation from all personnel, this is a more serious vice than snoring in a pup tent.

When an officer feels any temptation to monopolize the discussion, it is time to pray for a bad case of bronchitis.

CHAPTER TWENTY-TWO

YOUR RELATIONSHIPS WITH YOUR MEN

Inasmuch as most of this book has been directed toward covering the various approaches to this subject, there is need to discuss here only a relatively few points which could not conveniently be treated elsewhere.

This is the touchstone of success.

To any officer starting on a life career, it is impossible to overstate its importance. For the moment, we can forget the words duty and responsibility. The question is: "How do I get ahead?" And for a junior there is one main road open--he will strive to achieve such a communion of spirit with his subordinates that he will know the personality and character of every one of his men, will understand what moves and what stops them, and will be sympathetic to their every impulse.

This is the main course. The great principles of war have evolved from centuries of observation on how men react in the mass. It could not be otherwise than that any officer's growth in knowledge of when and how these principles apply to varying situations, strategical and tactical, come primarily of the acuteness of his powers of observation of individual men, and of men working together in groups, and responding to their leadership, under widely different conditions of stress, strain and emotion.

The roots of this kind of wisdom are not to be acquired from book study; books are a help only as they provide an index to what should be sought. The sage who defined strategy as "the art of the possible" (the art of politics has been defined in the same words) wrote better than he knew. The cornerstone of the science of war is knowledge of the economy of men's powers, of their physical possibilities and limitations, of their response to fatigue, hope, fear, success and discouragement, and of the weight of the moral factor in everything they do. Man is a beast of burden; he will fail utterly in the crisis of battle if there is no respect for his aching back. He is also one of a great brotherhood whose mighty fellowship can make the worst misery tolerable, and can provide him with undreamed strength and courage. These are among the things that need to be studied and understood; they are the main score. It is only when an officer can stand and say that he is first of all a student of human material that all of the technical and material aspects of war begin to conform toward each other and to blend into an orderly pattern. And the laboratory is right outside the office door. Either an officer grows up with, and into, this kind of knowledge through reflecting on everything that he can learn of men wherever he fits himself into a new environment, or because of having neglected to look at trees, he will also miss the forest.

By the numbers, it isn't a difficult assignment. The schools have found by experiment that the average officer can learn the names of 50 men in between 7 and 10 days. If he is in daily contact with men, he should know 125 of them by name and by sight within 1 month. Except under war conditions, he is not likely to work with larger numbers than that.

This is the only way to make an intelligent start. So long as a man is just a number, or a face, to his officer, there can be no deep trust between them. Any man loves to hear the sound of his own name, and when his superior doesn't know it, he feels like a cypher.

As with any other introduction, an officer meeting an enlisted man for the first time is not privileged to be inquisitive about his private affairs. In fact, nosiness and prying are unbecoming at any time, and in no one more than in a military officer. On the other hand, any man is flattered if he is asked about his work or his family, and the average enlisted man will feel complimented if an officer engages him in small talk of any kind. Greater frankness, covering a wide variety of subjects, develops out of longer acquaintance. It should develop as naturally and as easily as in civilian walks of life; rank is no barrier to it unless the officer is overimpressed with himself and bent on keeping the upper hand; the ranks are wiser about these things than most young officers; they do not act forward or presumptuous simply because they see an officer talking and acting like a human being. But they aren't Quiz Kids. Informal conversation between officer and man is a two-way street. The ball has to be batted back and forth across the net or there isn't any game. An officer has to extend himself, his thoughts, his experiences and his affairs into the conversation, or after his first trial or two, there will be nothing coming back.

It is unfortunately the case that many young officers assume that getting acquainted with their men is a kind of interrogation process, like handling an immigrant knocking for admission to the United States. They want to know everything, but they stand on what they think is their right to tell a man nothing. That kind of attitude just doesn't wash. In fact, the chief value of such conversations is that it permits the junior to see his superior as a man rather than as a boss.

An officer should never speak ironically or sarcastically to an enlisted man, since the latter doesn't have a fair chance to answer back. The use of profanity and epithets comes under the same heading. The best argument for a man keeping his temper is that nobody else wants it; and when he voluntarily throws it away, he loses a main prop to his own position.

Meeting one of his own enlisted men in a public place, the officer who does not greet him personally and warmly, in addition to observing the formal courtesies between men in service, has sacrificed a main chance to win the man's abiding esteem. If the man is with his family, a little extra graciousness will go a long way, and even if it didn't, it would be the right thing.

In any informal dealing with a number of one's own men, it is good judgment to pay a little additional attention to the youngest or greenest member of the group, instead of permitting him to be shaded by older and more experienced men. They will not resent it, and his confidence will be helped.

It should go without saying that an officer does not drink with his men, though if he is a guest of honor at an organizational party where punch or liquor is being served, it would be a boorish act for him to decline a glass, simply because of this proscription. Sometimes in a public cocktail bar an officer will have the puzzling experience of being approached by a strange but lonely enlisted man who, being a little high, may have got it into his head that it is very important to buy an officer a drink. What one does about that depends upon all of the surrounding circumstances. It is better to go through with it than create a scene which will give everyone a low opinion of the service. Irrespective of rules, there are always situations which are resolved only by good judgment. And, of course, the problem can be avoided by staying away from cocktail bars.

Visiting men in hospital is a duty which no officer should neglect. Not only does it please the man and his family; it is one of the few wide open portals to a close friendship with him. It is strange but true that the man never forgets the officer who was thoughtful enough to call on him when he was down. And the effect of it goes far beyond the man himself. Other men in the unit are told about it. Other patients in the ward see it and note with satisfaction that the corps takes its responsibilities to heart. If the man is in such shape that he can't write a letter, it is a worthy act to serve him in this detail. By the same token when a man goes on sick call, the officer's responsibility does not end at the point where the doctor takes over. His interest is to see that the man is made well, and if he has reason to think that the treatment he is receiving falls short of the best possible, it is within his charge to raise the question. The old saw about giving the man CC pills and iodine and marking him duty is now considerably outdated. But it is not assumed that every member of the medical staff serving the forces will at all times do his duty with the intelligence and reverence of a saint.

A birthday is a big day in any man's life. So is his wedding. So is the birth of a child. By making check of the roster and records, and by keeping an ear to the ground for news of what is happening in the unit, an officer can follow these events. Calling the man in and giving him a handclasp and word of congratulation, or writing a note to the home, takes very little time and is worth every moment of it. Likewise, if he has won some distinction, such as earning a promotion, a letter of appreciation to his parents or his wife will compound the value of telling the man himself that you are proud of what he has done.

Nothing is more pleasing or ingratiating to any junior than to be asked by his superior for his opinion on any matter--provided that it is given a respectful hearing. Any man gets a little fagged from being *told* all the time. When he is consulted and asked for a judgment, it builds him up.

There is absolutely no point in visiting kitchens or quarters and asking of the atmosphere if everything is all right. Men seldom complain, and they are loath to stick their necks out when there are other enlisted men within hearing. It is the task of the officer to *see* that all is right, and to take whatever trouble is necessary to make certain. If he is doubtful about the mess, then a mere pecky sampling of it will do no good. Either he will live with it for a few meals, or he won't find the "bugs" in it.

An officer should not ask a man: "Would you like to do such-and-such a task?" when he has already made up his mind to assign him to a certain line of duty. Orders, hesitatingly given, are doubtfully received. But the right way to do it is to instill the idea of collaboration. There is something irresistibly appealing about such an approach as: "I need your help. Here's what we have to do."

183

An officer is not expected to appear all-wise to those who serve under him. Bluffing one's way through a question when ignorant of the answer is foolhardy business. "I'm sorry, but I don't know," is just as appropriate from an officer's lips as from any other. And it helps more than a little to be able to add, "But I'll find out."

Rank should be used to serve one's subordinates. It should never be flaunted or used to get the upper hand of a subordinate in any situation save where he had already discredited himself in an unusually ugly or unseemly manner.

When suggestions from any subordinate are adopted, the credit should be passed on to him publicly.

When a subordinate has made a mistake, but not from any lack of good will, it is common sense to take the rap for him rather than make him suffer doubly for his error.

An officer should not issue orders which he cannot enforce.

He should be as good as his word, at all times and in any circumstance.

He should promise nothing which he cannot make stick.

An officer should not work, looking over his men's shoulder, checking on every detail of what they are doing, and calling them to account at every furlong post. This maidenly attitude corrodes confidence and destroys initiative.

On the other hand, contact is necessary at all times. Particularly when men are doing long-term work, or are operating in detachment at a remote point, they will become discouraged and will lose their sense of direction unless their superior looks in on them periodically, asks whether he can be of any help, and, so doing, gets them to open up and discuss the problem.

The Navy says, "It isn't courtesy to change the set of the sail within 30 minutes after relief of the watch." Applied to a command job, this means that it is a mistake for an officer, on taking a new post, to order sweeping changes affecting other men, in the belief that this will give him a reputation for action and firmness. The studying of the situation is the overture to the steadying of it. The story is told of Gen. Curtis E. LeMay of the Air Force. Taking over the 21st Bomber Command in the Marianas, he faced the worried staff officers of his predecessor and said quietly, "You're all staying put. I assume you know your jobs or you wouldn't be here."

The identity of the officer with the gentleman should persist in his relations with men of all degree. In the routine of daily direction and disposition, and even in moments of exhortation, he had best bring courtesy to firmness. The finest officers that one has known are not occasional gentlemen, but in every circumstance: in commissioned company and, more importantly, in contact with those who have no recourse against arrogance.

The traditional wisdom of addressing Judy O'Grady with the same politeness as one would the Colonel's Lady applies equally in all situations in life where one is at arbitrary advantage in dealing with another. To press this unnecessarily is to sacrifice something of one's quality in the eyes of the onlooker. Besides, there is always the better way.

CHAPTER TWENTY-THREE

YOUR MEN'S MORAL AND PHYSICAL WELFARE

To put it in a nutshell, the moral of this chapter is that when men are moral, the moral power which binds them together and fits them for high action is given its main chance for success.

There should therefore be no confusion about how the word is being used. We are speaking both of training in morals for every day living, and of moral training which will harden the will of a fighting body. One moment's reflection will show why they need not be considered separately, and why we can leave it to Webster to do the hairsplitting.

It is the doctrine of the armed establishment of the United States that when American men lead a personal life which is based on high moral standards, and when their aim is equally high as to physical fitness and toughness, under training conditions they will mature those qualities which are most likely to produce inspired leading and stout following within the forces.

There is nothing panty-waist about this doctrine. It was not pronounced to gratify the clergy or to reassure parents that their sons would be in good hands, even though these things, too, are important.

The doctrine came of the experience of the Nation in war, and of what the services learned by measuring their own men. But it happened, also, that the facts were consistent with a common sense reckoning of the case.

Let's figure it out. To be temperate in all things, to be continent, and to refrain from loose living of any sort, are acts of the will. They require self-denial, and a foregoing of that which may be more attractive, in favor of the thing which should be done. Granted that there are a few individuals who are so thin-blooded that they never feel tempted to digress morally, men in the majority are not like that. What they renounce in the name of self-discipline, at the cost of a considerable inner stress, they endeavour to compensate by their gains in personal character. Making that grade isn't easy; but no one who is anyone has yet said that it isn't worthwhile. In the armed services there is an old saying that an officer without character is more useless than a ship with no bottom.

In the summing up, the strength of will which enables a man to lead a clean life is no different than the strength of purpose which fits him to follow a hard line of duty. There are exceptions to every rule. Many a lovable rounder has proved himself to be a first-class fighting man. But even though he had an unconquerable weakness for drink and women, his resolution had to become steeled along some other line or he would have been no good when the pay-off came.

Putting aside for the moment the question of the vices, and regarding only the gain to moral power which comes of bodily exercise and physical conditioning, it should be self-evident that the process which builds the muscle must also train and alert the mind. How could it be otherwise? Every physical act must have as its origin a mental impulse, conscious or unconscious. Thus in training a man to master his muscles we also help him to master his brain. He comes out of physical training not only better conditioned to move but better prepared to think about how and why he is moving, which is true mobility.

In military organizations, "setting-up" and other formation exercises are usually a drag and a bore. Men grumble about them, and even after they are toughened to them, so that they feel no physical distress, they rarely relish them. The typical American male would much rather sit on his pants along the sidelines and watch someone else engage in contact sports. It's almost the national habit. Despite our athletic prowess, about 56 percent of American males grow to manhood without having ever participated in a group game.

But no matter how great the inertia against it, there must be unremitting perseverance in the physical conditioning of military forces. For finally, it is killing men with kindness to relax at this point. If life is to be conserved, if men are to be given a fair chance to play their parts effectively, the physical standards during training cannot be less than will give them a maximum fitness for the extraordinary stresses of campaigning in war.

When troops lack the coordinated response which comes of long, varied and rigorous exercises, their combat losses will be excessive, they will lack cohesion in their action against the enemy, and they will uselessly expend much of their initial velocity. In the United States service, we are tending to forget, because of the effect of motorization, that the higher value of the discipline of the road march in other days wasn't that it hardened the muscles, but that, short of combat, it was the best method of separating the men from the boys. This is true today, despite all of the new conditions imposed by technological changes. A hard road march is the most satisfactory training test of the moral strength of the individual man.

At the same time, to senselessly overload men for road marching hurts them two ways. It weakens their faith in the sense of the command, thereby impairing morale, and it breaks down their muscle and tendon. Enough is known about the average American male to provide a basic logistical figure. He stands about 5 feet 8 inches, and weighs about 153 pounds. The optimum load for a man is about one-third of body weight, the same as for a mule. That means that for a training march, approximately 50 pounds over-all, including uniform, blankets and everything, is the most that a man should be required to carry. If he gets so that he can handle that load easily, over let us say a 10-mile road march, then the thing to do, further to build up his power, is not to increase the weight that he carries, but to lengthen the march. Military men have known that this is the underlying principle for better than half a century. But the principle has not always been observed.

There is another not infrequent cause of breakdown--the leader who makes the mistake of thinking that every man's limit is the same as his own. Some come into the officer corps fresh from the stadia and cinderpaths of the colleges, in the pink of condition. They take charge of a group of men, some not yet seasoned, and others somewhat older and more wind-broke than themselves. They shag them all over the lot at reveille or take them on a cross-country chase like a smart rabbit trying to outrun hounds. The poor devils ultimately get back, some with their corks completely pulled, a few feeling too nauseated to eat their breakfast, and others walking in, feeling whipped because they couldn't keep up with the group.

When an officer does this kind of thing thoughtlessly, he shows himself to be an incompetent observer of men. When he does it to show off, he deserves to be given 10 days in the electric chair.

It is the steadiness and the continuity of exercise, not the working of men to the point of exhaustion and collapse, which keeps them upgrading until they are conditioned to the strain of whatever comes. To do it the other way around simply makes them hospital patients before their time, and fills them with resentment against the service.

In the nature of things, the officer who has been an athlete can fit himself into this part of the program with little difficulty and with great credit, provided he acts with the moderation that is here suggested. The armed services put great store by this. A man with a strong flair for physical training can usually find a good berth.

By the same token, the officer who has shunned sports in school, either because he didn't have the size or the coordination, or was more interested in something else, will frequently have an understandable hesitation about trying to play a lead hand in anything which he thinks will make him look bad. Of this comes much buck-passing. There is often a singular courtesy between officers within a unit, and they'll switch details, just to be friendly. So it frequently happens that the man who has no great knack at leading in exercise and recreation gets the mouse's share of it. And thereby the whole point is missed. For it should be perfectly clear that the man who has had the least active experience in this field is usually the one in greatest need of its strengthening effects. His case is no different than that of the enlisted man. If he has not kept himself in good physical shape, his nerves will not be able to stand the strain of combat, to say nothing of his legs.

It can be said again and again: *The highest form of physical training that an officer can undergo is the physical conditioning of his own men.* Nothing else can give him more faith in his own ability to stay the course and nothing else is likely to give him a firmer feeling of solidarity with his men. Study, and an active thirst for wider professional knowledge, have their place in an officer's scheme of things. But there is something about the experience of bodily competition, of joining with, and leading men in strenuous physical exercise, which uniquely invigorates one's spirit with the confidence: "I can do this! I can lead! I can command!" Military men have recognized this since long before it was said that Waterloo was won on the playing fields of Eton. Bringing it down to the present, Gen. Sir Archibald Wavell said: "The civil comparison to war must be that of a game, a very rough and dirty game, for which a robust body and mind are essential." Even more emphatic are the words of Coach Frank Leahy of Notre Dame, an officer of the United States Navy in World War II: "The ability to rise up and grasp an opportunity is something that a boy cannot learn in lecture rooms or from textbooks. It is on the athletic field primarily that Americans acquire the winning ways that play such an important part in the American way of life. The burning desire to emerge the victor that we see in our contact sports is the identical spirit that gave the United States Marines victory at Iwo Jima. If we again know war, the boys who have received sound training in competitive athletics will again fight until the enemy has had enough."

Men like to see their officers competing and "giving it a good college try" no matter how inept, or clumsy they may be. But they take a pretty dim view of the leader who perennially acts as if he were afraid of a sweat or a broken thumb. In team sports, developing around interorganized rivalry, the eligibility of an officer to participate among enlisted men is a matter of local ground rules, or special regulations. There is nothing in the customs of the services which prohibit it. To the contrary, it has been done many times, and is considered to be altogether within an officer's dignity. Where there is a flat ruling against it, it is usually on the theory that the officer, by competing, is robbing some enlisted man of his chance.

Need it be said that in any event, going along with the team, and taking an active interest in its ups-and-downs, is not only a service officer's duty, but a rewarding privilege, if he is a real leader? In this respect, he has a singular relationship to any group that represents his unit. He becomes part of their force, and his presence is important not only to the team but to the gallery. It is not unusual to hear very senior officers excuse themselves from an important social function by saying, "I'm sorry, but my team is playing tonight." That is a reason which everybody understands and accepts.

As for the ranks, even among those men who have had no prior acquaintance with organized sports, there is a marked willingness to participate, if given just a little encouragement. This is one of the effects of getting into military uniform. As someone said about gunpowder, "it makes all men alike tall," and provides a welcome release from former inhibitions. The military company is much more tightly closed than any other. When men are thinking and working together in a binding association, they will seek an outlet for their excess spirits, and will join together in play, even under the most adverse circumstance. During World War I, it was common to see American troops playing such games as duck-on-the-rock, tag and touch football with somebody's helmet in close proximity to the front. Because no other equipment was available, they improvised. So it is that in any situation, the acme in leadership consists, not in screaming one's head off about shortages, but in using a little imagination about what can be done.

The really good thing about the gain in moral force deriving from all forms of physical training is that it is an unconscious gain.

Will power, determination, mental poise and muscle control all march hand-in-hand with the general health and well-being of the man, with results not less decisive under training conditions than on the field of battle. A man who develops correct posture and begins to fill out his body so that he looks the part of a fighter will take greater pride in the wearing of the uniform. So doing, he will take greater care so to conduct himself morally that he will not disgrace it. He will gain confidence as he acquires a confident and determined bearing. This same presence, and the physical strength which contributes to it, will help carry him through the hour of danger. Strength of will is partly of the mind and partly of the body. In combat, fatigue will beat men down as quickly as any other condition, for fatigue inevitably carries fear with it. Tired men are men afraid. There is no quicker way to lose a battle than to lose it on the road for lack of preliminary hardening in troops. Such a condition cannot be redeemed by the resolve of a commander who insists on driving troops an extra mile beyond their general level of physical endurance. Extremes of this sort make men rebellious and hateful of the command, and thus strike at tactical efficiency from two directions at once. For when men resent a commander, they will not fight as willingly for him, and when their bodies are spent, their nerves are gone.

Looking after the welfare of men, however, does not connote simply getting them into the open air and giving them a chance to kick the ball around. The services are pretty well organized to provide their personnel with adequate sport and recreational facilities, and to insure an active, balanced program, in any save the most exceptional circumstance. Too, the provisions made for the creature comforts of men are ample, experience-tested, and well-regulated.

It is not so much that a young officer needs to have book instruction about the detail of these things. Such is the system that they can hardly escape his notice, any more than he can escape knowing where to get his pay check and by which path he goes to the barbershop.

What counts mainly is that he should fully understand the prime importance of a personal caring for his men, so that they cannot fail of a better life if it is within his power and wisdom to lead them to it.

Once the principle is grasped, and accepted without any mental reservation, time and experience will educate him in the countless meetings of situations which require its application.

There are times and situations which require that all men be treated identically, for the good of organization. There are also occasions when nothing else suffices but to give the most help, the most encouragement, the most relief to those who are most greatly in need. Grown men understand that, and the officer, approaching every situation with the question in his mind: "What does reason say about what constitutes fair play in this condition?" cannot go far wrong in administering to the welfare of those who serve under him.

It is moral courage, combined with practice, which builds in one a delicate sense of the eternal fitness of things.

One example: Under normal training conditions, it would be fair play, and the acceptable thing, to rotate men and their junior leaders to such an onerous task as guard duty. But if a unit was "dead beat" after a hard march, and an officer, pursuing his line of duty, walked among his men, inspecting their blistered feet and doing all he could to ease each man's physical discomfort, he would then be using excessively poor judgment if he did not pick out the men most physically fit to do whatever additional duty was required that night.

But infinite painstaking in attending to the physical welfare of men is not more important than thoughtful attention to their spiritual wants, and their moral needs. In fact, if we would give a little more priority to the latter, the former would be far more likely to come along all right.

The average American enlisted man is quite young when he enters service, and because he is young, he is impressionable. What his senior tells him becomes a substitute for the influence and teaching that he shed when he left his home or school. That need not mean a senior in age! *He looks to his officer, even though the latter may be junior in years, because he believes that the man with rank is a little wiser, and he has faith that he will not be steered wrong.*

Despite all the publicity given to VD, American kids don't know a great deal about its reality, and even though the greater number of them like to talk about women, what they have to say rarely reveals them as worldly-wise.

If an officer talks straight on these subjects, and believes in what he says sufficiently to set the good example, he can convince his better men that the game isn't worth the candle, and can save even some of the more reckless spirits from a major derail.

CHAPTER TWENTY-FOUR

KEEPING YOUR MEN INFORMED

Nobody ever told the South Sea savage about the nature of air in motion. He had never heard of wind and therefore could not imagine its effects. Thus when he heard strange noises in the treetops and there was a howling around certain headlands, while other headlands were silent, he could believe only that the spirits were at work. He would strain his ear to hear what they had to say to him, and never being able to understand, he would become all the more fearful.

It all sounds pretty silly. And yet civilization is a great deal like that. We pride ourselves today in saying, particularly within the western nations, that men and women are better informed than ever before in the history of the world. What we really mean by that is that they are overburdened with more kinds of fragmentary information than any people of the past. They know just enough about many major questions of the day that either they are driven to the making of fearful guesses about the unknown, or they try to close their minds to the subject, vainly seeking consolation in the half-truth, "What I don't know can't hurt me."

Therein lies a great part of the problem. For it is a fair statement that if all of the mystery could be stripped from such a complex topic as the nature of atomic power, so that men everywhere would understand it, universal fear would be displaced by universal confidence that something could be done, and society would be well along the road toward its control.

In World War I, the men who had the least fear of the effects of gas warfare were the gas officers who understood their subject right down to the last detail of the decontamination process and the formula for dichlorethylsulphide (mustard gas). The man to whom the dangers of submarine warfare seem least fearsome is the submariner. Of all hands along the battle line, the first aid man has the greatest calm and confidence in the face of fire, largely because he has seen the miracles worked by modern medicine in the restoring of grievously wounded men. The general or the admiral who is most familiar with the mettle of his subordinate commands will also have the most relaxed mind under battle pressure.

This leads to a point, which it is better to state here than anywhere else. In all military instruction pertaining to the weapons and techniques of war, the basis of sound indoctrination is the teaching that weapons when rightly used will invariably produce victory, and preventive measures, when promptly and thoroughly taken, will invariably conserve the operational integrity of the defense. It is wrong, *dead wrong*, to start, or carry along, on the opposite track, and try to persuade men to do the right thing, by dwelling on the awful consequence of doing the wrong thing. Confidence, not fear, is the keynote of a strong and convictive doctrine.

In war, in the absence of information, man's natural promptings alternate between unreasoning fears that the worst is likely to happen, and the wishful thought that all danger is remote. Either impulse is a barrier to the growth of that condition of alert confidence which comes to men when they have a realization of their own strength and a reasonably clear concept of the general situation.

Man is a peculiar animal. He is no more prone to think about himself as the central figure amid general disaster than he is to dwell morbidly upon thoughts of his own death. Left in the dark, he will get a certain comfort out of that darkness, at the same time that it clouds his mind and freezes his action. Disturbed by bad dreams about what might happen, he nonetheless will not plan an effective use of his own resources against that which is very likely to happen. Only when he is given a clear view of the horizon, and is made animated by the general purpose in all that moves around him, does he understand the direction in which he should march, and taking hold, begin to do the required thing.

It is almost gratuitous that this even needs to be stated. No high commander would think of moving deliberately into the fog of war if he was without knowledge of either the enemy or friendly situation. Even to imagine such a contingency is paralyzing. But in their nervous and spiritual substance, admirals and generals are no different than the green men who have come most recently to their forces. Such men can not stand alone any more than can the recruit. They draw their moral strength and their ability to contend intelligently against adverse circumstance largely from what is told them by the men who surround them. That is why they have their staffs. They could not command even themselves if they were deprived of all information.

Toward the assuring of competent, collected action, the first great step is to remove the mystery. This is a process which must be mastered in peacetime, if it is to stand the multiplied strains of war. What mystery? Let it be said that it surrounds the average file on every hand, even though the average junior officer does not realize it, while at the same time he himself is completely mystified by much that transpires above him. For example, we all like to throw big words about, to air our professional erudition; and we do not understand that to the man who does not know their meaning, the effect is a blackout which makes even the simplest object seem formidable. To illustrate, we can take the word "bivouac," common enough in military parlance, but rare in civilian speech. When green men are told, "We are going into bivouac," and they are not sufficiently grounded in the service to know that this means simply going into camp for the night without shelter, their instinctive first thought is, "This is another complex military process that will probably catch me short." Similarly if told that they are detailed "on a reconnaissance mission along the line of communications with a liaison function," they could not fail to be "flummoxed." And if then instructed to take a BAR up to the MLR and follow SOP in covering a simulated SFC party, they wouldn't be far from justified if they blew their tops, and ran shrieking from the place.

These are horrible examples, put forward only to illuminate a fairly simple point. Exaggerated though they may be, something of the same sort happens in almost every installation nearly every day. The difference is only in degree. *Every man in the service has an inalienable right to work and to think in the clear.* He is entitled to the why and the wherefore of whatever he is expected to do, as well as the what and the how. His efficiency, his confidence and his enthusiasm will wax strong in almost the precise measure that his superior imparts to him everything he knows about a duty which can be of possible benefit to the man. Furthermore, this is a two-way current. Any officer who believes in the importance of giving full information in a straight-forward manner, and continues to act on that principle, will over the long run get back more than he gives. But the chump who incontinently brushes off his subordinates because he thinks his time is too valuable to spend any great part of it putting them on the right track dooms himself to work in a vacuum. He is soon spotted for what he is, and if his superiors can't set him straight, they will shrug him aside.

These are pretty much twentieth century concepts of how force is articulated from top to bottom of a chain of command. Yet the ideas are as old as the ages. Ecclesiastes is filled with phrases pointing up that clarification is the way of strength and of unity. "All go unto one place." "Two are better than one." "Woe to him that is alone when he falleth." "A threefold cord is not quickly broken." "Whatsoever thy hand findeth to do, do it with thy might." "Folly is set in great dignity." "Truly the light is sweet." Great commanders of the past have reflected that knowledge is the source of the simplifying and joining of all action and have pondered how better to resolve the problem. But it is only in our time that this great principle in military doctrine has become rooted deep enough to stay, because the technological complexity of modern war is such as to permit of no other course.

It is folly to attempt to oversimplify that which is of its nature complex. War cannot be made less intricate by conjuring everyone to return to kindergarten and henceforth use only one-syllable words. No such counsel is here intended. The one thought worth keeping is that the military system, as we know it, will prove far more workable, and its members will each become a stronger link in the chain of force, if all hands work a little more carefully toward the growth of a common awareness of all terminology, all process and all purpose.

Once pronounced, the object also requires to be seen in due proportion. The principle does not entail that a corporal must perforce know everything about operation of a company which concerns his captain, to be happy and efficient in his own job. But it does set forth that he is entitled to have all information which relates to his personal situation, his prospects and his action which it is within his captain's power to give him. A coxswain is not interchangeable with a fleet admiral. To "bigot" him (make available complete detail of a total plan) on an operation would perhaps produce no better or worse effect than a slight headache. But if he is at sea--in both senses of that term--with no knowledge of where he is going or of his chances of pulling through, and having been told of what will be expected of him personally at the target, still has no picture of the support which will be grouped around him, he is apt to be as thoroughly miserable and demoralized as were the sailors under Columbus, when sailing on and on, they came to fear that they would override the horizon and go tumbling into space.

Lt. Gen. Sir Frederick Morgan wrote of the policy applied at his COSSAC planning headquarters during World War II: "Right down to the cook, they were told what had happened, what was happening, along with their part in it, and what it was proposed to do next."

Paraphrasing Montaigne, President Roosevelt told the American people during a great national crisis that the main thing they need fear was fear itself. In matters great and small, the fears of men arise chiefly from those matters they have not been given to understand. Fear can be checked, whipped and driven from the field when men are kept informed.

The dynamics of the information principle lies in this simple truth. We look at the object through the wrong end of the telescope when in the military service we think of information only as instruction in the cause of country, the virtues of the free society and the record of our arms, in the hope that we will make strong converts. These are among the things that every American needs to know, but of themselves they will not turn an average American male into an intelligent, aggressive fighter. Invigorated action is the product of the free and well-informed mind. The "will to do" comes of the confidence that one's knowledge of what requires doing is equal to that of any other man present.

This is the controlling idea and all constructive planning and work in the field of information is shaped around it.

CHAPTER TWENTY-FIVE

COUNSELING YOUR MEN

Among the ever-pressing problems of the commander, and equally of the young officer schooling himself to the ways of the service, is the seeking of means to break down the natural timidity and reticence of the great majority of men.

This he can never do unless he is sufficient master of himself that he can come out of his own shell and give his men a chance to understand him as a human being rather than as an autocrat giving orders. Nothing more unfortunate can happen to an officer than to come to be regarded by his subordinates as unapproachable, for such a reputation isolates him from the main problems of command responsibility as well as its chief rewards. So holding himself, he will never be able to see his forces in their true light, and will either have to exercise snap judgment upon the main problems within his own sphere, or take the word of others as to the factors on which promotions, rewards and punishments are based within the unit.

When the block is due to an officer's own reticence, mistaken ideas about the requirements of his position, or feeling of strangeness toward his fellows, the only cure for him is to dive head-first into the cold, clear water, like a boy at the old swimming hole in the early spring. Thereby he will grow in self-confidence even as he progresses in knowledge of the character of his men and of human nature in general.

If an officer is senior, and is still somewhat on the bashful side, by watching the manner of his own seniors when he gets counsel, and thawing toward his immediate juniors, thereby increasing his receptiveness toward them, there will occur a chain reaction to the bottom level.

The block, however, is not always of the mind and heart. No man can help his own face, but it can sometimes be a barrier to communication. One commander in European Theater was told by his Executive that his subordinates were fearful to approach him because of his perpetual scowl. He assembled his officers and he said to them: "I have been told that my looks are forbidding. The mirror reminds me of that every morning. Years ago I was in a grenade explosion, and a consequent eye injury and strain have done to me what you have to see every time we get together. But if you cannot look beyond the face, and judge my disposition by all else that you see of me in our work together, you do not yet have the full perception that is commensurate with your responsibility."

The too-formal manner, the overrigid attitude, the disposition to deal with any human problem by-the-numbers as if it were only one more act in organizational routine, can have precisely the same chilling effect upon men as came of this officer's scowl. Though no man may move wholly out of his own nature, a cheerfulness of manner in the doing of work is altogether within any individual's capabilities, and is the highest-test lubricant of his human relationships.

As a further safeguard against making himself inaccessible, the officer needs to make an occasional check on the procedures which have been established by his immediate subordinates. At all levels of command it is the pet task of those "nearest the throne" to think up new ways to keep all hands from "bothering the old man." However positive an order to the contrary, they will not infrequently contrive to circumvent it, mistakenly believing that by this act they save him from himself. Many a compassionate commander leads an unwontedly lonely life because of the peculiar solicitude of his staff in this matter and his own failure to discover what is happening to him. In this way the best of intentions may be thwarted. There is no sure cure for the evil but personal reconnaissance.

It is never a waste of time for the commander, or for any officer, to talk to his people about their personal problems. More times than not, the problem will seem small to him, but so long as it looms large to the man, it cannot be dismissed with a wave of the hand. Ridicule, sarcasm and the brush-off are equally inexcusable in any situation where one individual takes another into his confidence on any matter which does not involve bad faith on the part of the petitioner. Even then, if the man imparts that which shows that his own conduct has been reprehensible or that he would enlist the support of his superior in some unworthy act, it is better to hear him through and then skin him, than to treat what he says in the offhand manner. An officer will grow in the esteem of his men only as he treats their affairs with respect. The policy of patience and goodwill pays off tenfold because what happens to one man is soon known to the others.

In this particular there has been a radical change within the services during the current century, simply because of broader understanding of human relationships. In the Old Army, the man could get through to his commander only if he could satisfy the First Sergeant as to the nature of his business; this was a roadblock for the man who either was afraid of the First Sergeant, or was loath to let the latter know about his affairs. Custom dies hard and this one has not been entirely uprooted. But the distance we have traveled toward humanizing all command principles is best reflected by the words of General Eisenhower in "Command in Europe": "Hundreds of broken-hearted fathers, mothers, and sweethearts wrote me personal letters begging for some hope that a loved one might still be alive, or for additional detail as to the manner of his death. Every one of these I answered."

It is not necessary that an officer wet-nurse his men in order to serve well in the role of counsel. His door should be open, but he does not play the part either of a father confessor or of a hotel greeter. Neither great solemnity nor effusiveness are called for, but mainly serious attention to the problem, and then straight-forward advice or decision, according to the nature of the case, *and provided that from his own knowledge and experience he feels qualified to give it.* If not, it is wiser to defer than to offer a half-baked opinion. To consider for a time, and to seek light from others, whether higher authority or one's closer associates, is the sound alternative when there is a great deal at stake for the man and the problem is too complex for its solution to be readily apparent. The spirit in which this work should be undertaken is nowhere more clearly indicated than in the words of Schuyler D. Hoslett who in his book, "Human Factor in Management," said this: "Counseling is advising an individual on his problem to the extent that an attempt is made to help him understand it so he may carry out a plan for its solution. It is a process which stimulates the individual's ability for self-direction."

Family affairs, frictions within the organization, personal entanglements which prey upon the mind, frustrations and anxieties of varying kind, the sense of failure and other nameless fears which are rooted deep in the consciousness of nearly every individual, are the more general subjects in counseling.

Whatever impairs the man that he wishes to take up with his officer becomes ipso facto the officer's rightful business. Equally so, on the positive side, when his only desire is to bring forward something that he believes would serve the interests of organization, he should be heard.

In either case, the perfecting of counsel develops around two controlling ideas, stated in the order of their importance: (1) what is in the best interests of the unit, and (2) what is for the good of the man. In this particular, the officer as counselor is rarely in the role of a disinterested party. Unlike the preacher, the lawyer, the teacher or the best friend, he has to look beyond what is beneficial simply to the spiritual, mental and moral need of one individual. There is an abiding necessity to equate the personal problem to the whole philosophy within which a command operates. *To keep in mind that every individual has his breaking point is everlastingly important. But to remember that the unit is also made of brittle stuff is not less so.*

When undue personal favors are granted, when precedents are set without weighing the possible effects upon all concerned, when men are incontinently urged, or even sympathetically humored by their superiors toward the taking of a weak personal course, the ties of the organization are injured, tension within it mounts and the ranks lose respect for the manhood of their leaders.

All things are to be viewed in moderation, and with compassion, but with a fine balance toward the central purpose. Let us take one example. Within a given command, at a particular time, leaves have been made so restricted, for command reasons, that there must be a showing of genuine urgency. One man comes forward and says that he is so sick for the sight of home that he can no longer take duty. As certainly as his superior tries to facilitate this man's purpose because of fear that he will break, the superior will be harassed by other requests with no better basis, and if they are not granted, there will be general discontent. On the other hand, suppose another man comes forward. A wire from home has informed him that his mother is dying. If the superior will not go to bat on such a case, he will win the deserved contempt of the same men who were ready to take advantage of the other opening, but in this instance would seek nothing for themselves.

To know the record, the character and the measure of goodwill of the subject is all-important in counseling. It puts the matter in much too dim a light to say that after the call comes, the officer should check up on these points so that he can deal knowledgeably with the man. That is his first order of business within the unit--to learn all that he can about the main characteristics of his men. This general duty precedes the detail work of counseling. Under normal circumstances, no officer is likely to have more than 250 men in his immediate charge. There are exceptions, but this is broadly the rule. It is by no means an excessive task for one individual to learn the names and a great part of the history of the men he sees daily, when not knowing them means that he has neglected the heart of operations.

What the man says of himself, in relation to the problem, deserves always to be judged according to his own record. If he has proved himself utterly faithful, action can be taken on the basis of his word. If he is known to be a corner-cutter and a cheat, his case, though listened-to with interest and sympathy, needs to be taken with a grain of salt, pending further investigation.

World War II officers had to abide by this standard in dealing with the general malaise which arose out of redeployment. When a man came forward and said that he couldn't take it any more, and the commander knew that he had always been a highly dutiful individual, it became the commander's job to attempt to get the man home. But when a second man came forward with the same story, and the record showed that he had always shirked his work, the question was whether he should be given the final chance to shirk it again. To favor the first man meant furthering discipline; his comrades recognized it as a fair deal. To turn back the second man was equally constructive to the same end. In a general situation of unique pressure, commanders found that these principles worked.

Many of the problems on which men seek advice of their officers are of a legal nature; unless an officer is versed in the law, the inquiry must be channeled to a qualified source. Other problems are of a kind that use should be made of the home services of such an organization as the Red Cross. A knowledge of the limits beyond which the help of a special office or agency must be sought is therefore as important to the officer-consultant as an ability to give the man full information about the whereabouts and use of these facilities.

The Red Cross is usually an effective agent in checking the facts of a home situation and returning the data. But at the end of the line where officer and man sit together, its resources for helping the individual (when what is needed mainly is advice on a human equation) are not likely to be any better than what his military superiors can do for him. In any time of crisis, the normal human being can draw strength and composure far more surely from a person he well knows than from a stranger.

There is this illustration. During World War II, many a man overseas got word that his home had been broken up. The counselor could talk the thing out with him, learn whether a reconciliation was the one most important thing, or whether the man was groping his way, looking for a friend who could help him see the matter in proportion, and weigh, among other things, his duty to himself. The Red Cross could check the facts of the home situation. But the man's readjustment depended in the main on what was done by those who were closest to him.

Sooner or later every commander has to deal with some refraction of this kind of problem. When it comes, moralizing and generalizing about the weakness of human nature does no good whatever. To call the man a fool is as invidious as to waste indignation upon the cause of his misfortune. Likewise, any frontal approach to the problem, such as telling the man, "Here's what you should do," should be shunned, or used most sparingly. The more effective attitude can be expressed in these words: "If it had happened to me instead of to you, and I were in your same situation, here are the things I would consider, and here are the points to which I would give greatest weight." To tell any subject to brace up and be a man is a plain inference that he is not one. To reflect with him on the things which manhood requires is the gentle way toward stirring his self-respect. So doing, a counselor renews his own character. *Also worth remembering is that in any man's dark hour, a pat on the back and an earnest handclasp may work a small miracle.*

There is much counseling over the subject of transfer. Herein lies an exception to a general rule, for in this case the good of the man takes precedence over the good of organization. No conscientious officer likes to see a good man depart from his organization. Nevertheless, the service is not in competition with itself, and it advances as a whole in the measure that all men find the niche where they can serve most efficiently, and with the greatest satisfaction. There are officers who hold to every able subordinate like grim death, seeing no better way to advance their personal fortunes. This is a sign of moral weakness, not of strength, and its inevitable fruit is discontent within the organization. *The sign of superiority in any officer, at whatever level, is his confidence that he can make another good man to fill any vacancy.* When it is self-evident that a man can better himself and profit the service through transfer, it is contrary to all principle to deny him that right. This does not mean that the unit's exit door should be kept open, but only that it should be ready to yield upon a showing of competent proof. It is not unusual that when the pressure mounts and war danger rises, many a man develops a sudden conviction that he would be more useful in a noncombat arm. The officer body itself is not unsusceptible to the same temptation. Unless the great majority are held to that line of duty which they had accepted in less dangerous circumstance, the service would soon cease to have fighting integrity. But it makes no point to keep men in a combat arm or service who are quite obviously morally and physically unequipped for its rigor, and it is equally wasteful to deny some other arm or service the use of a specialist whose skills fill it particularly. Some of the ablest commanders in our service have abided by this rule: They never denied the man who had a legitimate reason for transfer, and they never shuffled off their lemons and goldbricks under a false label. Though seemingly idealistic, the rule is also practical. The time wasted in excessive worry over a discard is sometimes better spent by concentrating on the value of trumps.

Men tend to seek officer counsel when they feel discriminated against by lesser authority. When that happens, it is the duty of the officer to get at the facts, and act according to them. Complaints against any junior are always unpleasant to hear because of their air of intrigue. Tactlessly handled, without due weighing of the case from both sides, they turn one blunder into two. But no officer is well-advised if he believes that his duty automatically is to uphold the arm of a subordinate when the facts say that the latter is dead wrong. His duty is to reduce friction wherever it is caused by a misuse of power. This implies dealing discreetly with the offender instead of directly discountenancing him.

There are a few broad, common-sense rules which, when followed, will enable any officer to play his part more effectively in the counseling of men.

Privacy is requisite and the interview should not be held at an hour when interruptions are likely.

A listless manner spoils everything, diminishes the force of reason and discourages confidence.

To put the man at ease immediately by some personal gesture is more important than observing forms.

Thereafter the situation is best served by relaxation of bearing rather than by tension:

All excess of expression is a failing, but above all in the man to whom another looks for guidance.

To listen well is the prelude toward pondering carefully and speaking wisely.

No counsel is worthy that has any lower aim than one's own ideals of self-respect.

Early enough is well; quickly done can be quickly undone.

To refuse with kindness is more winning than to acquiesce ungraciously.

To note another man's mood, and to become congenial to it, is the surest way to engage his confidence.

Decisions which are wholly of the heart and not of the mind will ultimately do hurt to both places.

No man will talk freely if met by silence, but an intelligent question encourages frankness above all else.

When one man loses possession of himself it is the more reason that the other should tighten his reserve.

Affectation in one's own manner gives the lie to one's own credit and destroys it with others.

To express pity for a man does not serve to restore him and put him above pity.

When a man is so burdened by a personal problem that it shuts out all else, he must be led to something else.

Imprudent tactics can undo the wisest strategy.

While these dispositions have particular value in relation to the counseling of one's subordinates, they also have some application to any situation in which men work and commune together. Men at any level do not mistake the touch of sincerity, nor fail to mark as unworthy of trust the man who pays only a superficial regard to a matter which they deem important.

For the officer already burdened with other duties, counseling may seem like a waste of time, and an activity that more properly belongs to the chaplain. The wise and understanding "padre" may sometimes counsel men on their material problems and thereby assist the officer who is over troops. But so doing, he is committing a trespass unless he acts with the commander's knowledge and consent. The commander is the foster father of the men in his organization. When he renounces this role, he neglects a trust.

That neglect cuts the fighting efficiency of the unit at its root. Finally, counseling, like all else in military life, has a combat purpose. Other things being equal, the tactical unity of men working together in combat will be in ratio to their knowledge and sympathetic understanding of each other. Whatever the cause, aloofness on the part of the officer can only produce a further withdrawal on the part of the man. Finally, the cost comes high. In battle, and out of it, the failure to act and to communicate is more often due to timidity in the individual than to fear of physical danger.

Described in cold type, the counseling process probably appears a little sticky. Actually, it is nothing of the sort. For it has been going on ever since man became civilized. It is a force in all organized human relationships, beginning in infanthood and lasting through old age. Because of the nature of a military group, and particularly because of the deriving of united strength from well-being in each of the component parts, there is much more need to regularize it and to qualify all men in a knowledge of those things which will enable them to assist a fellow in need of help. But in the military society, far more than in civil life, confidence is a two-way street. It would be almost impossible to express the collective gratitude of tens of thousands of lieutenants and ensigns who in times past have learned to rely on the friendly counsel of a veteran sergeant or petty officer, and have usually gotten it straight from the shoulder, *but with respect*. The breaking-in of most young officers, and the acclimating of them to their role in a command system, is due, in large measure, to support from this source. Nor are senior commanders reluctant to receive moral comfort of this same kind in periods of crisis.

When the planes of the First Tokyo Raid under Col. James H. Doolittle, crashed among the mountains and along the sea-coast of Eastern China, after one of the most valiant strokes in our military annals, their commander was among the few who had the added misfortune of coming to earth within the Japanese lines. By fate's mercy, he just happened to escape by walking between the enemy outposts. Farther along, he saw the wreck of another of his planes. Then he came to a third; it was smashed beyond hope. But its crew had already heard from several other parties. They too had lost their B-25's to the fog, the night and the crags. Doolittle realized then that everything was gone, lives saved yes, but otherwise the expedition was a total ruin.

The Commander sat for a long time in the cockpit of the wrecked plane, terribly depressed, thinking only of how totally he had failed.

At last one of the younger men, Sgt. Paul Leonard walked up to him and said: "What's the matter, Colonel?"

Doolittle said: "It couldn't be worse. We've lost everything. We've let the country down."

The kid said: "Why, Colonel, you've got this all wrong. You have no idea how this looks to the United States. Don't you realize that right now they're getting ready to make you a general? Why I'll make you a bet they give you the Congressional Medal."

Doolittle thanked him. He thought it was a nice thing for the boy to say. That kind of loyalty was worth having in a bad hour. The boy started to walk away; he could tell that Doolittle didn't believe a word of it. Then suddenly he turned and came on back.

"Colonel," he said, "I'd like to make a deal with you. Suppose I'm right about it and you're wrong. So they give you a star and the Congressional Medal. If that happens, will you agree to take me with you wherever you go?"

Doolittle made him a solemn promise. Fresh courage came to him out of the boy's tremendous earnestness.

And of course the boy was right, and the contract was kept, and all things went well until, by a savage irony, Sgt. Leonard was killed in the last German raid against Doolittle's headquarters in Europe shortly before the war ended.

CHAPTER TWENTY-SIX

USING REWARD AND PUNISHMENT

One of the illusions having greatest currency among our people is that any green member of the fighting establishment is merely an American civilian in a uniform, and that therefore, his spirit is nourished to the extent that accommodations and usages of the service most nearly duplicate what he has known elsewhere.

This belief is especially prevalent during wartime when every mother's son puts on a new suit; it is natural to think that everything in the service will better suit the boy if it smells like home. The corollary of this rather quaint idea is that military organization is therefore most perfect when it operates in the same way as the civil society.

Earlier in this book it has been suggested that these ideas need to be questioned on two broad grounds: Do not both of them run counter to the facts of encharged responsibility, and to human nature itself?

To emphasize it once again, the military officer is not alone an administrator: *he is a magistrate.* There are special powers given him by the President. It is within these powers that he will sit in judgment on his men and that he may punish them when they have been grievously derelict. This dual role makes his function radically different from anything encountered in civil life--to say nothing of the singleness of purpose which a fighting service is supposed to move forward.

Moreover, the military officer is dealing with men who are submitted to him in a binding relationship which by its nature is not only more compelling but more intimate than anything elsewhere in society. As much as the parent in the home, and far more than the teacher in the school or the executive in business, he is directed to center his effort primarily on the building of good character in other individuals.

One need only compare a few points of advantage and disadvantage to see why a better balanced sense of justice and fair play is required of the military officer than of his brother in civil life, and why the aim would be far too low if the fighting services did not shoot for higher standards of personnel direction than are common in the management of American business. Here are the points:

> If any subordinate in the civilian vineyard feels that he is getting a bad deal from his boss, and has become the object of unfair discrimination, it is his

royal American privilege to quit on the spot, be he a policeman, a government factotum or a hod carrier.[1] He can then maintain himself by carrying his skill into a new shop. But an enlisted member of the armed establishment cannot quit summarily, and finally, if his commander is just wrong-headed and arbitrary, it can be made almost impossible for him to transfer out. However bad his fortune, he's stuck with it.

Nepotism is so general in our business and political life that the people who suffer from its effect accept it more or less as the working of nature; the results are therefore less destructive of efficiency than they might be otherwise. It is common to see the boss's nephew or his son get a good spot in the office and then rise like a rocket, even though he is a third-rater. And it is not less common to see a straw boss in a factory favor the man whom he thinks might grease the wheels for him on the outside. But in the armed establishment, favoritism on any grounds, and particularly on such treacherous grounds as these, will destroy the foundations of work and of control.

The armed establishment has its own body of law. Therein, too, it differs from any civilian autonomy except the state itself. The code is intended to enable a uniform standard of treatment to all individuals in the regulating of all interior affairs. The code is not rigid; its provisions are not absolute. It specifies the general nature of offenses against society, and special offenses against the good of the service. But, except for the more serious offenses, particularly those which by their nature also violate the civil code, it does not flatly prescribe trial and punishment. Military law, in this respect, has more latitude, and is more congenial, than civil law covering minor offenders. Rarely arbitrary in its workings, it premises the use of corrective good judgment at all times. It regards force as an instrument only to be used for conserving the general good of the establishment. The essential power behind the force is something spiritual--the will and conscience of the great majority, expressing itself through the action of one or several of their number. Its major object is not punishment of the wrong-doer but protection of the interests of the dutiful. This view of military law is four-square with the basic principle of all action within the armed services--*that in all cases the best policy is one which depends for its workings on the sense of duty in men toward each other, and thereby strengthens that sense through its operations.*

Put in these terms, the attitude of the service toward the problem of correction as a means of promoting the welfare of the general establishment obviously reposes a tremendous burst in the justice and goodwill of the average officer. It would be useless to blink the fact. But there is this to be said unalterably in favor of the military system's way of handling things: If the organization of the whole human family into an orderly

---

1. A "hod" is a three sided box sitting atop a stick used by workers to transport bricks and mortar.

unit is ever to be made possible, it will be done only because many men, of all ages and working at many different levels, develop this faculty for passing critical, impartial judgment on the conduct and deserts of those whom they lead, instead of regarding it as a special kind of wisdom, given only to the few anointed. Nor is that all. Not only the knowledge but the sense of duty in men is imperfect. In every society are men who will not obey the law of their own accord. Unless the authority which receives and interprets the law will also impose it, by force if necessary, the reign of law soon ceases. Whether an ordered society is to exist thus depends upon whether there are citizens enough, fixed with a sense of duty, to obey it and to enforce it.

At first glance, the responsibility seems extraordinarily heavy and difficult. But with broadening experience, it becomes almost second nature to an officer quickly to set a course by which to judge individual men in relation to the affairs of organization, provided that he has steered all along in the light of a few elementary principles.

Concerning reward, and equally with respect to punishments, no more pertinent words could be said than those uttered long ago by Thomas Carlyle: "What a reflection it is that we cannot bestow on an unworthy man any particle of our benevolence, our patronage or whatever resource is ours--without withdrawing it, and all that will grow out of it, from one worthy, to whom it of right belongs! We cannot, I say; impossible; it is the eternal law of things."

He said a number of important things in this one brief paragraph. There is first the thought that when any reward, such as a promotion, a commendation or a particularly choice assignment is given other than to the man who deserves it on sheer merit, some other man is robbed and the ties of organization are weakened.

Next, there is this proposition: if, in the dispensing of punishment, undue leniency is extended to an individual who has already proved that he merits no special consideration, in the next round a bum rap will be given some lesser offender who is morally deserving of a real chance. The Italians have an epigram: "The first time a dog bites a man, it's the dog's fault; the second time, it's the man's fault."

According to Carlyle, these things have the strength of a natural law. Nor is it necessary to take his word for it. Any wise and experienced military administrator will say approximately the same thing and will tell of some of the bad examples he has met along his way.... The commander who was afraid to punish anybody and by his indecision punished everybody.... The lieutenant who had such a bad conscience about his own weak handling of a bad case of indiscipline that he threw the book at the next offender and thereby spoiled a good man and gained the ill will of the company.... The old timer who smarted under excessive punishment for a trivial offense, broke under it, got into worse trouble, and became a felon.... The officer who promoted his pets instead of his good men and at last found that there were no good men left.... The skipper who condoned a small case of insolence until it swelled into a mutiny.... The fool who handled every case alike, as if he were an animal trainer instead of a builder of human character ... and so on, ad infinitum. It is a long and sorry list, but the overwhelming majority of dutiful executives in the armed services avoid these stupid blunders by following a Golden Rule policy toward their men.

If lack of obedience is the most frequent cause of service men being brought on the carpet, then as obedience is a moral quality, so should punishment be employed as a moral act, its prime purpose being to nourish and foster obedience. Before meting punishment, it is necessary to judge a man, and judgment means to think over, to compare, to weigh probable effects on the man and on the command, and to give the offender the benefit of any reasonable doubt. Before any punishment is given, the questions must be faced: "What good will it achieve?" If the answer is none, then punishment is not in order. Punishment of a vindictive nature is a crime; when it is given uselessly, or handed out in a strictly routine manner, it is an immoral act.

But when punishment has to be awarded, the case must be handled promptly, and its issue must be stated incisively, so that there is no room for doubt that the officer is certain about his judgments. Men know when they are in the wrong, and even when it works to their disadvantage, they will feel increased respect toward the officer who knows what should be done, and states it without hemming and hawing. The showing of firmness is the first requirement in this kind of action. It is as foolish to go back on a punishment as to threaten it and not follow through. The officer who is always running around threatening to court martial his subordinates is merely avowing his own weakness, and crying that he has lost all of his moral means. Even the dullest men do not mistake vehemence and abuse for signs of strength.

To punish a body of men, for offenses committed by two or three of their number, even though the offense is obnoxious and it is

211

impossible to put the finger on the culprits, is the act of a sadist, and is no more excusable within military organization than in civilian society. Any officer who resorts to this stupid practice will forfeit the loyalty of the best men in his command. There is no reason why it should be otherwise.

As a general rule, it is a serious error to reprimand a subordinate in the presence of any other person, because of the unnecessary hurt to his pride. But circumstances moderate the rule. If the offense for which he is being reprimanded involves injury of any sort to some other person, or persons, it may be wholly proper to apply the treatment in their presence. For example, the bully or the smart-aleck who wantonly humiliates his own subordinates is not entitled to have his own feelings spared. However, in the presence of his own superior, an officer is always ill-advised to administer oral punishment to one of his own juniors, since the effect is to destroy confidence both up and down the line.

It is always the duty of an officer to intervene, toward the protection of his own men against any manifest injustice, whatever its source. In fact, this trust is so implicit that he should be ready to risk his professional reputation upon it, when he is convinced beyond doubt that the man is being unfairly assailed, or that due process is not being followed. Both higher authority and civil authority occasionally overreach; an officer stands as a shield protecting his men against unfair treatment from any quarter. *But it is decidedly not his duty to attempt to cheat law or thwart justice for the sake of his men simply because they are his men.* His job, as Shakespeare puts it, is "to unmask falsehood and bring truth to light, to wrong the wronger till he render right."

Finally, the best policy on punishments is to eliminate the frictions which are the cause of most transgressions. When a ship is happy, men do their duty. Scarcely anything will cross them up more quickly than to see rewards given with an uneven hand. Even the stinker who has no ambition but to duck work can recognize a deserving man, and will burn if that man is bypassed in favor of a bootlicker or some other lightweight.

Nothing is more vain than to give a promotion, or any reward, in the hope, or on the promise, that the character who receives it will hit the sawdust trail and suddenly reform.

Duty is the only sure proving ground. Men, like motors, should be judged on their all-around performance. There is no other way to generate the steady pull over the long grind.

CHAPTER TWENTY-SEVEN

FITTING MEN TO JOBS

In civilian society, what amounts to a cult has developed around the idea that the average person has a natural bent for some particular job or profession, which if thwarted will fill him with those frustrations which are conceded to be the cause of most of the mental and moral disorders of mankind.

Therefore if all men could become rightly placed, we would have Utopia tomorrow.

This theory of what humanity mainly cries for is perforce rejected by the military establishment, for several eminently practical as well as ideal reasons.

It discounts man, his plastic and impressionable nature, his response to all that goes on around him and his marked ability to adjust to any environment. He is not like a bolt fitted into a hole by a riveter, nor merely clay in the hands of the potter. What he becomes is mainly of his own making.

Further, the theory does not meet the needs of the situation, since in the services, as elsewhere, there are not enough better holes to go around, and no man is ready to say that he is good for nothing but life as a file-closer.

But the last and main reason why the theory is no good is that it doesn't square with human experience. A narrow classification system invites the danger of overspecialization and lessens the team play which is so indispensable to all military enterprise. It is possible for the machine to break down totally from lack of interchangeability in its parts.

We learn much from war, but some of the most obvious lessons are disregarded. One of the things that it should teach us is the tremendous adaptability of the average intelligent man, his ability to take hold of work altogether remote from any prior experience, master it, and find satisfaction in it, provided he is given help and encouragement by those who already know.

This is the great phenomenon of war--greater than the atomic bomb or supersonic flight. Former bookkeepers emerge as demolitions men. Divinity students become pharmacist's mates. School teachers operate tanks. Writing men turn into navigators. Woodsmen become lecturers. Longshoremen specialize in tactics. And all goes well.

Then when it is all over, and everyone gets back in his well-worn groove, the social scientists explain that these miracles occurred because under the stimulus of great fear and excitement which attends a period of national emergency, individuals will sublimate their main drives, and adjust temporarily to what would be otherwise an onerous personal difficulty. Sheer poppycock! Normal men do not feel pressed by fear simply because a state of war exists; their chief emotions change scarcely at all. These transformations occur only because the man had the potential all along, and with someone backing him up *and giving him the feeling of success*, his incentives became equal, at least, to anything he had known in his peacetime occupation.

That is the long-and-short of it. If our average man couldn't become a jack of many trades, and a master of several, the United States would never be able to meet a major war emergency.

For these reasons, service concepts of how men should be fitted to jobs do not develop around the simple notion that it is all a matter of putting a square peg in a square hole--which is the one best way to deny the peg any room for expansion. The doctrine is that *men are many sided, that they learn their own powers and likes through experiment, that they are entitled to find what is best for them, and that having found it, their satisfactions will still derive mainly from intelligent and interested treatment by their superiors.*

Every officer arrives sooner or later at the point where he has a direct hand in the placement of men. By way of preparation for that responsibility he should do two things mainly--learn all that he can from his superiors about its technical aspects, and in his own thinking, concentrate on principles to the exclusion of detail.

The fundamental purpose of all training today is to develop the natural faculties and stimulate the brain of the individual rather than to treat him as a cog which has to be fitted into a great machine.

The true purpose of *all* rules covering the conduct of warfare and all regulations pertaining to the conduct of its individuals is to bring about order in the fighting machine rather than to strangle the mind of the man who reads them.

Thus in the assignment of men to work within any military organization, no amount of perfection in the analysis of skills and aptitudes can compensate for carelessness in their subsequent administration. The uniformed ranks are not mechanics, storekeepers and clerks primarily, but fighting men. This makes a difference. The optimum over-all results do not come from the care exercised in seeing that every man is placed at exactly the right job but from the concern taken that in whatever job he fills, he will feel that he is supported and that his efforts are appreciated. There is scarcely a good man who has served long within the profession without filling a half-dozen roles requiring vastly different skills. And looking back, what would the average one say about it? Not that he was happiest where the nature of the task best suited his hand, but happiest where his relations with his superiors gave him the greatest sense of accomplishment.

That is the human nature of the equation. We can let the economist argue that what a man puts into a job is largely dependent on what he takes out of it. And we can let the philosopher answer him that the fault in his proposition is that he has turned it the wrong way 'round. Regardless of which man has put the cart before the horse, there are two basic truths which outweigh the merits of the argument.

First. *All human progress has come of the willingness of a man at a particular time to undertake a job which no one had ever done before.*

Second. *The main reward of any job is the knowledge that worthwhile work has been accomplished.*

This last may sound like a corny maxim, but it's true. The reason maxims become corny is because they're true.

Despite all of the present-day emphasis on paycheck security as the mainspring of human action, the far stronger force which moves man as a social being is his desire for a secure place in the respect and affections of his associates, including his chief or his employer. Gary Cooper, playing in "The Cowboy and the Lady," used the line, "I aims, ma'm, to be high-regarded." Except for the few wrong-headed people, he was speaking for the whole human family.

The man who can get along without wanting or needing words of approval from other people is fit for a cell by himself, either padded or barred.

Loyalty in the masses of men waxes strong in the degree that they are made to believe that real importance is attached to their work and to their ability to think about their work. It weakens at every point where they consider that there is a negative respect for their intelligence; the dignity in any work is not inherent in the job itself but in the attitude of others toward it. Cabinet ministers, college presidents and industrial magnates will quit their jobs when they feel they no longer have the confidence of those to whom they are responsible. That experience is as demoralizing to great men as to the mine-run. Equally, the feeling of compensation which comes with any token of recognition is one of those touches of human nature which make all men akin. If men of genius and good works did not find Nobel prizes and honorary college degrees highly gratifying, this custom would have faded long ago. It is as rewarding to them to be called good at their job as it was to the New Jersey street sweeper who pushed his broom so diligently that he swept halfway into the next town before discovering his mistake.

The far inferences of these things should be reasonably clear to every officer of the fighting establishment. It makes little difference whether a man is digging a ditch or is working up a loading table for an invasion: what he thinks about his work will depend in large measure upon the attitude of his superiors. He will develop no great conviction about what he is doing except as it is transmitted to him. *The fundamental cause of any breakdown of morale and discipline within the armed service usually comes of this, that a commander or his subordinates transgress by treating men as if they were children or serfs instead of showing respect for their adulthood.*

The requirements of modern war are such that we certainly do not want to turn out one man exactly like another, or turn the majority into mechanical men, capable of one set function. But the rule applies to officers as well as men. The greater freedom which is needed has nothing to do with social behavior or privilege. It is the freedom to think boldly and originally for the common good, for, to quote Kant again: "What one learns the most fixedly and remembers the best is what one learns more or less by oneself."

Thus in the matter of sizing up men, judging of their capacities and trying to get them rightly placed, the need is not a formula, since no formula will work. It is only by keeping principles uppermost in our thoughts that the greatest measure of common sense will prevail in our actions. That is what is needed, rather than clairvoyant powers, or a master's degree in psychology, if the service officer is to handle personnel efficiently. There are no great wizards in this field: there are only men who know more about the human nature of the problem than others because they have had a zest for meeting humanity and have built a text out of what others have told them.

The job begins by the search for data on the individual--all of the data that may be obtained. It goes on from that to sitting down with the subject, getting him to open up and talk freely about himself, what he has done, what he would like to do with his life, and his reasons for so feeling, et cetera. But the information from all sources has to be balanced against one's impression of the outer man, not just what he says but how he talks, the degree of his attentiveness, his bearing, his eye, his self-control. The decision is made on the basis of all these reckonings. This is common sense in action, and the only alternatives to it are to act upon a hunch or purely emotional grounds; one might, with better reason, determine another man's fortune by the flip of a coin.

Let's see briefly how the method works out in practice.

If the record shows that a man is a bad speller, careless about punctuation, not interested in writing, non-experienced at clerkship, and something of a rough diamond in his nature, he would be a bad bet for the administrative side, or in supply work, or in a communications role, though with a little polishing, and provided that he seems self-assured and is what we would call a "likeable" man, he might become a capital leader of a tactical group.

On the other hand, the man who says he had tried in vain to develop a manual skill, but has always been clumsy with his hands, and is supported in what he says by the records of his service, isn't necessarily excluded from becoming a good weapons or demolitions man, if he seems strong in body and nerve, though he would hardly do for a mechanic's berth, or a carpenter's assistant or as a radio repairman. Weapons and demolitions require strength, carefulness and good sense rather than great dexterity.

Take the man who is uncommunicative, or morose or unusually shy. From the day that he starts his service, his superiors should do their best to help him to change his ways; these ingrown men are roadblocks to group cooperation. But if he does not pick up and become outgiving, he hasn't the quality of a junior leader and there is no point in wasting space by sending him to any school or course out of which it would be expected that duties as an instructor would devolve upon him.

However, there is one word of extreme caution on this point. For as long as 6 months after entering service, some men are under abnormal constraint because they are in a new element, and feel a little frightened inside. Whether this is the case is to be judged best by getting full information on the man. If the record shows that he had led his class in college, managed an athletic team, headed a debating team in high school, been the main wheel in a boy's club or a Scout troop, or led any kind of group, this is to be taken as a sign that the potential is there and that he is a sleeper. The most common error made in the services is that we are prone to underscore that a man was a lieutenant in a cadet company while taking no note of the file who had greater prestige in other activities because of his natural qualities as a leader.

These are only a few average samples of personnel handling, and of elementary reasoning. As Mother Goose might say, if the list had been longer, the case still wouldn't have been stronger. Far more profitably, we can dig a little deeper into the subject of principles.

In two senses, every decision as to the placing of men in the armed service is a moral decision, and therein it differs from average civilian responsibility. What is best for the man has always to be measured against the ultimate security and fighting objects of the establishment.

For example, it is dead wrong, even in time of peace, to commit tactical leadership to the hands of the man whose moral force clearly falls short of what is required on the field of war, no matter how congenial he may be. And it is just as wrong to let a blabbermouth work his way into security channels, even though the hour is such that he can do no immediate harm.

What importance should be attached to a man's estimate of his own capabilities? It is always pertinent, but it is by no means decisive. This is so for two reasons, the first being that the majority of men tend to over-sell themselves on the thing they like to do, and the second, that very few men know their own dimensions. Almost consciously, men resist the thing that they do not know, because of premonitory fears of failure. When the Armored Force School was first organized in 1941, a private from a unit stationed in Georgia was arbitrarily assigned to take the radio course. He protested, saying that he did not like anything about the field and therefore had no talent for it. But his commander sent him along. Within 1 week after arriving at Fort Knox, he was operating at a faster rate than any man in the history of the Army. Every service could tell stories of this kind; they are not miracles; they are regular features of the daily show.

At the same time, the man who volunteers for a particular line of duty--especially if it is a hard duty--already has one mark in his favor.

The fact that he wants to do it is one-half of success. Before turning him down, there must be a substantially clear showing that he lacks the main qualifications. It must be a *compelling* reason, rather than the overweening excuse that it is more convenient to keep him where he is. In any case, he should be thanked for coming forward, and earmarked as a good prospect for the next likely opening.

There is a slack saying in the services that "the good man never volunteers." That is an outright canard. The best men still do.

In job placement, mistakes are inevitable. Any authority in this work will say so. Every experienced man who has had conspicuous success in picking the right men, and in getting scores of individuals started up the right ladder, will also shudder a little as he recalls his particularly atrocious blunders. Outward appearances are so greatly deceiving! The prior estimates placed on men are so frequently highly colored or outright dishonest!

As to the making of mistakes, it is just not enough to comment that they have value, provided one has sufficient breadth to learn from hard experience. What is vastly more important is that the mistake, once made, will not be needlessly compounded. That is a normal, human temptation. The attitude, "I don't care if he is a chump; he's my chump," has nothing in its favor. Yet it becomes a point of pride in some men that they will not admit their judgments are fallible. Consequently, having chosen the wrong man for a given responsibility, they will sustain him there, come hell or high water, rather than make public acknowledgement of error.

With what result? Mainly this, that for the sake of the point, they win, with it, the contempt of their other subordinates. For there is something very childish about this form of weakness, though it is a failing not unknown in many men otherwise qualified for high responsibility. To put it plainly, *no man* has the moral right to suffer this upon any organization he is professing to serve.

The advice of one's subordinates, as to the placement and promotion of men with whom they are in close contact, is not to be followed undeviatingly. Men play favorites: they will sometimes back an individual for no better reason than that they "like the guy." Too, each small group leader, even the best one, will work to advance the interests of his own men, because so doing is part of his own buildup. Unless decisions are made from a central point of view, the subordinate who talks the most convincingly will get an extra portion of favor for his men, and jealousies will wrack the organization.

There is one last point. No officer can progress in fitting men to jobs except as he becomes better informed about job requirements. This is an essential part of his education. There is no administrative technique which is separate and apart from knowledge of how basic work is performed in the fields which have to be administered. A great many officers resist this truth, but it is nonetheless valid.

What is eternally surprising in the fighting services is how the aggressive questing for knowledge continues to pay large dividends, and leads, in the average case, to a general forgiveness of one's little sins and vices.

CHAPTER TWENTY-EIGHT

AMERICANS IN COMBAT

The command and control of men in combat *can* be mastered by the junior leaders of American forces short of actual experience under enemy fire.

It is altogether possible for a young officer his first time in battle to be in total possession of his faculties and moving by instinct to do the right thing, provided that he has made the most of his training opportunities.

Exercise in the maneuvering of men is only an elementary introduction to this educational process. The basic requirement is a continuing study, first of the nature of men, second of the techniques which produce unified action, and last, of the history of past operations, which are covered by an abundant literature.

Provided always that this collateral study is sedulously carried forward by the individual officer, at least 90 percent of all that is given him during the training period becomes applicable to his personal action and his power to lead other men when under fire.

Each service has its separate character. The fighting problem of each differs in some measure from those of all others. In the nature of things, the task of successfully leading men in battle is partly conditioned by the unique character and mission of each service.

It would therefore be gratuitous, and indeed impossible, to attempt to outline a doctrine which would be of general application, stipulating methods, techniques, etc., which would apply to all Americans in combat, no matter in what element they engaged.

There are, however, a few simple and fundamental propositions to which the Armed Services subscribe in saying to the officer corps what may be expected of the average man of the United States under the conditions of battle. Generally speaking, they have held true of Americans in times past from Lexington to Okinawa. The fighting establishment builds its discipline, training, code of conduct and public policy around these ideas, believing that what served yesterday will also be the one best way tomorrow, and for so long as our traditions and our system of freedoms survive. These propositions are:

I

When led with courage and intelligence, an American will fight as willingly and as efficiently as any fighter in world history.

II

His keenness and endurance in war will be in proportion to the zeal and inspiration of his leadership.

III

He is resourceful and imaginative, and the best results will always flow from encouraging him to use his brain along with his spirit.

IV

Under combat conditions he will reserve his greatest loyalty for the officer who is most resourceful in the tactical employment of his forces and most careful to avoid unnecessary losses.

V

He is to a certain extent machine-bound because the nature of our civilization has made him so. In an emergency, he tends to look around for a motor car, a radio or some other gadget that will facilitate his purpose, instead of thinking about using his muscle power toward the given end. In combat, this is a weakness which thwarts contact and limits communications. Therefore it needs to be anticipated and guarded against.

VI

War does not require that the American be brutalized or bullied in any measure whatever. His need is an alert mind and a toughened body. Hate and bloodlust are not the attributes of a sound training under the American system. To develop clearly a line of duty is sufficient to point Americans toward the doing of it.

VII

Except on a Hollywood lot, there is no such thing as an American fighter "type." Our best men come in all colors, shapes, and sizes. They appear from every section of the Nation, including the territories.

VIII

Presupposing soundness in their officer leadership, the majority of Americans in any group or unit can be depended upon to fight loyally and obediently, and will give a good account of themselves.

IX

In battle, Americans do not tend to fluctuate between emotional extremes, in complete dejection one day and in exultation the next, according to changes in the situation. They continue, on the whole, on a fairly even keel, when the going is tough and when things are breaking their way. Even when heavily shocked by battle losses, they tend to bound back quickly. Though their griping is incessant, their natural outlook is on the optimistic side, and they react unfavorably to the officer who looks eternally on the dark side.

X

During battle, American officers are not expected either to drive their men or to be forever in the van, as if praying to be shot. So long as they are with their men, taking the same chances as their men, and showing a firm grasp of the situation and of the line of action which should be followed, the men will go forward.

XI

In any situation of extreme pressure, or moral exhaustion, where men cannot otherwise be rallied and led forward, officers are expected to do the actual physical act of leading, such as performing as first scout, or point, even though this means taking over what normally would be an enlisted man's function.

XII

The normal, gregarious American is not at his best when playing a lone-handed or tactically isolated part in battle. He is not a kamikaze or a one-man torpedo. Consequently, the best tactical results obtain from those dispositions and methods which link the power of one man to that of another. Men who feel strange with their unit, having been carelessly received by it, and indifferently handled, will rarely, if ever, fight strongly and courageously. But if treated with common decency and respect, they will perform like men.

XIII

Within our school of military thought, higher authority does not consider itself infallible. Either in combat or out, in any situation where a majority of militarily-trained Americans become undutiful, that is sufficient reason for higher authority to resurvey its own judgments, disciplines and line of action.

XIV

To lie to American troops to cover up a blunder in combat rarely serves any valid purpose. They have a good sense of combat and an uncanny instinct for ferreting out the truth when anything goes wrong tactically. They will excuse mistakes but they will not forgive being treated like children.

XV

When spit-and-polish are laid on so heavily that they become onerous, and the ranks cannot see any legitimate connection between the requirements and the development of an attitude which will serve a clear fighting purpose, it is to be questioned that the exactions serve any good object whatever.

XVI

On the other hand, because standards of discipline and courtesy are designed for the express purpose of furthering control under the extraordinary frictions and pressures of the battlefield, their maintenance under combat conditions is as necessary as during training. Smartness and respect are the marks of military alertness, no matter how trying the circumstances. But courtesy starts at the top, in the dealing of any officer with his subordinates, and in his decent regard for their loyalty, intelligence, and manhood.

XVII

Though Americans enjoy relatively a bountiful, and even luxurious standard of living in their home environment, they do not have to be pampered, spoon-fed and surfeited with every comfort and convenience to keep them steadfast and devoted, once war comes. They are by nature rugged men, and in the field will respond most perfectly when called on to play a rugged part. Soft handling will soften even the best men. But even the weak man will develop a new vigor and confidence in the face of necessary hardship, if moved by a leadership which is courageously making the best of a bad situation.

XVIII

Extravagance and wastefulness is somewhat rooted in the American character, because of our mode of life. When our men enter military service, there is a strong holdover of their prodigal civilian habits. Even under fighting conditions, they tend to be wasteful of drinking water, food, munitionment and other vital supply. When such things are made *too* accessible, they tend to throw them away, rather than to conserve them in the general interests. This is a distinct weakness during combat, when conservation of all supply is the touchstone of success. The regulating of all supply, and the preventing of waste in any form, is the prime obligation of every officer.

XIX

Under the conditions of battle, any extra work, exercise, maneuver or *marching which does not serve a clear and direct operational purpose* is unjustifiable. The supreme object is to keep men as physically fresh and

225

mentally alert as possible. Tired men take fright and are half-whipped before the battle opens. Worn-out officers cannot make clear decisions. The conservation of men's powers, not the exhaustion thereof, is the way of successful operation.

XX

When forces are committed to combat, it is vital that not one unnecessary pound be put on any man's back. Lightness of foot is the key to speed of movement and the increase of firepower. In judging of these things, every officer's thought should be on the optimistic side. It is better to take the chance that men will manage to get by on a little less than to overload them, through an over-cautious reckoning of every possible contingency, thereby destroying their power to do anything effectively.

XXI

Even a thorough training and long practice in weapons handling will not always insure that a majority of men will use their weapons freely and consistently when engaging the enemy. This is particularly true of Americans. In youth they are taught that the taking of human life is wrong. This feeling is deep-rooted in their emotions. Many of them cannot shake it off when the hour comes that their own lives are in danger. They fail to fire, though they do not know exactly why. In war, firing at an enemy target can be made a habit. Once required to make the start, because he is given personal and intelligent direction, any man will find it easier to fire the second and third time, and soon thereafter his response will become automatic in any tactical situation. When engaging the enemy, the most decisive task of all junior leaders is to make certain that *all* men along the line are employing their weapons, even if this means spending some time with each man and directing his fire. Reconnaissance and inspection toward this end, particularly in the early stages of initial engagement, are far more important than the employment of weapons by junior leaders themselves, since this latter tends to distract their attention from what the men are doing.

XXII

Unity of action develops from fullness of information. In combat, all ranks have to know what is being done, and why it is being done, if confusion is to be kept to a minimum. This holds true in all types of operation, whatever the service. However, a surfeit of information clouds the mind and may sometimes depress the spirit. We can take one example. A commander might be confronted by a complex situation, and his solution may comprise a continuing operation in three distinct phases. It would be advisable that all hands be told the complete detail of "phase A." But it might be equally sensible that only his subordinates who are closest to him be made fully informed about "phase B," and "phase C." All plans in combat are subject to modification as circumstances dictate; this being the case, it is better not to muddle men by filling their minds with a seeming conflict in ideas. More important still, if the grand object seems too vast and formidable, even the first step toward it may appear doubly difficult. Fullness of information does not void the other principle that one thing at a time, carefully organized all down the line, is the surest way.

XXIII

There is no excuse for malingering or cowardice during battle. It is the task of leadership to stop it, by whatever means would seem to be the surest cure, always making certain that in so doing it will not make a bad matter worse.

XXIV

The Armed Services recognize that there are occasional individuals whose nervous and spiritual makeup may be such that, though they erode rapidly and may suffer complete breakdown under combat conditions, they still may be wholly loyal and conscientious men, capable of doing high duty elsewhere. Men are not alike. In some, however willing the spirit, the flesh may still be weak. To punish, degrade or in any way humiliate such men is not more cruel than ignorant. When the good faith of any individual has been repeatedly demonstrated in his earlier service, he deserves the benefit of the doubt from his superior, pending study of his case by medical authority. But if the man has been a bad actor consistently, his officer is warranted in proceeding on the assumption that his combat failure is just one more grave moral dereliction. To fail to take proper action against such a man can only work unusual hardship on the majority trying to do duty.

XXV

The United States abides by the laws of war. Its armed forces, in their dealing with all other peoples, are expected to comply with the laws of war, in the spirit and to the letter. In waging war, we do not terrorize helpless non-combatants, if it is within our power to avoid so doing. Wanton killing, torture, cruelty or the working of unusual and unnecessary hardship on enemy prisoners or populations is not justified in any circumstance. Likewise, respect for the reign of law, *as that term is understood in the United States*, is expected to follow the flag wherever it goes. Pillaging, looting and other excesses are as unmoral where Americans are operating under military law as when they are living together under the civil code. None the less, some men in the American services will loot and destroy property, unless they are restrained by fear of punishment. War looses violence and disorder; it inflames passions and makes it relatively easy for the individual to get away with unlawful actions. But it does not lessen the gravity of his offense or make it less necessary that constituted authority put him down. The main safeguard against lawlessness and hooliganism in any armed body is the integrity of its officers. When men know that their commander is absolutely opposed to such excesses, and will take forceful action to repress any breach of discipline, they will conform. But when an officer winks at any depradation by his men, it is no different than if he had committed the act.

XXVI

On the field of sport Americans always "talk it up" to keep nerves steady and to generate confidence. The need is even greater on the field of war, and the same treatment will have no less effect. When men are afraid, they go silent; silence of itself further intensifies their fear. The resumption of speech is the beginning of thoughtful, collected action, for self-evidently, two or more men cannot join strength and work intelligently together until they know one another's thoughts. *Consequently, all training is an exercise in getting men to open up and become articulate even as it is a process in conditioning them physically to move strongly and together.*

XXVII

Inspection is more important in the face of the enemy than during training because a fouled piece may mean a lost battle, an overlooked sick man may infect a fortress and a mislaid message can cost a war. In virtue of his position, every junior leader is an inspector, and the obligation to make certain that his force at all times is inspection proof is unremitting.

XXVIII

In battle crisis, a majority of Americans present will respond to any man who has the will and the brains to give them a clear, intelligent order. They will follow the lowest-ranking man present if he obviously knows what he is doing and is morally the master of the situation, but they will not obey a chuckle-head if he has nothing in his favor but his rank.

XXIX

In any action in which the several services are joined, any American officer may expect the same measure of respect from the ranks of any other service as from his own, provided he conducts himself with a dignity and manner becoming an American officer.

For all officers, due reflection on these points, relating to the character of our men in war, is not more important than a continuing study of how they may be applied to all aspects of training, toward the end that we may further strengthen our own system. This is the grand object in all military studies. That service is most perfect which best holds itself, at all times and at all levels, in a state of readiness to move against and destroy any declared enemy of the United States.

APPENDIX ONE

RECOMMENDED READING

Army Historical Division
        Okinawa: The Last Battle, 1949.
        Omaha Beachhead, 1946.

H. H. Arnold--Global Mission, 1949.

Basil Bartlett--My First War, 1941.

William Liscum Borden--There Will Be No Time, 1946.

David L. Brainard--The Outpost of the Lost, 1929.

Bernard Brodie
        A Guide to Navy Strategy, 1944.
        The Absolute Weapon, 1946.

Vannevar Bush--Modern Arms and Free Men, 1949.

Winston S. Churchill
        The World Crisis, 1931.
        The Unknown War, 1931.
        The River War, 1933.
        Marlborough: His Life and Times, 1933-35.
        A Roving Commission, 1939.
        The Second World War, 1948.

Hugh M. Cole--The Lorraine Campaign, 1950.

W. F. Craven and J. L. Cate--The Army Air Forces in World War II, 1948.

Edward S. Creasy--Decisive Battles of the World, 1862.

James P. S. Devereux--The Story of Wake Island, 1947.

Giulio Douhet--Command of the Air, 1927.

Clifford Dowdey--Experiment in Rebellion, 1946.

Theodore Draper--The Six Weeks' War, 1944.

Dwight D. Eisenhower.

230

    Crusade in Europe, 1948.

    Report by the Supreme Commander, 1946.

George Fielding Eliot--The Ramparts We Watch, 1938.   If Russia Strikes, 1949.

Charles W. Elliott--Winfield Scott, 1937.

Cyril Falls--The Nature of Modern Warfare, 1941.

Ferdinand Foch--The Principles of Warfare, 1913.

J. F. C. Fuller.

    Decisive Battles, 1940.

    The Generalship of Ulysses S. Grant, 1929.

    Armament and History, 1946.

    The Second World War, 1948.

    Armored Warfare, 1943.

Douglas F. Freeman--R. E. Lee, 1934.

William A. Ganoe--History of the United States Army, 1942.

James M. Gavin--Airborne Warfare, 1947.

Joseph I. Greene--The Living Thoughts of Clausewitz, 1943.

Russell Grenfell--The Bismarck Episode, 1949.

U. S. Grant--Personal Memoirs, 1885.

Augustin Guillaume--Soviet Arms and Soviet Power, 1949.

Francis de Guingand--Operation Victory, 1947.

W. F. Halsey--Admiral Halsey's Story, 1947.

Gordon A. Harrison--The Cross-Channel Attack, 1950.

B. H. Liddell Hart.

    Sherman, 1934.

    The Future of Infantry, 1934.

    The German Generals Talk, 1949.

G. F. R. Henderson.

    Stonewall Jackson and the American Civil War, 1898.

    The Science of War, 1905.

Pendleton Herring--The Impact of War, 1941.

R. D. Heinl, Jr.
> The Defense of Wake, 1947.
> Marines at Midway, 1948.

John Hersey--Into the Valley, 1943.

Russell Hill--Desert War, 1942.

Max von Hoffmann--The War of Lost Opportunities, 1925.

Ralph Ingersoll--The Battle Is the Pay-Off, 1943.

Douglas Wilson Johnson--Topography and Strategy in the War, 1917.

Melvin M. Johnson and Charles T. Haven--Automatic Arms, 1941.

Walter Karig, Russell L. Harris and Frank A. Manson--Battle Report, 1944-1949.

George C. Kenney--General Kenney Reports, 1949.

Roger Keyes--Naval Memoirs, 1933.

Alexiei Kuropatkin--The Russian Army and the Japanese War, 1909.

Lee J. Levert--Fundamentals of Naval Warfare, 1947.

Bert Levy--Guerilla Warfare, 1942.

Charles B. MacDonald--Company Commander, 1947.

A. T. Mahan--Influence of Seapower Upon History.

George McMillan--The Old Breed, 1949.

George C. Marshall--General Marshall's Report, 1946.

S. L. A. Marshall.
> Island Victory, 1944.
> Bastogne: The First Eight Days, 1946.
> Men Against Fire, 1948.

Giffard Martel--An Outspoken Soldier, 1944.

Walter Millis.
> The Last Phase, 1946.
> This Is Pearl, 1947.

John Miller, Jr.--Guadalcanal: The First Offensive, 1949.

Drew Middleton--Our Share of Night, 1946.

Samuel Taylor Moore--America and the World War, 1937.

Samuel Eliot Morison--History of United States Naval Operations in World War II (14 vols.), 1947--.

W. F. P. Napier--History of the War in the Peninsula (6 vols.) 1828.

James R. Newman--The Tools of War, 1942.

Frederick Palmer.
America in France, 1921.
John J. Pershing, 1921.

George S. Patton, Jr.--War As I Knew It, 1947.

Thomas R. Phillips--Roots of Strategy, 1940.

Frederick Pile--Ack-Ack, 1949.

Fletcher Pratt.
Ordeal by Fire, 1935.
Road to Empire, 1939.
The Marine's War, 1948.
Navy: A History.

Leonard Rapport and Arthur Northwood--Rendezvous With Destiny, 1948.

Roland Ruppenthal--Utah Beach to Cherbourg, 1947.

W. T. Sherman--Memoirs, 1886.

Robert E. Sherwood--Roosevelt and Hopkins, 1948.

Milton Shulman--Defeat in the West, 1948.

Holland M. Smith--Coral and Brass, 1949.

E. L. Spears.
Liaison 1914, 1930.
Prelude to Victory, 1939.

Joseph W. Stilwell--The Stilwell Papers, 1948.

Alfred Vagts--The History of Militarism, 1937.

Yorck von Wartenburg--Napoleon as a General.

Archibald Wavell.
      Allenby, 1941.
      Generals and Generalship, 1941.

John W. Wheeler Bennett.
      The Forgotten Peace, 1939.
      Munich: Prologue to Tragedy, 1948.

Kenneth P. Williams--Lincoln Finds a General, 1949.